FOUR PIECES OF LUCK

A PHYSICIAN'S JOURNEY

BY

PETER TOGHILL

ISBN No: 1.903172.64.0

Publishers: Barny Books
                Hough on the Hill,
                Grantham,
                Lincolnshire
                NG32 2BB

                Tel: 01400 250246
                Email: Barnybooks@hotmail.co.uk

Introduction

I began this story, and indeed it is a story rather than an autobiography, as an informative read for my daughters, Claire, Helen and Joanna. They know little or nothing of their distant family, my childhood and education or even of my life as a young doctor. As the story unfolded, my physician's journey became entwined with happenings elsewhere in Britain and the rest of the world, with our family life in middle England and in the development of a new medical school here in Nottingham. I have not attempted to disentangle the various strands.

As well as being an informative and, I hope, entertaining read, it is very much an individual story. Whether we lead humdrum lives or have scaled the dizzy heights to fame we all have a unique story to tell. Because of that it is worth telling. This is my personal tale of growing up, of experiences and adventures, of disappointments, of struggles and failures, of crusades and successes. I have made no attempt to be comprehensive, either in my own narrative or when dealing with others. The story is light hearted and anecdotal in style and I hope that I have not offended any old friends, colleagues or patients by omission or perhaps by commission. I am most grateful for their friendship and support for so many years

I was fortunate in being born in the pre-war days and, as a child of World War II, I was able to observe the war from the sidelines without being exposed to its full horrors. As a doctor I had lived through what has been perhaps the most momentous half-century of medical achievement so far. It was a time when medicine was transformed from an art to a science. So much has happened that it has been impossible to deal with all aspects of medicine, so I have dealt with the passing scene as I saw it and as it affected me.

So far as I know, none of my clinical colleagues in Nottingham have written about the Queen's Medical Centre, Nottingham or about the new Medical School. Dr Frank Jacob published "A History of the General Hospital Nottingham" in 1951 and John Bittiner and David Lowe produced "Nottingham General Hospital - Personal Reflections" in 1990. At the other end of the town Paul Swift and David Lowe celebrated the centenary of the City Hospital with "The People's Hospital" in 2003. Paul Swift also wrote about the Nottingham Medico-Chirurgical Society in "Sawbones to Keyholes" in 2003. There are, of course, more official records written, under the aegis of the University, recording the history of the Nottingham Medical School. My contribution is meant to be another small piece in the jigsaw.

In these reflections I have drawn from some "Personal Views" and "Materia non Medica" written by me in the British Medical Journal over the years. I take personal responsibility for what I have said in these but none of the comments are particularly controversial. My colleague Mr David Daly FRCS has allowed me to transcribe his graphic account of the Kegworth disaster from the British Medical Journal of the time. Other memoirs are from my own papers and from research carried out for my Presidential Lecture "Clinical Apprentices" given to the Nottingham Medico Chirurgical Society in 1987.

My good friend and relative by marriage, John Dawes, gave me the incentive to tell my story by giving me his own account of a peripatetic life in shipping in the Far East to read. I hope that my story will be as entertaining as his. I am indebted to him.

My dear wife Rose has patiently read and corrected all the contents. To her, for this and everything else, I am more than grateful.

Peter Toghill

Burton Joyce,
Nottinghamshire.
2006.

Contents

Introduction

Chapters

Part 1 A Long Apprenticeship

Part 2 A Professional Life

Part 3 A Change of Tempo

Part 1 A Long Apprenticeship

Chapter 1

The Telephone Rang……..

On my first Saturday evening as a consultant physician the phone rang. The voice at the other end spoke in an urgent Southern Irish brogue.

"Tom O'Grady here. Thank God you're in, I've tried five physicians already and you're the only one at home."

I felt flattered that I was so high on his list!

"I'm out here in the Vale of Belvoir," he said, "and one of the guests at the big house has chest pains, probably a coronary. He's not very keen to go to hospital." With few diagnostic and therapeutic options available in 1968, coronary thrombosis did not always merit immediate admission to hospital. "I'll meet you at the house in half an hour," said Tom.

I had recently been appointed consultant physician to the General Hospital, Nottingham. The deposit on a mortgage for a new house had cleared out my savings and it was essential to start earning additional money to supplement my NHS salary. One of the ways of doing this was by visiting patients in their homes at the request of their General Practitioners or undertaking private practice. Most consultants at that time were offered either full time or maximum part-time contracts. The working week was divided into eleven sessions, each corresponding to a half day's work. If you elected to give up payment for two sessions, then you could do what you wanted with the spare time. This could be playing golf, bird watching or just taking it easy! Most of us undertook the realistic option of working 9/11ths for the NHS and doing 2 sessions of private work.

Sean O'Grady's reputation had preceded him. Like many Irishmen his great love was horses. He lived in style in an old vicarage with extensive stabling and kept a string of hunters. His life style attracted wealthy patients from far and wide to his patch on the Nottinghamshire/Leicestershire borders. He may not have been the most academic general practitioner in the county but he knew when a patient was ill and when he needed help. When I had seen more of him, I confirmed that he was a sound doctor who knew the backgrounds of all his patients, particularly those with horsy connections. One old farmer's wife declared to me,

"Dr O'G. is a real gentleman - he always gets off his horse to examine you!"

So off I went in my rusting two-tone Triumph Herald car. A misty enveloping dusk was falling over the Vale of Belvoir as I drove up the impressive avenue of elms leading to the "big house." This was the heart of English hunting country with its tidy undulating fields neatly surrounded by low jumpable hedges.

Sean O'Grady was already there sitting waiting in his shooting brake, the nineteen sixty's equivalent of the four by four. He was wearing dirty corduroys, a checked shirt, hacking jacket and cap. His weathered nutmeg face crumpled into a relieved and welcoming smile.

"Good of you to come," he said. I realised again that I couldn't have refused!

He swung himself out of his car and explained that this was where the local squire, very much the landed and titled local gentleman, ruled with benevolent but wholly autocratic style, more in keeping with the 19th than the 20th century. There had been a shooting party at the house and one of the guests, an Honourable no less, had been seized with chest pain whilst returning to the house. The pain was regressing but there seemed to be little doubt on clinical grounds that it was due to a coronary thrombosis. The problem was that he wouldn't go into hospital without consultant advice. Hence my required presence, even though I was the sixth choice!

Tom was all for going round to the back through the Tradesmen's entrance. My hackles rose. I might be new but I was determined to enter through the front door. We rang the bell and a stony faced butler ushered us up to one of the guest rooms to see the patient. He had indeed had a coronary, confirmed by my unreliable ECG and, although his condition was stable, I thought it would be safer to transfer him to hospital. He proved an agreeable patient and accepted my advice.

"Best have a word with Her Ladyship before we make the arrangements," said Tom.

The family and weekend guests were dining. A couple of uniformed flunkeys were in attendance and the men were wearing black ties. Her ladyship presided from one end of the impressively laden table. Aristocratic, yes. Beauty, no. That aquiline nose formed the leading edge of a hatchet face that must have been responsible for a thousand character assassinations. But she was duly attentive to me and agreed with my suggestion. She thanked me effusively for coming out on such a dreary evening and then, as a generous offer, suggested that I might join them all for dinner - they were only on the soup course. As an afterthought, she added

"But then I'm sure that your little wife will have dinner waiting for you when you get home."

I daren't say that as I left, my wife had said, "Get some fish and chips on the way home."

I realised then that henceforth I should be prepared to deal with dukes and dustmen and that a new life awaited me!

Chapter 2

Early Days

Three Pieces of Luck

Life had moved on a long way since I had been born in the early thirties. At that time Britain and the Empire was at ease with itself and the prospect of another World War was unthinkable. A few farsighted politicians had warned of the inevitable consequences of Hitler's insatiable appetite for territorial expansion. Few listened. But within the first few years of my early childhood we were at war again. Few had any real concept of the duration and the turmoil that was to come. At the age of seven I became a child of the war.

But in those confused and uncertain days I had three pieces of luck.

My first was that our family held together. My father, then in his forties and a sergeant in the Metropolitan police, was in a reserved occupation. This meant that he was not eligible for call-up into the armed Forces. So, apart from my being evacuated to the Midlands during the worst of the Blitz, I was able to live at home during the war years with my parents at Bushey in Hertfordshire. It was then a rural Hertfordshire village sufficiently far north of London to avoid the worst of the bombing and many of the deprivations of wartime inner city life.

My second piece of luck was that I had a father, well educated in the University of the World, who always expected me to seize the best available opportunities. Ours was a family firmly anchored in the working class and although father always had his feet on the ground (perhaps a good thing for the family) he urged me to scramble up the educational ladder as far as I could go.

My third stroke of good fortune was the eleven plus exam. I scraped through in the scholarship list to Watford Grammar School for Boys; it was hardly with distinction as I was 26th in a list of 31. Nevertheless I got in. Watford Grammar School was well known locally and it had a national reputation for scholarship and sporting prowess.

I have said that these were pieces of luck; but this was how my early life worked out. As a child of the war, there was an inevitability to my early life - infant school at the end of our road, council school down the lane and then secondary education determined by the results of a somewhat hit or miss eleven plus examination. Our family held together because there was no real alternative. In addition to his job as an established police sergeant, knowing the Hertfordshire scene well, my father was much in demand for advice and practical help. And it wasn't all police work. My mother, like all housewives in the war, took on extra jobs: serving dinners at the local schools, helping in shops and serving behind the bar at The Stag, our local. There was no prospect of a move or change, barring unexpected disaster.

Over subsequent years I followed my father's advice to seize what I regarded as the best options available. I was not always right, but my early background gave me advantages over those whose feet were not so firmly grounded in the mud of the real world.

My Family

I have to accept that all autobiography is merely one's own version of life, but we cannot change our antecedents and at some time it is necessary to talk about the family. I have to say that I find genealogists who spend all their time researching their boring families unutterably tedious. My family background is tedious too, in that we have no landed gentry, no bishops, no politicians, no Nobel Prize winners and no generals to boast about. Nor are there any murderers, forgers, thieves or bigamists existing as skeletons in the cupboard. At least if there are I don't know them.

My father in 1909 with Great Grandfather Field on the Thurnscoe farm, South Yorkshire

The Toghill side of our family came from Gloucestershire. There is a local viewpoint called Tog Hill on the way from Chipping Sodbury to Bath. The census of 1881 records 134 Toghills then living in the UK with the largest proportion resident in the Gloucestershire or Somerset areas. Grandfather Frances John Toghill was born in Wick, Gloucestershire in 1877. He was proud of his West

9

Country origins and there was always a large photograph of the famous Gloucester cricketer, W.R.Hammond, hitting a superb cover drive, hanging in the living room of his house at Widmerpool, and later at Keyworth. He became a railwayman and, when I first knew the Toghill grandparents, was a signalman at Widmerpool station between Loughborough and Nottingham. Being a railwayman in the first half of the 20th Century was considered to be a good, steady and respectable job. That was of course before Dr Richard Beeching savaged the Railway Network in the early 1960s. He married Mary Elizabeth Field, daughter of a tenant farmer of Thurnscoe, South Yorkshire in 1902.

They set up house in Ilkeston where my father, John Walter (Jack), was born on 16th February 1903. He was the second of non-identical twins; his brother was Frances Thomas (always known as Frank). Times were hard, money short and Grandma Toghill must have had problems coping with the two boys. Being the weaker twin Jack was sent away to be brought up by his maternal grandmother and her two unmarried daughters, Berthe and Clara, on their farm in Thurnscoe. No one has ever talked about the reasons for this separation of the twins but I know that my father resented being sent away because Frank was always the favoured son. But though father was regarded as the weakling he grew up in robust health and survived into his late 80s. Sadly Frank suffered an incapacitating stroke in late middle age.

After leaving school at the age of 13, in the middle of the First World War (WWI) when he was little more than a child, my father worked on the Thurnscoe farm. Life was grim for ordinary folk living in South Yorkshire. The slaughter of the War was appalling: wives lost their husbands, sweethearts their fiancés, and parents their sons. Of the 8,000,000 men who were mobilised 850,000 soldiers were killed, 2,000,000 were wounded; many crippled, blinded and deeply traumatised survivors were never able to work again. Father admitted to me that he had been lucky - he had been born too soon to fight and not old enough in the early 1920s to have to carry the responsibilities of family life. For most lads who had been at school with him in a mining village the only realistic employment was "down the pit." He didn't fancy that!

Farming was hard physical work for a young lad but, living on a farm, the family was insulated from some of the hardships of the outside world. They had enough to eat and could keep themselves warm. Father told me how, as a sideline, he became an expert thatcher. In the evenings he would frequently return home with his hands bleeding and raw, like pieces of raw steak, from pushing the sharp wooden staves into the straw. But he enjoyed the farming life and, as an older man, particularly during the Second World War (WWII), helped the local farmers at harvest time.

Sadly there wasn't much money or much of a future in farming in South Yorkshire in the 1920s. By 1921 the post war euphoria had faded and the country was in severe depression with high unemployment. But he was fit, enthusiastic and intelligent though without academic qualifications. A career in the police appealed but at the time (1924 - 25) neither the Yorkshire nor the Nottinghamshire Forces were taking on new recruits. But the "Met" accepted him and he joined the Metropolitan Police as a Constable on 6th July 1925 subsequently retiring as a sergeant on 9th January 1955.

He had met my mother, Lena Mary Jow, whilst living in Thurnscoe. She was the third and youngest daughter with two younger brothers in a family of five. They lived in Bolton on Dearne, surely one of the grimiest and most unattractive of all the mining villages in the South Yorkshire coalfield. James Jow, her father was a miner and, in those days when wages were determined largely by the whims of the mine owners, the family was desperately poor. Mum's mother, Lizzie, was widowed early when her husband James, the grandfather I never saw, was killed by a rock fall in the pit leaving the family in abject poverty. Such pit accidents were commonplace and simply accepted as fate by the local community. There was no compensation and the widow's pension was a pittance.

My mother in 1917 on the milk round at Bolton on Dearne

My father and mother married in the Parish Church of Bolton on Dearne on Boxing Day 1927. They moved to lodgings in New Barnet the next day. For my mother it must have been sheer heaven to have swapped the cringing poverty of a miner's widow's family for the relatively affluent suburbs of North London. I was, I fear, often critical of her scrimping and saving when I was young but the ingrained habits of her early life must have been hard to shake off. After some early moves in

11

rented accommodation and with promotion to sergeant at Bushey Police Station my parents moved to Rosebery Road.

Rosebery Road

During the late '20s the nation reached one of the low points. Wall Street crashed in 1929 and the Great Depression was upon us. Unemployment in England was unacceptably high and showed every prospect of getting worse. During the summer of 1931 the first Labour government was overturned and a National Government was drawn together by the Prime Minister, Ramsey MacDonald, denounced as a traitor by the Labour Party.

The High Street, Bushey Village, Hertfordshire, circa 1900

On 16th June 1932 the Times reported on its news page the conviction of the Egyptian drug smuggler and trafficker Mohamed Mustapha Nafei, Mr Winston Churchill urged the need for higher commodity prices and Percy Holmes and Herbert Sutcliffe made a world record opening partnership of 555 for Yorkshire against Essex. It was also the day on which I was born at 44 Rosebery Road, Bushey in Hertfordshire. In those days home births were the accepted routine amongst ordinary folk. No matter how hard you look you will find no blue plaque on the house.

Rosebery Road was composed of a string of unattractive houses built in the early days of the century and added to piecemeal over the years. It was presumably named after Lord Rosebery, who was never elected to Parliament but was Gladstone's Foreign Secretary and later, in 1895, a singularly ineffective Prime Minister. Our semi-detached house was built before WWI in the standard three up/three down style with a kitchen, living room and front room downstairs and three bedrooms upstairs. Between the wars the back bedroom was converted to make a bathroom and toilet. The outside lavatory was at the back behind the kitchen.

It was all fairly basic, no central heating of course; in the winters we huddled round a coal fire in the living room in the middle of the house. Mother had a routine of clearing out the ashes first thing and getting the fire going with twisted rolls of newspapers and a few sticks. In the depths of winter, and indeed the winters always seemed marrow-chilling in their severity, we tried to keep the fire smouldering overnight with nutty slack, which was mainly coal dust. The Government issued instructions as to how you could make coal bricks from coal dust but they never seemed to work properly in our house. The coal fire was the only real source of heat in cold weather and was the focal point of, not only the living room, but for the whole house. In the winter I changed into my pyjamas in front of the fire and scuttled upstairs to bed. The bed was warmed by an ochre coloured stone hot water bottle, put in the bed an hour or so earlier. Gas geysers heated the water in the kitchen and bathroom. Both were noisy and smelly and exploded into activity when the water was turned on. My mother nearly gassed herself once in the bathroom when the flue was blocked by a bird's nest.

The living room was where we had our meals, sat round the fire, and listened to the radio in the evenings and where I did my homework when things were quiet. With two armchairs, a square dining table with chairs and a sideboard, there wasn't too much elbow room. The chiming wall clock made so much noise that my father took out its striking mechanism. My wife Rosemary and I have kept it for sentimental reasons and it is still in our family house now. When it went to the local clockmaker recently he was highly puzzled as to why it had been eviscerated!

The kitchen was on the north side of the house and was always cold. This was the reason, I presume, why food never went bad despite having no refrigerator. Washing machines and dishwashers were unheard of in working class homes.

We were lucky to have a garden with lawns and six apple trees. At the bottom of the garden were sheds in which my father kept his gardening tools, my rabbits and guinea pigs, our bicycles and anything else that might come in useful for the future. He was a handy joiner and fashioned shelves, tables and toys that were hard to come by in the war years. I suspect that he retired to the shed to escape from my mother when she was suffering from one of her many hypochondriacal bouts.

Most working class folk at that time rented their accommodation and our family was no exception. Our landlord was a man called Price who owned several other properties in the area. He always came to collect the rent on Monday mornings and payment was recorded in a dog-eared Rent Book kept by my mother.

When I was at home I was always encouraged to take out the rent of 12s 6d in cash. This was not to employ me usefully but in the hope that Mr Price would return the odd sixpence as pocket money! He sometimes did. In the 1950s after the War my father bought the house for £1,300 and so became a homeowner. It doesn't seem much now but when my parents moved to Burton Joyce in 1988 they were able to sell it for £36,000, a handsome profit indeed.

Early Memories

I know little of my very early days, except that I must have been a difficult baby. Mother was driven to distraction by my constant and inconsolable crying. She told me that, time and time again, I was taken to the bottom of the garden and shut in the garden shed out of earshot. Looking back I suspect that I wasn't getting enough to eat - or to be more accurate enough to drink. Breast feeding in the 1930s and 40s was measured by time at the breast rather than by amount taken. I suspect that the midwives were more concerned with the concept of overfeeding than the risk of underfeeding. Such were the difficulties I created that mother vowed that she would have no further children. I was to grow up an only child.

Those early memories tend to be blurred and it is impossible to attach specific dates to most of them. However I am in no doubt that I heard and understood Edward VIII's Abdication broadcast on 10th December 1936, when I was four and a half. We had gone to visit the Dixons, who owned the corner shop at the end of the road. In those days corner shops sold everything but not very much of anything. I doubt if this one made much money as it was run by Mrs Dixon whilst Mr Dixon was away supplementing the family income serving as a Petty Officer in the Merchant Navy. Nevertheless the Dixons were marginally above us in the social scale and we valued their friendship. We crowded round the crackling radio to hear the expected and momentous message. Children are highly impressionable and I was aware that the King's decision to give up the throne was a result of scandalous behaviour in wanting to marry a twice-divorced American woman. I vaguely remember those in the room bitterly criticising the King for being so selfish and all expressed support for Stanley Baldwin, the Prime Minister, in forcing the King to go.

At Christmas we sang; -

> Hark the herald angels sing
> Mrs Simpson's got our King.

The clouds of war were gathering but in many ways concerns about the future of the monarchy suppressed the unease about the rise of Nazi Germany. Families were enjoying a better standard of living, many were living in their own or rented homes and holidays by the sea were becoming the norm. Travel abroad was still restricted to the wealthy.

Riding on the back of a heifer, at the age of seven, provided me with my first formal introduction to the medical profession. It was a dare, of course, because I was confident that cows could be ridden as easily as donkeys. I was soon to be proved wrong and a quick kick of the back legs landed me on my outstretched left arm, which then adopted an unusual bend. The sister at our local Cottage Hospital put it in a splint overnight. There was no question of organising emergency X-rays. Over the next few days our local GP had two or three attempts to reduce it. Failing to achieve an acceptable result I was transferred to the Stanmore branch of the Royal National Orthopaedic Hospital for an open reduction. My memories of this are hazy but I certainly remember that chloroform anaesthesia was frightening. A cloth mask went over your nose and chloroform was dripped on to it from a bottle. There was a pounding in the ears with the feeling that one's head was exploding - then oblivion. The surgery went well and my surgeon Karl Nissen was, many years later, to be the catalyst for my own medical aspirations.

The family on a Bournemouth seaside holiday in the mid 1930s. In those halcyon summers, few imagined that we would soon be at war.

15

We hear much about the psychological trauma of childhood admissions to hospital. One memory was of a row of other children in Gloucester Ward of the Royal National Orthopaedic Hospital confined to bed in whole length plaster casts with a hole in the bottom area for toileting. In hindsight I suspect these were children with tuberculous spines. My other memory, and lasting humiliation, was being visited by the vicar (I was a choirboy) when I was performing business on the bedpan. We forget what embarrasses children!

The run up to War

My early schooldays, from Infants' School, through Ashfield Boys' Council School and into the first years at Watford Grammar School, straddled WWII, from 1939 to 1945.

Until the beginning of 1939 I had no real awareness of the war clouds that were looming. But during the summer of 1939, even as children, we realised that Britain was edging inexorably towards war. I remember asking my best friend and mentor Ray Miller, all of eleven months older, if he thought that we were going to win. Summoning up all the confidence of an eight-year-old, he declared,   "Of course we are." I know now that our families and friends did not share that innocent confidence. Nevertheless the circumstances of the outbreak of war on the 3rd of September 1939 are as clear to me now as they were then on that sunny Sunday morning.

Now, some 65 years on my children, and certainly my grandchildren, would be pressed to describe and explain the sequence of events that led to the War that was to engulf much of the world. After the Great Depression of 1929 Adolf Hitler's Nazi Party had built up a massive following. Its extreme nationalism and anti-communism won widespread support across Germany. By 1932, the year of my birth, the Nazi Party was the largest in the German Reichstag and, by 1933, Hitler was Chancellor. His initial stated goal was to incorporate all ethnic Germans into a Greater German State. During the mid 1930s he began to escalate an aggressive re-armament campaign which allowed him to assuage his seemingly insatiable appetite for more territories. In 1938 he annexed Austria and encroached into Czechoslovakia. The Baltic ports and the Polish Corridor were absorbed into Greater Germany and the State of Czechoslovakia ceased to exist. The Jews were persecuted openly and relentlessly. Poland was the next country in Hitler's sights. On 1st September German tanks crossed the Polish border and German bombers began pounding Warsaw and Polish airfields.

Neville Chamberlain, the Prime Minister who had earlier sought to appease Herr Hitler's territorial demands, could no longer renege on his guarantee that, in the event of a German attack, Britain and France would come to Poland's defence.

We waited anxiously for the Prime Minister's voice on the radio on that fateful morning to report the response of Herr Hitler to his warning that, "if Germany did not stop all aggressive action against Poland then ......a state of war would exist between us." By 11.15 am the Prime Minister announced that, "no such undertaking had been received (from Germany) and that consequently this country is at war with Germany."

A Child of the War

The Prime Minister's announcement was not unexpected. What was unexpected, within minutes, was the wailing of the newly installed sirens announcing an air raid. No one knew what to do. Many put on their gas masks. Some rushed to the air-raid shelters, others, paralysed with fright and fear, did nothing. My friend Ray Miller and I were playing in the yard of the Police Station, where his family had a flat, when the siren sounded. Bewildered, we dived for the nearest cover. It happened to be the kennel used for stray dogs, fortunately empty at the time. It must have been smelly, dirty and flea ridden, but to us it seemed to be a suitable haven. Needless to say we were quickly extracted by the grown-ups and scolded for our stupidity. The immediate crisis, both local and national, was quickly resolved when it was discovered that it was a false alarm and that the plane spotted crossing the coast was one of ours.

Nevertheless the next few years were to be very different from what had gone before.

The country had not been entirely unprepared for war and the Government had already set about protecting civilians from the twin threats of gassing and bombing. We were all issued with gas masks and were urged to practice wearing them at home and at school. They were truly frightening; the cylinder in the front looked like a huge pig's snout. I hated wearing mine and always felt as though I was going to suffocate. But some of the lads enjoyed the rehearsals as they discovered that they could make vulgar farting noises by blowing out hard through the side rubber of the facepiece.

"Can't help it, Miss," they would protest when admonished by the teacher. We were expected to carry our gas masks everywhere in a special cardboard box fitted with a shoulder strap. Despite the public being urged to look after their masks, hundreds were lost or thrown away.

A blackout was imposed with street lamps being turned off and householders had to use heavy blackout material for curtains.

"Put that light out," was a frequent call from the Air Raid Wardens if they detected the merest chink of light escaping round the curtains. In our house, like thousands of others, we criss-crossed the windows with adhesive tape as this was said to limit the glass shattering with bomb blast. Sandbags were everywhere, neatly stacked as additional protection round the entrances and windows of schools, shops and public buildings. We converted one of our sheds to an air raid shelter by surrounding it with sandbags and fitting it out with wooden bunks.

Later on we were issued with a Morrison shelter. This was named after the Home Secretary, Herbert Morrison, and was an enormously strong iron cage-like structure with a 6 ft x 5ft top on legs 2ft high. Father erected ours in the front room and I remember doing my homework on it. In air raids we scrambled under it and tried to get some sleep. Fortunately it was never "combat tested". Morrison was one of the senior figures in the Labour Party who had been appointed to Churchill's new coalition war cabinet. He lacked charisma but was a shrewd political manoeuverer. He was unpopular with his colleagues even from the Labour Party. One of Morrison's staff, seeking to explain his unpopularity to the doughty trade union leader, Ernest Bevin, said,

"Herbert Morrison is his own worst enemy."
"Not while I'm alive 'e ain't!" Bevin responded.

Many families had Anderson shelters, named after Sir John Anderson, the Home Secretary and another member of the War Cabinet. They were made of arched strips of corrugated iron and were partly dug into the ground. We never had one and they were not all that popular. They were always damp and it was difficult to prevent water from seeping in at the bottom. However some families contrived to make them reasonably habitable and lived in them during the height of the Blitz. It made one realise the appalling conditions the soldiers suffered in the trenches in WW1. It has to be said that they were built to last and I have seen a few of them recently in existence in suburban gardens.

In those early months even we as children were aware that the war was going badly. What we did not appreciate fully was the country's dissatisfaction with our tired, ailing and obviously ineffective Prime Minister, Neville Chamberlain. On 8th May 1940 a senior Tory MP, Leo Amery, criticised him vehemently in the House of Commons declaring,

"You have sat too long for any good you have been doing. Depart, I say, and let us be done with you. In the name of God, go!"

Angry words indeed; they were used three centuries before by Oliver Cromwell to the Long Parliament. A petulant Prime Minister left the House. With a hostile Conservative Party he had no option but to resign. On 10th May, the King sent for Winston Churchill who had emerged as the most credible candidate, to form a new government. Three days later Churchill addressed the House of Commons.

"I have nothing to offer but blood, toil, tears and sweat," was his rallying cry.

18

The Blitz

For a small boy of eight the war became a reality in April 1940 when the aerial bombardment of London began in earnest. The mood of the country was sombre. Our School headmaster, Mr Herbert Brothers, told us that if the Germans invaded England there was little we could do to defend the country. For the first time I began to have fears. Would we be bombed? Would the family be split up? Would I be sent away? Would we be killed?

The Blitz was concentrated on central London, the docks and other strategic targets. It was a desperate time for those living in central London but other cities such as Liverpool and Coventry were targeted. Thousands were killed and swathes of houses and flats destroyed by the bombing or fire. Many Londoners bedded down each night on platforms at Underground Stations. In October 1940 nearly 200,000 people were spending the night at 79 different stations. As an example of other hopefully safe havens, hundreds of Londoners went to live in the Chislehurst caves, which were equipped with electric lights, a canteen and a sick bay.

Warnings of air raids were given by the fluctuating wailing of sirens on the roofs of police stations. My friend Ray, whose father was a police sergeant, lived in the police station flat and I remember how the wailing siren shook the whole building, causing ornaments to fall off the mantelpiece. Sometimes during the "Battle of Britain" we could watch the dogfights from the relative safety of the shed at the bottom of the garden. Such was the weight of the sandbags on the roof that the planks were bowed - the mildest tremor would have collapsed the lot!

Those of us living to the north of London were fortunate to miss the heaviest of the bombing. Nevertheless the eldritch wail of the sirens was heard night after night as we settled down to try to sleep. The crackle of anti-aircraft guns, the crump of falling bombs and the rattle of the windows as the blast hit them, seemed to be all around us. On bad nights we could see the red glow from the fires over north London, with the anti-aircraft shells bursting above us as we looked across Harrow and Wealdstone. When dawn broke we would hear the continuous wail of the all-clear sirens. Tired families crept out of their shelters to try to get an hour or two's sleep before going about their business. Air raid wardens and fire fighters rubbed their eyes and prepared for a full day's work. Daytime raids were less frequent, but at school there were underground concrete shelters into which we scuttled when the sirens went. We enjoyed this diversion from lessons and were all issued with Horlicks tablets to suck.

We soon heard where the bombs had fallen and we kids scoured the craters looking for shrapnel which was eagerly traded at school. There was often an unexploded bomb roped off and surrounded, at a distance, by police and soldiers awaiting the arrival of the brave bomb disposal teams of the Royal Engineers to make it safe.

This was the summer and autumn of the Battle of Britain when Goering's Luftwaffe was thwarted in its bid to establish air supremacy over southern England. Even in our part of the world we were able to watch the daytime dogfights and attacks on the bombers. We were of course expected to take cover but became braver and/or more foolhardy as time went on. We cheered on the Spitfires and Hurricanes and hurrahed like mad when one of the Jerries went down with a streamer of smoke to hit the ground with a thud that was heard a few seconds later.

In the war we had, for a while, two lodgers, Peter Abdey and his mother. During the worst of the Blitz, Peter and I slept under the stairs for extra safety. As the stairs creaked and groaned on climbing them I can't think that they would have provided much additional protection if a bomb had fallen! The protection was of the same order as our shed at the bottom of the garden.

We were further crowded out, later in the war, with servicemen and women billeted on us. They were usually WAAFs (Women's Auxiliary Air Force) - and an interesting group they turned out to be. The first was a schoolteacher in civilian life and I am grateful to her for my precocious knowledge of geography. She bought a large world map, which was pinned on the wall. This allowed us to follow the progress of the war day by day. Each evening I was tested on world cities and have, to this day, remembered all that I was taught. The most popular lodger was a blonde WAAF called Julie. She was pretty and extroverted. One day looking in her cupboard for some of my clothes I chanced upon some of her love letters. I need not have read them but curiosity took the better of me and I did. Her boyfriend's explicit description of their recent lovemaking pushed up my admiration for her enormously. Her stamina, athleticism, gymnastic ability and animal enthusiasm were high on the Richter Scale. And I learnt a few things that weren't in the sex education pamphlets we were issued with from school!

Like many others at that time Father had an allotment on the edge of the village. Two or three times a week he wheeled his tools there in a home-made barrow to "Dig for Victory" as we were encouraged to do by the Government propaganda machine. Many of the locals became expert vegetable gardeners producing potatoes, leeks, onions, cabbages and Brussel sprouts to supplement our boring diet. I suspect they enjoyed getting out of the house too. One of father's annual jokes was to scratch the face of Hitler on his tiny marrows and to bring then home fully-grown with Hitler's face a foot in diameter.

A Lucky Evacuee.

In August 1939, nearly a million and half children had been evacuated from London to rural England and Wales. In retrospect this proved to be something of a panic measure. During subsequent months, in the "Phoney War," many of these children trickled back to their homes, some having reluctant, unsympathetic or even cruel foster parents, some being inappropriately housed. The majority were just homesick. When the Blitz began in earnest a better organised evacuation scheme got under way with hundreds of thousands of children being moved away from the principal targets of the bombing. Many children had to go where they were sent. It was as simple as that. Others, more fortunate, went to relatives or friends in the country.

Thousands of children were sent overseas to Canada, the United States and South Africa. Those who stayed in Blitz-targeted Britain viewed this with some disapproval. Some felt that it was mainly the children from wealthier families who could afford to head for safer shores. Others taking the higher moral ground took the view that the children were deserting what, at the time, seemed to be a sinking ship.

I was lucky in that it was arranged for me to go to stay with my paternal grandparents in a tiny hamlet near Widmerpool on the Leicestershire/ Nottinghamshire border. My grandfather was an exiled west countryman who worked as a signalman on the old London, Midland and Scottish railway nearby. He was a stern, paternalistic figure with a bald head and a monkish rim of white hair. His large white moustache yellowed in the mid-line through his habit of drinking his tea from a saucer and sucking it through his whiskers. He was a stickler for routine and insisted on meals being served on the dot, to coincide with the beginning of the eight, twelve and six o'clock news. He always had his own personal plate, knife, fork and spoon. When he came in at the end of the day he would put his feet up on a stool and expect grandma to unlace his boots, take them off and put his slippers on. Grandma didn't seem to mind this, accepting it as part of her wifely duties. I was never able to get particularly close to him but to be fair he was never unkind or cruel. He was a real hypocrite always adopting high principles but avidly reading "The News of the World" from cover to cover on a Sunday. But there were times when he could be a bit of a pig to Grandma. She was a dear and looked after me like a son. Perhaps this was to make up for the fact that my father had been sent away as a baby.

Grandpa and Grandma lived frugally in a fairly primitive semi-detached cottage. Water had to be fetched from a pump in the yard and the toilet was a reeking, dark and dingy earth closet outside. The bucket was emptied when it was full and the contents collected regularly by a verminous scoundrel, who came round pulling a revoltingly smelling cart. Not surprisingly everyone knew him as Lavender Joe. Cooking and heat for the living room was from a huge iron oven fuelled by railway sleepers provided, but not sawn up, by the railway. Grandfather and I had to split them with wedges. In spite of the oven it was very cold in the winter, with toothbrushes frozen stiff inside the ice-covered windows. I always slept in socks, pants and vest, as well as pyjamas, in the depths of the winter.

But we didn't go hungry; there were vegetables from the garden, eggs from the chickens and the occasional rabbit or pigeon. In these days of supermarkets, with overloaded trolleys being pushed through the checkouts by grossly obese overfed housewives, it is salutary to think of Grandma returning from her once-weekly shopping in Nottingham. All the provisions were contained in one basket. As a treat in the school holidays I was taken into Nottingham with her when we had dinner (poshly now called lunch) at a British Restaurant for eight pence. These were restaurants set up to by the Government to provide a simple, cheap, nutritious meal, usually meat and two veg, to bolster the wartime diet.

Today there are many who seek to emphasise the emotional upsets generated by wartime restrictions and separations. I have to say that I do not recall any significant homesickness or deprivation resulting from my spell away. Perhaps I was fortunate in that I was with relatives but most of the other evacuees I mixed with, mainly from the ports of East Anglia, did not seem to be unduly disturbed by the experience. The local children accepted me and we did what most other country children did in their spare time. We roamed the surrounding fields, splashed about in the ditches, played in the nearby farmyard and made camps in the woods. At threshing time, amidst all the dust and clatter, we gleefully watched the terriers chase and grab the escaping rats by their necks, toss them into the air to catch them again as they fell, squealing and screeching. In the depths of winter we played on the frozen farm pond; no one seemed to worry then about the dangers of falling through thin ice. I was only walloped once by Gran - for falling over in the fresh dung of the cowshed and ruining my new raincoat!

When it was clear that the Blitz was more or less over, I returned safely to Bushey to the arms of my family. I spoke with a Midland accent and my classmates were most impressed by my brown country boots, then rarely worn by southern schoolboys.

Wartime Hardships

As the war dragged on, food rationing became an accepted feature of life. The ration book was one of the most important domestic documents, containing vouchers entitling us to prescribed amounts of foods that were in short supply. This meant nearly everything except bread and vegetables. In 1940, for example, we were allowed 4oz of bacon and ham, 1oz of cheese and 1 shilling and 10 pence worth of meat per person per week. All sorts of new food became part of the nation's diet: Spam, an American import - quite a delicacy I thought; whale meat, tough, purplish black, greasy and quite disgusting; dried eggs, fried like an omelette - one of my favourites; snoek - we were never quite sure what that was; and dried milk - always instantly recognisable in tea or coffee. In fact rationing continued until 1954 when butter, sweets, meat and eggs were last to come off.

Even bread, our staple food was rationed in 1946 for two years after the end of the war. Lord Woolton, a Manchester businessman, was put in charge of our diets and, as Minister of Food, his became a household name.

There was a black market in food, cigarettes and spirits. Some of the unscrupulous shopkeepers always had "a bit of this or that" under the counter for their favourites. It has to be admitted that favours in kind rather than money were often exchanged both ways! A new word, spiv, was introduced into the language to describe those engaged in black market dealings. Those of us who became addicts of "Dad's Army" in the 1970s, easily recognised L/Cpl Jones (Clive Dunn) as the devious butcher with "a bit under the Counter" and Pte Walker as the spiv.

We children were provided with school dinners at 4d per day. I seem to recall that they weren't too bad, but we were always suspicious of the constituents. We recited: -

"Dead dogs' giblets, Green cats' eyes
All mixed together in snot and bogie pies
Horses' skin all green and thick
All washed down with a cup of cold sick."

Clothes were also rationed and we had to trade-in clothing coupons when we wanted to buy something new. There was a complex scheme for school children. We were all weighed and measured and our shoe sizes noted. Those above certain standards for their age were awarded extra coupons. Unfortunately someone in Whitehall got the average shoe size wrong. For a year or two virtually everyone received extra coupons because of their alleged big feet. Mothers and Grandmothers became expert patchers and menders. I was embarrassed having to wear socks mended with ankles and feet of a different shade of grey. On reflection, though, people were a good deal less scruffy that some of today's youngsters with their patched jeans and sweaty T shirts.

Keeping warm in the winter became a problem as fuel stocks dwindled. Most households, like ours, kept warm by a coal fire in the living room. Other rooms had fireplaces but the fires were rarely lit, as there wasn't much spare fuel. Wooding was a regular pastime during the colder months. This meant pushing a wheelbarrow along the lanes and through the woods collecting fallen or dead branches to cut up and burn. Central heating was a great luxury, certainly not for the likes of us.

There was of course no television, that centrepiece of modern domestic life and entertainment. During the long dark evenings most families were cooped up, like us, in the one room, which acted as a dining/living room. The wireless was turned on when we all settled down after the evening meal had been cleared away and homework done. There were two channels, the Home Service and the Forces. Most wirelesses (note that they weren't called radios then) could pick up other foreign stations but the reception was awful - humming, crackling, waxing and waning and then fading altogether. A treacherous Englishman, William Joyce (Lord Haw Haw), broadcast propaganda from Germany. It was listened to as it was so laughable. After the war cricket enthusiasts like myself used to get up before breakfast to try to get the Test Match commentaries from Australia, but even with an ear to the wireless it was often impossible to get the score.

Some of the programmes became mandatory listening for us:

Much Binding in the Marsh - about an accident prone RAF station.
ITMA (It's That Man Again) with Tommy Handley, a nationally known figure and a celebrity if ever there was one - surely one of the most popular comedy programmes ever.
Variety Bandbox - good all round entertainment for everyone on Sunday evenings.
Educating Archie - however could a ventriloquist and his dummy become popular on the air?

Then there were the serials: -
Dick Barton - with its exciting ratta-tat-tat musical introduction.
And later, The Archers - and it's still going strong!

Going out for the evening meant the cinema. Going out for a meal was almost unheard of for ordinary families. And in any case the food wasn't worth it! Our local cinemas were in Watford. There were five in the town, from the Gaumont at the top of the range to the Plaza at the bottom, very much a fleapit. We often went as a treat after school, clutching our sandwiches to be eaten in the interval between the second feature and the main film during the News. At the posher Gaumont cinema there was a theatre organ and the organist, Tommy Dando, rose up from below the stage to sink down again after playing, waving goodbye as he went. Animal films, including cartoons were hugely popular both to adults and children. It didn't seem to matter that they were over-sentimental; perhaps this was a happy break from the harsh realities of the world outside. Dumbo, Bambi, Mickey Mouse, and later Lassie were all family favourites. It is an indication of their quality that Casablanca, In Which We Serve, This Happy Breed, Brief Encounter and The Bells of St Mary's are still being shown in black and white on afternoon television now.

The progress of the war engulfed us all. We listened to the news bulletins avidly and most families posted world maps on the wall, with pins and stickers to record changes in the various fronts. It was all gloomy news until October 1942, when General Montgomery defeated Rommel at El Alamein in the North African desert. This was, I think, the turning point. Monty was to become one of the Great War heroes with his name a household word. I met him in later years when I was doing my National Service and have to say that I found him extraordinarily vain, self-opinionated and overbearing. But then, I suppose, he had many reasons to be so. We followed all the campaigns - the invasion of Italy, the bombing of the German cities, D-Day, the advance across Europe and then the war in the Far East.

Even as a boy, I listened to Winston Churchill's speeches on the wireless, almost hypnotised by the mastery of his words. Who else put our thoughts into such poignant phrases "Never..... was so much owed, by so many, to so few." Who else would speak of Italy as "the soft underbelly of Europe" and who else would forecast with hope of "the end of the beginning." Conversation next morning would be

"Did you hear Winnie last night? But it wasn't all complimentary "I wish he'd get some new false teeth!" someone was always bound to say.

As the war ground on to its conclusion, new threats to the home front emerged, first the unmanned flying bombs, V1 Doodle bugs and secondly the V2 rockets. The frightening thing was that so little could be done about them.

We began to identify the characteristic drone of the Doodlebugs launched from France and the Low Countries. They were safe whilst the engines were still going but we knew we had to dive for cover as soon as the engine cut out. It was impossible then to define the direction of its dive. We had several explode on our village, one on the cricket pitch. No one was playing at the time.

We heard the drone of another doodlebug once when father and I were helping Charlie Jones, a neighbouring farmer, with the harvest. We looked into the distance and saw this ugly grey hornet spurting fire from its tail and approaching low and fast in the shimmering blue afternoon sky. As it passed over us the engine cut out. Charlie, red faced, sweating and immensely corpulent yelled out,

"The bugger's going to drop on us, get down!"

"Not much point in you doing that" yelled father, "you're the same height lying down as you are standing up." We all laughed, but then a huge blast shook the ground. Charlie's belly quivered as he buried his head in the stubble and some clods of earth flew over our prone bodies.

"Sod it," said Charlie heaving himself to his feet, "I think I've shit myself."

As the war dragged on to its inevitable conclusion Hitler threw his last secret weapon at us, the V2 rockets. These were more frightening than the doodlebugs as they struck without warning, wreaking much havoc with their one-ton high explosive warheads. It was a hit or miss campaign; many of these dreadful weapons exploded harmlessly off target.

A Scramble up the Educational Ladder. The First Rungs

Much is talked now about the emotional turmoils children undergo when starting school. Perhaps this is so for those going away to boarding school but for me, going to Merryhill Infants School at the end of the road, it was merely just another day in 1937. Mrs Stride took the reception class and had been at the school forever - as far as we could tell. From the low level of a five year-old, she was a tall, grey-haired lady smelling strongly of Lifebouy soap. The only other teacher that I remember was Miss Kinselly. Her only distinction was to be the object of what, to us, was a very rude couplet: -

"Miss Kinselly's
got a big fat belly"

It was the first introduction I had to robust vulgar humour.

After two or three years at the infants' school the sexes were segregated and the boys moved down School Lane to Ashfield Boys' School, a cluster of grey stone buildings backed by an asphalt playground. The Headmaster was Mr Brothers, a short, wiry, white-haired man with a Wiltshire burr to his voice. He was a music enthusiast and his great joy was conducting the boys for singing lessons. His favourites were "Shenandore" and, for the older boys, "Old Man River." He delighted in joining in but we all avoided standing in the front row as he showered everyone with saliva. He could wield a cane to good effect. Before very long I was to be whacked by him for arguing with our form mistress about the spelling of words in a test.

Why people make so much fuss about corporal punishment in schools I don't know, though I am sure that there are sadists at large who need to be kept in check. We had to bend over and received six of the best on the bum. I really don't remember any pain and it was a matter of some pride to recount to my parents what had happened. Other male teachers in the school, but not the lady teachers, used to cane boys regularly. One I remember well, Mr Bodley, specialised in a two or three step run up before bringing the cane down smartly on the outstretched hand. Now that really did sting. One overgrown, gangling youth in our class, Titus Ward, squared up to him after a caning but discretion took the better of him at the last moment, much to the disappointment of the rest of the class, silently egging him on. Other punishments at the school were writing out lines or standing in the corner with hands on one's head. A few minutes of the latter were much more physically unpleasant than the caning.

My argument-provoking form mistress proved to be the most memorable teacher at the school. She took responsibility for the class taking the 11-plus examination. She was a large, plump, bespectacled forty-year-old spinster, with a faint moustache, who sailed through the school like a galleon in full sail. We all suspected her of being frustrated as she often talked of her "gentlemen friends" though we never saw any. Note that even at the age of 11 we all were fully aware of adult relationships. Our suspicions of sexual frustrations were all confirmed when she sent Peter Humphreys to the Headmaster, for caning, for drawing dirty pictures in the margin of his workbook. Peter swore that they were just doodles and none of the class could see or understand what she could object to in them. Sadly Peter, one of the brightest in the form, died over one weekend from pneumonia following 'flu. They were pre-antibiotic days.

Nevertheless this conscientious and very able teacher taught the three Rs well. She widened our horizons by talking about her holidays, walking in Bavaria before the war, in reading books like Tom Sawyer and Huckleberry Finn and in taking us on rambles round her home in rural Boxmoor.

Young cricketers. The beginnings of a life-long addiction to cricket. Ray Miller, my life-long friend, is on the right.

Whilst in her form we took the 11-plus examination to determine whether we were good enough to go on the local Grammar schools. When I took it, eight of us got through - a record for Ashfield School. I don't remember much about it except that we had to write an essay on "A Day in the Life of ...." The choice of the subject was ours and I wrote about one of the local farmers. Having cleared the first hurdle we went to the local Grammar School, in my case Watford Boys' Grammar School, to be interviewed by the Headmaster and the Form master of the scholarship class, 111C1. I was asked about my favourite period of history, which I claimed to be the Victorian Era because it was the first one that came to mind. This was followed by an equally abortive attempt to talk about the Industrial Revolution. I came 26th in the list of 31 places but it enabled me to get my feet onto the next rung of the educational ladder. And to record this academic triumph my name, with the 7 others, was inscribed on the Scholarship Honours Board at Ashfield.

We didn't have much opportunity for sport during the war but I learned my cricket in the field adjacent to the school where we used a milk churn as the wicket. The resounding "bong" if the ball hit the wicket left decisions in no doubt. We were scarcely embryonic Don Bradmans, hitting a tennis ball against a wall with a cricket stump, but Ray Miller, my best friend and I, played for hours in the Police Station Yard on an asphalt makeshift wicket. Sadly a strong lofted on-drive through the recreation room window put an end to all that. Our only sport at Ashfield was stoolball, an ancient game played with heavy oval bats about a foot in diameter. The bowler aimed at a square board at head height. I have never heard of anyone else playing it.

There were better opportunities for sport in the years to come

The next scramble up the educational ladder

By 1943 Britain had grown weary of the war but mercifully the tide was beginning to turn. The Allies had invaded Italy, Mussolini had been deposed and Italy had surrendered. The RAF was bombarding Germany night after night and Hamburg had been razed to the ground. On other fronts the Russians were marching inexorably towards the west with a thrust towards Kiev and the Australians and the Americans were beginning to loosen the Japanese stranglehold in the Pacific.

These were momentous world events but, in my small corner of England, I was beginning a further scramble up the educational ladder. My minuscule academic triumph at Ashfield School earlier in 1943 entitled me to join the Scholarship Class at Watford Grammar School for Boys in the September. This was the oldest and the best school in the area. Elizabeth Fuller of Watford had founded in 1704 a charity school on land adjoining the parish churchyard. In the original building, known as The Free School, forty boys and twenty girls were taught to read, write and "cast accounts." With the help of endowments and gifts Elizabeth Fuller's original school survived until the 1880s. The school moved to newly built premises, now the Central Primary School, in 1881. The two Endowed Schools remained there in Derby Road until the early days of the 1900s, by which time the buildings could not contain the numbers of pupils. With the help of County funds the boys moved in 1912 to a large impressive building in the Rickmansworth Road which was the school I joined in 1943. In the following year it was to take up Voluntary Controlled Status.

Watford Grammar School for Boys

There is no doubt that even then Watford Boys' Grammar School offered some of the finest educational opportunities in the country. It went comprehensive in the 1970s but crucially retained a partially selective admissions policy - despite opposition from government appointed school adjudicators. In 2004 the school was named as the country's top comprehensive in the Financial Times 1,000-league table. Fame of a different kind came when it was selected as the setting for the film version of Alan Bennett's award winning play, The History Boys, about Oxbridge hopefuls. Currently, in the early 21st Century, it sends several pupils a year to Oxford and Cambridge.

I have to be honest and say that I have no over-riding impression of my first day there. School started each day with formal assembly when nearly everyone was expected to attend. The school was predominantly Church of England but other religions, mainly Jewish boys and the very few other ethnic groups, were excused the prayers and hymns. The multicultural society was still 20 years away. We assembled under the eagle eye of the second master, Fanny Lister, a red headed ball of fire, renowned for his explosive temper and fierce punishments. Why his nickname was Fanny no one knew. We were all terrified of him. Strangely, when he retired he metamorphosed into a "Mr Chips" figure much beloved by Old Boys. Whilst the boys gathered, the gowned masters slid into their seats on the stage and with everyone in place the prefects noisily marched in from the back of the Hall. The stage was set.

The Prefects with the Headmaster, Percy Bolton,
at Watford Grammar School for Boys in 1950 (PJT front row, 2nd from R)

Then God appeared. God was the Headmaster. Percy Bolton MA was a grey, lean, ascetic looking man with pale skin, silver framed spectacles, and snowy hair skirting a bald pate. He always wore a dark grey suit and a sober tie. The nostrils of his aquiline nose were pinched in and seemed to quiver as though there was always the smell of "dirty little boys" under them. Percy Bolton was indeed an awe-inspiring figure. A strict disciplinarian, he had a profound influence on the school and his leadership was primarily responsible for the school's superb academic tradition. He had been a Senior Wrangler at Cambridge and took the sixth form advanced mathematics class himself. Needless to say the school always won Oxbridge Scholarships.

Hymns sung, prayers said, announcements made, congratulations offered to those achieving academic prowess and to those triumphing on the games field, the Headmaster swept off the podium and we filed out to our classrooms to start the real work of the day.

My companions in 111C1, the Scholarship Class were a hotch potch of untidy 11 and 12 year olds thrown together as the result of a questionable selection process. I do not have a comprehensive follow up of all the boys, but in later life this patch-arsed group threw up a High Court Judge, an admiral, a professor of physics, a consultant anaesthetist, a consultant physician and an actuary. There must be others that I do not know about but the selection for the Grammar School training can't have been too wrong. Our form-master Mr A E Merritt was a kindly father figure and was known to all as "Dreamy." This was because his head nodded as though he was dropping off to sleep, though he never did! Rumour had it that it was due to shell shock in WW1, but with hindsight as a doctor I diagnosed it as an idiopathic senile head tremor. We all owed much to his guidance and benevolence, though I fear we didn't show it at the time.

This began seven happy and productive years. There were of course ups and downs but I cannot remember any serious deliberate unkindness by the staff, bullying by older boys, overt homosexuality, sexual abuse or petty crime. At times we wrote on the lavatory walls, trained binoculars on the Grammar school girls using our swimming pool, ate ice creams in the street and smoked dog ends in the cycle sheds. No doubt we deserved our Headmaster's condemnation as "dirty little boys." I can only write from my own experience but we were not plagued by the problems that seem to trouble today's youngsters.

I prospered in this environment. Within a week of starting, a stern English master, Rocket Stevenson, had taught me to learn and work on my own. His incisive questioning, and a good old rollocking for sloppy work, clearly demonstrated that I was not going to get away with drifting along with the tail-enders. I was not particularly bright but I discovered that I had mental stamina and could write quickly which was a great advantage when doing examinations. Soon I was in the topflight and remained there as I moved on up the school.

After three years at Watford Grammar School the war in Europe came to an end. On May 8th 1945 hostilities in Europe ceased. Mr Churchill the Prime Minister announced

"The German war is at an end. Advance Britannia! Long live the cause of freedom! God save the King!"

I listened to those fine words on our wireless not quite understanding what they really meant. I could scarcely remember a world without war. For me there was the frustration of having a puncture and having to walk the best part of five miles home - and it was mostly uphill too! The next day was a holiday with bonfires throughout the country at night.

Back at school, life continued much as before. All of us had to take, in addition to the standard subjects, French, Latin and Greek or German. Latin lessons were eagerly anticipated as they were taken by an attractive and demure young teacher with peaches and cream complexion. She often sat, with less than perfect propriety, on a raised dais at the front of the classroom. We were always dropping our pencils in the hope of a glimpse of white thigh!

I took a long while to decide on a career though it was always to be some sort of science. I found my way into the main science stream and had, as form-master in the upper remove, dear old Inky Knight. He taught chemistry with a light touch and a degree of buffoonery but inspired us all and produced some future FRSs on the way. Such was the excellence of teaching that virtually everyone in our science stream passed the old General Schools Certificate with Distinctions in Ordinary and Advanced Mathematics, Physics and Chemistry with credits in other subjects too. Those were the days when passing exams meant more than regurgitating junk from the Internet!

So far it must sound all work and no play. The tradition was that everyone took part in compulsory games unless they were medically unfit. It was rugger in the autumn term, hockey in the spring term and athletics and cricket in the summer. I loved the sport never quite reaching the top but being good enough to be vice-captain of rugger and cricket (and incidentally deputy head boy).

I felt I never quite made it. Sport was taken very seriously. We had a dedicated cricket master and professional cricket coach, Tarbox of Worcester who enjoyed telling us with monotonous regularity how in 1932 he had performed the double of 1000 runs and 100 wickets. Our cricket master lived for school cricket. After a win he was a delight with a huge satisfied grin that never left his face - until we lost a game. Then we knew that we were in for a highly critical and punishing analysis of our lamentable performance. He ran the cricket highly effectively, was popular and much admired. But he had a fault. He was undoubtedly fonder than he should have been of the boys and would hang around the changing rooms putting arms round shoulders and patting bottoms affectionately. He did no more than that but with today's climate of opinion he would have certainly been dismissed.

We all accepted this as no more than a quirk of his personality. He was a first rate history teacher too and his contribution to school life was immense. I am sure that the common sense attitudes that prevailed then to individual cases were more sensible than those of today and that no serious harm was done.

With a career in biological science in mind, I joined the Biology Vlth Form with a dozen others, most planning careers in medicine, dentistry or veterinary science. We were taught by the only biologist on the teaching staff, Willy Wyles. He had a pawkish sense of humour and managed to work us hard with a light touch. He also turned slow leg breaks and bowled me out first ball in the Staff Student cricket match in my last year at school. The Biology Vlth all took Higher School Certificate after one year in the Vlth Form (most schools took two years over it) and this allowed us to repeat our special subjects at Scholarship level in the final year.

By now I had decided on medicine as a career and applied to Clare College, Cambridge. As the time for the entry exams and vivas drew near it became clear that the prospect of six years of medical studies, three at least at Cambridge and three more at a London Teaching Hospital, would impose a financial strain on the family.

So it was agreed that I would opt for the shorter London course. Luckily a good Higher School Certificate Examination result and a London Inter-collegiate Exhibition for £15 per year, was boosted by Hertfordshire County Council to State Scholarship level. The way was clear to enter University College London as a preclinical medical student

Cricket was almost a religion at school. PJT ready to go out to bat for the School against the Gentlemen of Hertfordshire.

Chapter 3

Medical Student Days

Anatomy, Physiology and all That

After leaving school, most of my contemporaries had to do their National Service - either 18 months initially but later 2 years. This provided the first opportunity for many to get abroad to Germany, the Suez Canal, Aden, Palestine, as it was then, Hong Kong and Malaya. Others didn't get any further than Catterick or Aldershot. As the Forces badly needed doctors, potential medical students were deferred until they had qualified. I was in that category.

I began my medical training in October 1950 at University College London (UCL). I was to spend five academic terms there learning about anatomy, physiology and pharmacology before crossing Gower Street to enter University College Hospital Medical School (UCHMS) as a clinical student.

UCL is still referred to sarcastically as the "Godless Institution of Gower Street." At the beginning of the 19th Century the benefits of a university education in England were restricted to men who were members of the Church of England. UCL was founded in 1828 to challenge that discrimination and was the first university to be established in England after Oxford and Cambridge. It thus provided a progressive alternative to the religious restrictions, academic constraints and upper class preferences of the older universities.

The imposing main building flanks a quadrangle opening on to Gower St with its entrance directly opposite the old University College Hospital (UCH), with which it was linked inextricably in its development. Its handsome façade is easily recognisable as it has appeared on countless films and television programmes, seeking to present an imposing backdrop to their plots. The 2nd MB course, which I joined, was housed in dignified but fusty old buildings fronting on to the southern stretch of Gower Street. There were about 60 of us of whom less than a quarter were women. Even in 1950 UCL was virtually a university in itself with over 7000 students and faculties in every subject.

All the 2nd MB students had visited the Faculty of Medical Sciences before, as we had to pass entry interviews for admission. A novel feature for those times was a psychological assessment. A plump untidy, straggle-haired lady wearing owl-like spectacles carried this out; she mystified us by the long pauses after our answers. Vulnerable and nervous as we were, we thought she was delving deeply into our subconscious. Knowing what I know now about psychologists I suspect she didn't really know what to ask next!

Arriving there on the first morning we were greeted in the Anatomy Lecture Theatre by Jack Aitken, the Senior Lecturer who was also Sub Dean. He was a tall, balding distinguished, business-like Glaswegian, who spelt out the dos and don'ts of being a medical student. Amongst the dos we were told where to get our white coats, what books we would want, what we would need for dissecting tools, and who would teach us. Amongst the don'ts we were told not to display our illustrated anatomy books on the underground, not to bring friends into the dissecting room for vicarious thrills and not to chatter loudly about our medical work in public places. He informed us, what we knew already, that medical students had a low reputation with the public. We were not to lower that reputation still further. That reputation had been fostered by generations of medical students roistering, playing rugby, drinking beer and avoiding hard work (except when the exams grew near).

As long ago as 1830, Henry Acland had described the students of St George's Hospital disparagingly: -

" everything wears the air of low men, of low habits, such as I have never hitherto come into contact with...... they are the most bearish I have ever beheld as a mass. "

I don't think that we were that bad.

In fact most of us were straight from school and were pretty overawed by the prospect of five years' hard work in a new environment. Most were getting our first taste of life in the world outside. We were a relatively conventional lot. Some were from public schools, most from Independent or Grammar schools; a handful had been in the Forces for National Service. There were two or three postgraduates from other disciplines. One of the most popular of these was a plump, laid back Jewish graduate, Joseph Sandler, who already had a PhD in psychology and worked in a private psychiatric clinic nearby. He was full of worldly advice. In later years he was to become Professor of Psychoanalysis at the Freud Centre in the Hebrew University of Jerusalem. Another who stood out from the crowd was Tsewang Pemba. Always cheerful and hard working, he was the first Tibetan ever to undertake medical training in the West. Years later he was to become the Physician and Surgeon to the King of Bhutan.

Much of the anatomy teaching was undertaken in that Holy of Holies, the dissecting room. A pale, white-coated, cadaveric technician, Joe, with a macabre sense of humour was in charge of this sanctuary. His main purpose in life seemed to be to keep unauthorised persons out of his domain and to make sure that we medical students behaved with appropriate decorum. We had probably moved on since William Dale wrote in 1840:-

"Drinking, smoking and brawling were the very rational occupations of the dissecting room. In those days it was no uncommon thing to see a regular battle among the students, parts of the human body forming their weapons. "

Fifty years on, I can still capture the smell, which engulfed us when we went through the swing doors of that cold, sepulchral, unwelcoming room. It clung to clothes, hair and skin hours later but was impossible to describe – formalin, disinfectant, carbolic soap and death all mingled together. On the "slabs," not unlike those seen in the mortuary scenes in popular TV dramas, the corpses were laid out, mottled marble white, stiff and long ago launched into eternity. To us, I fear, they were but a vehicle for our learning.

Here we were expected to study anatomy, then regarded, with physiology, as the basic grammar on which the vocabulary of clinical medicine was based. We were required to assimilate anatomy in great detail: muscle attachments, the courses of blood vessels, nerve tracts in the central nervous system and the ramifications of the lymphatic vessels. Our Bible was Gray's Anatomy, a truly huge tome, which was supplemented by Jamieson's Illustrations of Regional Anatomy. We all now agree that this degree of detailed anatomy is largely unnecessary. It can be mugged up by those specialists who require it at a later stage in their careers. But I also believe that the pendulum has swung too far in the opposite direction. The amount of anatomy that is now taught is too limited. Our students in Nottingham now have little more than a First Aider's knowledge of general anatomy. Indeed a surgical colleague suggested to me recently that if a student, in an examination, called the knuckles the metacarpophalangeal joints he would be a candidate for honours!

Now just as the use of human tissue for research purposes has become controversial, the use of cadavers for dissection and the teaching of anatomy are beset with ethical difficulties. Indeed the new Peninsular Medical School in the Southwest of England has decided to abandon cadaver dissection entirely. An indication of how many attitudes have changed comes from Thailand, where donors offer their bodies for dissection. In return the medical students regard these body donors, whose names are well known to them, as honoured teachers. As such the dissection courses are given elaborate Buddhist ceremonies and rites.

In my days as a medical student a group of five or six students was allocated to dissect each body. Under those conditions we soon got to know each other well. Peter Sutton, my room mate, was perhaps the most serious and hardworking of our group. He was anxious to live up to his father's high academic standards. Graham Sutton (later Sir Graham) was then Professor of Mathematics at the Royal Military College at Shrivenham; he later became the Astronomer Royal. Sometimes he would call in for tea in our Hall of Residence to amaze and amuse us by reciting the contents of a page from Gray's Anatomy after a casual read through. James Hall, newly arrived from Oundle, then a boys' only public school, greatly appreciated his newfound freedom. He quickly pitched in to his new extra-mural student life by earning a rowing purple for London University. In later life he became an Air Commodore in the Medical Branch of the RAF and earned a CBE. Another buddy was Gerry Scott. He was very laid back and had the unusual distinction in those days of owning a car. He later became a hepato-biliary surgeon in Canada. Molly Wakeley, a serious and loyal friend, also trained later to be a surgeon and moved to missionary work in Lahore, Pakistan. The last member of our group, Michael Galton, a likeable but bumptious and over confident ex-City of London schoolboy, sadly died in a road crash at an early age. We were therefore a mixed gang with differing potentials.

Demonstrators, young men or women who were studying for the Primary FRCS (Fellowship of the College of Surgeons) examination, undertook the day to day supervision of our dissecting. For the privilege of looking after us they received a nominal salary. The Head of the Department, which had a formidable research reputation, was Professor J Z Young FRS. Known to everyone as JZ, he was a distinguished neuro-anatomist and was the only Professor of Anatomy in the UK without a medical degree. Tall, slightly stooping, with a mop of uncontrolled black hair, a beak-like nose, and protruding teeth, he was everyone's idea of the eccentric professor. He would breeze into the dissecting room from time to time to see what we were doing but was really a research scientist who yearned to get back to a research institute in Italy each summer to study nerve conduction in the nerve fibres of the giant squid.

We spent a term dissecting each region of the body: head and neck, arm, thorax, abdomen and leg. Each week we sat around the body to have a viva on the section that we had been studying in the previous week, the demonstrators picking up bits of tissue for us to identify and talk about. There was no way of avoiding this and at the end of the term we were allocated marks which we had accumulated during the year. No worries about elitism then!

A team of high-powered scientists whose primary interest was neuro-muscular transmission taught physiology and pharmacology. Some were European émigrés whose accents were so fruity that it was, at times, virtually impossible to understand them. Prominent amongst them was Bernard (later Sir Bernard) Katz FRS who became a Nobel Prize winner in 1970. In our practical classes we played around with dog, cat and frog organ preparations in water baths trying to get them to twitch, contract or pulsate. The recordings were on rotating smoked drums - a far cry from modern electronic apparatus. All I remember of pharmacology was testing the effects of sedatives on our calculating abilities and noting that the inhalation of nitrous oxide made you woozy but didn't make you laugh.

It wasn't all hard work. The male standard uniform was sports coat and flannels. It was fashionable to wear leather patches at the elbows and edges of our jackets when they began to wear. A long light blue and dark blue UCL scarf was *de rigeur* to identify your origins, not to keep warm. The really snazzy dressers, were the Slade Art School students. They appeared in paint daubed garb and fostered a reputation of being non-conformist, risqué and permissive. When I took one out after a Fresher's dance she was quite the reverse!

I shared a room with Peter Sutton in Bentham Hall, Cartwright Gardens. This was a five-minute walk from UCL and provided us with bed and breakfast and an evening meal. Cartwright Gardens was a Bloomsbury Square that had known better days but was saved from dereliction by being bought by London University, tarted up and used as a Hall of Residence. The room that Peter and I had was just big enough to take two single beds, two chairs and a table. Peter slept with my feet a few inches from his head - but didn't complain! We were as poor as church mice and had to eke out our weekly cash allowance. Bentham Hall had no central heating in the bedrooms and we allowed ourselves sixpence worth of gas fire each night in the winter months.

Money was in short supply everywhere, not only for medical students. We managed to save enough to go to the cinema every fortnight or so. Peter and I saw "The African Queen" in a fleapit near St Pancras Station. It made a big impression. Everyone shuddered at the leeches being burnt off Lauren Bacall's legs but only a few months later the Chief Pharmacist at UCH, Mr Whittet, showed us similar leeches kept in the Pharmacy. He had to admit that they hadn't been used for therapeutic purposes for some years! As well as the cinema providing a cheap source of entertainment, we students frequented Lyons Corner Houses where you could take your girlfriend out for a bowl of soup, salad and music for 1s 6d.

In the late winter of 1952 the King died suddenly and unexpectedly. The nation was shocked but the expressions of sadness, though heartfelt, came nowhere near the mass outpouring of sorrow and hysteria that followed Princess Diana's death 50 years later. By the late 20th Century it had become much more fashionable to wallow in grief.

George VI had been a popular monarch and his decision to stay in London with his family throughout the war, when he could have sheltered in safety in exile in Canada, reassured the nation during those dark days. He had increased in confidence from the shy, diffident young Duke of York, who had endured the misery of a dreadful stammer, to a devoted family man who stepped forward, duty bound, to take the throne at the time of his brother's abdication.

In recent years his health had been poor and was aggravated by a lifetime of heavy cigarette smoking. Sadly he suffered three complications of tobacco abuse: peripheral vascular disease causing intermittent claudication of the legs, carcinoma of the bronchus and finally a myocardial infarct which was to prove fatal. At the time of his operation for carcinoma, the medical profession was astonished and dismayed by the news that such major surgery was to be performed in a converted suite in Buckingham Palace. Even in 1950 it seemed old fashioned and foolhardy. Now it would be unthinkable. However all went well. The story that went round the medical profession at the time was that the surgeon, Mr Clement Price-Thomas of the Westminster Hospital performed the pneumonectomy successfully but nearing the end of the operation, stripped off his gloves and gown and went to leave the theatre, calling out to his senior registrar assistant,

"Finish sewing him up."

"But this is the King" protested the assistant. Price-Thomas countered

"I haven't sewn up a chest myself for twenty years, and I'm not going to start practising on the Monarch."

In the early morning of 6th February after a day spent shooting hares, the King died in his sleep. Several obituarists described his death as being due to cancer but it was a heart attack, yet another complication of his smoking. The link between smoking, heart attacks and lung cancer had yet to be firmly established by the medical profession.

We watched the King's funeral cortege move slowly and solemnly down Gower Street led by the four Royal Dukes; the two young dukes, Edinburgh and Kent upright and purposeful; the two older dukes Windsor and Gloucester trudging manfully but mournfully. The Duke of Windsor, still not forgiven by the public, cut a sorry figure in his Field Marshall's uniform, now seemingly several sizes too big for him. It was the end of one era - and the beginning of another.

And so it was for us in our minor way. At the end of our five terms at UCL we took the 2nd MB exams. James Hall and Gerry Scott failed and had to re-take in six months. Peter Sutton and Michael Galton passed and elected to take intercalated BSc degrees. Molly and I passed too and could move on to become clinical students at University College Hospital.

Walking the Wards

University College Hospital, London pictured in 1906

On 1st April 1952 I joined a group of 43 eager beavers, 36 men and 7 women, starting their clinical training. The majority were from UCL but six Oxford graduates, who had elected to undertake their clinical work at UCH joined us. This was a new phase in our lives and we all felt rather important when we were kitted out with stiffly starched short white coats and brand new stethoscopes. We displayed the latter as prominently as we could; either hanging them from our pockets or dangling them round our necks. It was of no importance that we hadn't the slightest idea what to hear through them. All I remember was the advice to keep the tubes at least 18 inches long -

"that's the maximum distance a flea can jump!"

The immediate object in life was to "walk the wards." This meant learning our trade by being a clinical apprentice. We would watch how our bosses did their jobs, follow their examples and then try to become expert ourselves. For the first time we would have direct contact with patients. We soon learned that for those patients, we were their proper doctors - they didn't seem to mind too much if we weren't fully qualified. They confided their worries and fears to us without reservation and asked us questions we had no idea how to answer.

The public, in those post-war years, was less knowledgeable, more trusting and certainly less litigious than today's well-informed and sometimes hostile patients. One reason for this was that they remembered health care in the pre- NHS era when they paid family doctors and consultants directly or indirectly for their services. Many families, including my own, were visited once a week by a man from a Friendly Society who collected a small contribution, filled in a well thumbed notebook, had a chat and then got on his bike to collect from the next person down the road. We knew that these contributions could, in times of trouble, be a godsend to offset the disastrous effects of chronic illness. Going to a teaching hospital meant that you could be treated freely by the best consultants and have excellent nursing care.

"He's in Harley Street, of course", the patients would say knowingly to friends. Being prodded and poked by medical students was a small price to pay in exchange for their care. Indeed it was most unusual to hear a patient refuse to cooperate.

Looking back we were fortunate to deal individually with ill patients. Now there are so many doctors in training that there aren't enough patients to go round. I cannot believe that teaching videos, actors simulating patients' diseases and even realistic models are effective alternatives.

However we were awakened quickly from our dreams of self-importance on the first day in medical school when we were told to report for a six week nursing course. This meant bed- making (hospital corners and all that), learning to give injections, cleaning up incontinent patients, giving enemas, emptying bedpans and finding one's way around the sluice room. We were quickly brought down to earth. In those days Sister was in charge of the ward and knew everything that was going on. And she looked the part too. "Carry on Sister" really came to life! A frilly bonnet pinned to silver grey hair, stiff white collar and bow, trimly upholstered figure, dark blue dress all fronted by a stiff blindingly white apron that crackled and swished as she moved. All was held together by a belt tightly linked by the UCH emblem.

But even 'frilly bonnet' allowed herself a tight-lipped smile from time to time. One of our patients was a confused ex-cabinet minister, who needed an enema to get his bowels moving. The students were invited to watch this performance. Within seconds the megaphonic and bellicose politician's voice echoed through the ward.

"Whatever are you doing, Sister?"

"I have to get you to pass a motion," Sister explained. Our patient, though demented, had some of his parliamentary instincts left.

"Before you pass a motion you have to have a debate," he bellowed. Collapse of all of us!

Our subsequent training on the wards, both in medicine and surgery, was undertaken in firms of students, each firm of about six students being supervised by two or more consultants. We were called clerks on the medical side and dressers in the surgical wards. It was very much an apprenticeship system being with the chiefs, as they were known, in the wards, outpatients or in the operating theatre. Bedside teaching was the traditional method of demonstrating diseases and many of the chiefs integrated the patients themselves into the discussions. It was on the medical wards that I met Professor Max Rosenheim, the Professor of Medicine, who was to become my first medical hero.

At first sight Max, as everyone knew him, looked an unlikely hero. He had been a Brigadier in the RAMC in the war and a more unlikely military figure you would never meet. Short and stout, he stumped around the hospital leading a large entourage of white-coated staff, students and hangers-on. His large head and heavy jowls were apparently mounted on his shoulders without any obvious intervening neck. He carried, even then, the warning signs of atheromatous disease - a prominent arcus senilis of the pupil and ear lobe clefts. Then, little credence was given to these physical signs but sadly, fatal vascular disease was to overtake him at a relatively early age. But in spite of his somewhat forbidding appearance he was a kindly man with a throaty chuckle and grunt and, in all the years I was to know him, I never saw him angry. His genius was in simplifying medical science so that even the most complex concepts were understood by all, including the patients.

Years later when I was his registrar, he came back to UCH in the evening after giving a lecture at the Royal Free Hospital. He had understood that it was to be for the medical students and prepared accordingly. When he arrived he found that he was to address an important audience of consultants and academics. There was little time to change the lecture or the slides. Afterwards he told me, he was showered with congratulations on "a most brilliant lecture." Clarity and simplicity are appreciated by all!

Lord Rosenheim, as President of the Royal College of Physicians. My first hero.

(Photo of his portrait, courtesy of the RCP)

To learn about surgery we became "dressers" attached to consultant surgeons. Ostensibly, as a dresser, one was responsible, with the nurses, for dressing the surgical wounds. In fact the experience was to teach us all a strict aseptic technique which was far stricter than the casual aseptic techniques that developed in the subsequent decades. In the 1950s it was hoped that antibiotics would deal with all infections. The emergence of the multiple resistant organisms has been the result. As student dressers we spent far too long acting as third assistants hanging on to retractors in the operating theatres. Several of our batch went green round the gills and keeled over at their first sight of blood. All in all, this time could have been better spent.

Doctor in the House

Round about this time I became involved, albeit in a minor way, with the film "Doctor in the House", and its sequelae. This was the first of a series of light-hearted films based on Richard Gordon's delightful books about the medical goings-on in a teaching hospital. Richard Gordon, a consultant anaesthetist in real life, based his books on his own experiences of working in hospitals.

The reason why I became involved was that Betty Box, the producer of the first film in the series, decided that University College Hospital, or to be more accurate, University College London, was an ideal location. Real live medical students were readily available for bit parts and as extras - hence my opportunity for fame on the big screen. Perhaps not surprisingly that fame did not materialise!

Betty Box had recruited a talented group of actors to take part. Dirk Bogarde (later Sir Dirk) was of course the star. He was suave, handsome but enigmatic and was the major box office attraction. With him were Donald Sinden (later Sir Donald), Donald Houston and Kenneth More who took the parts of extroverted, boisterous, nurse chasing, beer swilling, long-term medical students who were forever getting into scrapes. Hattie Jacques was everyone's idea of Matron and Sir Lancelot Spratt, played by James Robertson Justice, was the rumbustuous surgeon. It was rumoured that Sir Lancelot was based on George Brownlee, a larger than life New Zealander, who was a surgeon at the General Hospital Nottingham where I was to work later. Whenever I taught students by the bedside I was always mindful of Sir Lancelot's loud, gruesome and graphic description of what was going to happen to his patient on the operating table the next day.

"Don't worry, my man, you won't understand what I'm talking about" he reassured his terrified patient.

I was lucky in that I had to help coach Dirk Bogarde in the rugger skills that he was required to show. As a result I learned something about the man behind the mask. Of all the actors in the "Doctor films" he was the one who was the perfectionist. The others were "Hail fellow, well met " types for whom acting was fun, convivial and an easy way of earning a living. Dirk Bogarde was a loner for whom every performance had to be perfect, no matter how trivial it might be in relation to the rest of the film. Naturally I followed his subsequent career, his move to France and his brilliant performances in such films as "The Servant" and "Death in Venice." His 15 books glowing with self-analysis, humour and poignancy entranced me. Reading those books I was uncertain how much they were generated by his hyperactive imagination or his fantasies. He was nevertheless an extraordinarily talented man.

A Dabble in the Specialities

It is not sufficient for a medical student to have a firm grounding in general medicine and surgery. He or she must have a reasonable knowledge of the specialist subjects such as dermatology, ear, nose and throat, obstetrics and gynaecology, paediatrics, psychiatry and health care of the elderly. A few weeks in each speciality is scarcely enough before being thrust out into the real world. Each consultant regards his own speciality as essential and basic.

"What I teach is core knowledge," claimed one North American specialist possessively, "What the others teach is crap!"

A bewildering battery of new symptoms and physical signs assaulted our eyes, ears and brains.

Perhaps the most exciting, dramatic and frightening for the medical student was, and still is, obstetrics. In theory we were required to conduct at least twenty deliveries under supervision, before being let loose on the unsuspecting public as qualified doctors. Remember that in the post-war years many general practitioners delivered mothers in their homes and were not required to take any special postgraduate training. Because UCH did not have sufficient births in the London hospital we were sent out on the district with the midwives to bolster our theoretical knowledge. Some of us were sent to non-teaching hospitals.

I was lucky enough to go to Norwich where a kindly and maternal Senior Hospital Medical Officer took me under her wing and allowed me to get extra experience. But it wasn't too easy. I was issued with a rusty bike and expected to cycle over to the West Norwich Hospital when there was some action - which was most nights. We had no disasters but I don't think that I must have made much impression as I was never asked to give my Christian name to the child - more's the pity because the first child I delivered was to be called Clint!

Another period of banishment from the *Alma Mater* came when we were sent to Neasden Hospital, an antiquated isolation hospital in the Northern suburbs of London. Once through the gate we were incarcerated there for a fortnight, in the mistaken assumption that we would spread dreadful diseases if let out. In spite of our protestations that most of the diseases we would be in contact with had significant incubation periods, it was deemed safer for us to stay put. In defence of the Physician Superintendent's unreasonable argument for us staying put, it has to be said that, in the 1950s, there were many disagreeable and potentially fatal infectious diseases in the community. During our stay we saw poliomyelitis, diphtheria and meningococcal meningitis.

Dr Twining MacMath, the superintendent, took his responsibilities seriously, not the least being the moral welfare of the medical students foisted onto him. The nurses as well as the medical students were incarcerated in the hospital and, of course, a degree of fraternisation occurred. After a rather noisy party one evening we were reported for going into the nurses quarters - a dreadful sin - and were reprimanded in his office next day. The following day a pair of knickers fluttered from the hospital flagpole in defiance. This led to us being paraded before the Dean on our return to UCH. He rebuked us but, secretly I think, saw the funny side of it as he had had dealings with our Scottish Presbyterian superintendent before.

Alas, or is it alas, the archetypal medical figures of yesteryear no longer seem to exist. Perhaps as the years passed ex-students conjured up these characters and exaggerated their traits. I suspect that the curse of political correctness suppresses the eccentricities too. Nevertheless UCH in the 1950s spawned a few unforgettable consultants.

Whilst I was a student the veteran urological surgeon, F J F Barrington, (known to everyone as Snorker) was brought out of retirement to undertake a long-term locum. A bachelor with short-cropped grey hair and a permanently disapproving expression, he always reminded me of a cartoonist's caricature of a turn of the century Prussian officer. His conversation with patients was limited to a few grunts, and snorts. His teaching was limited to grudging axioms. His operating was always at breakneck speed and he was often peeling off his gloves at the end of an operation before we students had finished scrubbing up! In one of his not infrequent outbursts against the nursing staff in theatre he handed theatre sister the 12th rib which he had removed during a nephrectomy.

"For God's sake don't make any more women with it," he growled.

Lord Amulree was physician in charge of the Geriatric Unit for UCH at St Pancras Hospital. He was a tall benevolent silver-haired patrician with snaggly teeth and a formidable stutter. His father had been a member of Lloyd George's Cabinet in WWI and had been elevated to the peerage for his services to the war. His son, the Hon. Sholto Douglas, who later inherited the title, had been a popular Resident Medical Officer at UCH in his younger days and had joined the Department of Health in 1930 where he became interested in the problems of old age. He was appointed in 1949 to set up a Geriatric Department at UCH but, by that time "The Lord", as he was known to everyone, had forgotten all the day-to-day medicine required to look after patients. But he gathered round him a team of medical, nursing and administrative experts to provide care for the old and infirm. When I was a student these elderly patients were housed in two dismal draughty barns of wards with rows and rows of beds. By today's standards the set up would be regarded as degrading and impersonal, but geriatrics was then a Cinderella speciality and basic care was better than nothing.

The Lord was a kindly man who mixed easily with all classes of society though he was not averse to winding down the window of his Rolls Royce when he took us on domicilliary visits to patients' foul smelling and dismal homes, to give obstructing motorists and cyclists a volley of costermonger expletives. The stutter always disappeared on these occasions as he bellowed

"Out of the f…..g way." He always entertained royally at his home in Egerton Gardens when there always seemed to be ageing Russian princesses in attendance.

There were of course a number of committed Harley Street types who used their position on the staff at UCH as a status symbol. Kenneth Harris, the senior physician, referred to his brother as "also a famous physician" in a lecture. Modesty indeed! A few consultants were delivered at the front door of the hospital by their chauffeurs and, without looking or speaking, handed bowler hats and umbrellas into the care of the waiting and expectant porters. One morning a senior registrar asked an obsessional surgeon, a stickler for timekeeping, if he could have a few words before the start of the ward round.

"Certainly, Allen," said the chief, "let me just telephone my home to say that I will be a few minutes late for dinner."

I was a medical clerk on the neurological firm under Drs Blake Pritchard and William Gooddy. They couldn't stand each other and Sister always had to ensure that they weren't on the ward together. Blake was precise, slim, erect, grey haired with steel-rimmed spectacles. He was an excellent teacher, being able to mimic every neurological disorder himself. He had us round to his house near Harley Street once a fortnight where, over half a pint of beer, he would tax us with obscure philosophical arguments; he loved the sound of his own voice. Every few weeks he would invite the firm for the weekend to his country house in Godmanchester, driving there in his Bentley. When we arrived we discovered that we were an imported gardening squad, fed and watered accordingly! His colleague Bill Gooddy was young, suave and elegant with hair that was undoubtedly too long for a neurological consultant in those years. He had a double existence: in London during the week and in Sussex at the weekends where he was on the staff of local hospitals. Visitors were told "Please accept my domestic arrangements as you find them." For those days it was a racy lifestyle, which we all admired.

The End of the Beginning

As we entered our final year life became more serious. There had been class exams and prize exams at various times during the course but the final MB BS exams were concentrated in the last six weeks of the course. In those exams it was necessary to pass all the four disciplines: - pathology, medicine, surgery, and obstetrics and gynaecology. Failure in one or more of these subjects meant a further six months' study in the referred discipline, followed by a retake. This usually had financial implications, which worsened with each retake, with our grant-giving bodies,

One option, which many of us took, was to take the Conjoint Examination as an insurance policy. This was a professional based qualification offering Licentiateship of the Royal College of Physicians of London (LRCP) and Membership of the Royal College of Surgeons of England (MRCS). This was a costly business but it did mean that if one passed Conjoint, but failed in the MB

BS, it was possible to start work. Rumour had it that the Conjoint was easier than the MB BS. I now know that it provided welcome additional income for the Royal Colleges.

Being chronically hard up I borrowed some money and passed the Conjoint exam, first go. I was then comfortable in the knowledge that I would not have to suffer a period of unemployment. I learned subsequently that the numbers of letters after one's name, impressed the public rather than their importance!

But the real hurdle was still to come and this involved intensive revision with much burning of the midnight oil. As well as the written examinations there were clinicals where we were required to assess real patients. Many of these were drawn from panels of patients with chronic illnesses. Most were well used to the routine and welcomed the day out with, what was for some, fun in seeing the to and fro exchanges between students and the examiners. Many were old lags who were inclined to romanticise and to garble their histories. Many knew their diagnosis as did the gentleman I was given to examine.

"Now young man " he said confidentially "I have a syphilitic aortic aneurysm and you will be expected to demonstrate expansile pulsation over the chest and to hear an aortic diastolic murmur." Cheered and relieved I noted what he had said and carefully confirmed the physical signs in the heart. Later when my interrogation about the case began my spirits were to sink.

"I know that Mr Brown will have told you the diagnosis" said my examiner "Let's talk about the changes you will have found in his legs."

Enormous effort and discussion has gone into the validity of qualifying clinical examinations in medicine the last 20 or 30 years. This form of assessment is, of course, subjective and attempts are being made to produce (using the modern jargon) a level playing field. Now with a lifetime of experience behind me, I believe that two skills must be tested before students can be allowed to call themselves doctors.

Firstly, they must be able to communicate with their patients, to take an accurate history of the condition and to perform a careful clinical examination. Talking to patients is an essential skill that some never master in a lifetime. How dreadful to hear from a patient,

"I knew he must be an important specialist because he wouldn't let me talk to him."

Doctors have to be crystal clear that they understand what patients really mean. The use of terms such as dizziness, palpitations and blackouts mean different things to different people; their precise meaning has to be ferreted out. Many patients do not understand what is meant when asked about eructation, expectoration or passing flatus. Words like belch/burp, spit or fart will often bring a, "Now I know what you mean doctor," smile to the patient's face.

Secondly, newly qualified doctors need to be safe and to show common sense. Not every child with a fever needs to be given antibiotics, not every lass with indigestion needs immediate endoscopy and not every forgetful 85-year-old needs a brain scan. But every middle-aged man with recent onset severe central chest pain needs urgent admission to hospital for assessment as a possible case of myocardial infarction.

But I am wandering. I need to return to my own experience of trying to get my feet on to the first rung of the professional ladder. After our written exams, vivas and clinicals there were some anxious days before, on the appointed date, the results of the examinations in medicine for the whole of the University of London were posted on the railings of Senate House. It was an apprehensive crowd, which had gathered, ten or twelve deep. We all chattered nervously. Then the porter arrived with the lists. A surge forward and those patiently waiting in the front searched frantically for their own and other familiar names. I was well to the back but John Dalton, my own lookout close to the front, looked back for familiar faces. He spotted me, and raised his thumb. That sign was enough. I was through.

Chapter 4

A Clinical Apprentice

The paper qualifications, exciting as they were, did no more than unlock the door to the next stage of learning my trade. I was to become a clinical apprentice and for my first year, the pre-registration year, I would technically be on probation before the General Medical Council (GMC) let me loose on the public at large.

My immediate ambition on qualifying was to get Professor Max Rosenheim's house physician post. This was the "blue ribbon" pre-registration job at UCH, which was strenuously contested, so much so that a mini-examination and interview was organised for the several applicants. Accordingly I put my name down and found myself in the last two, only to be beaten at the post by the better man, my good friend Clifford Floyd. This was a bitter disappointment at the time as I had set my heart on the job. I was destined to wait another five years before I returned to UCH as Max's registrar.

Nottingham Beckons

Having failed to get the plum UCH job I didn't fancy any of the others that were available. What to do? There was a surfeit of newly qualified doctors waiting for work on the market. So I did what everyone did. I scoured the advertisement columns of the British Medical Journal for vacancies. One job that caught my eye was a house-surgeon's post at the General Hospital, Nottingham. Well, for a start I knew Nottingham from my days as an evacuee. It had the reputation of being a "warts and all" city with a busy industrial base built on Raleigh cycles, Players cigarettes, a lace market, Boots the Chemists and coal mines to the north of the city. For entertainment there were two theatres, two football teams and, for me, the attraction of Trent Bridge, a cricket ground, second only to Lords as a first class venue.

At that time the University of Nottingham had no intention of setting up its own medical school. D.H. Lawrence, one of Nottingham's most famous sons, obviously didn't think too much of his home town and sneered at its academic aspirations: -

In Nottingham, that dismal town,
Where I went to school and college,
They've built a new University
For a new dispensation of Knowledge

He could have been better disposed to the University because by the end of the 20th Century it was one of the most rapidly expanding and successful educational institutions in the UK. Nevertheless even at that time I was certain I would get an abundance of medical experience working in a large hospital at the hub of England. So in went my application.

A few days later I was walking up Park Row from the City Square for an interview. The wards of General Hospital Nottingham scrambled up the hill to the huge iron gates enclosing the hospital courtyard flanked by the original hospital buildings and entrance hall. The courtyard was obviously the hub of hospital activity with nurses, doctors and porters scurrying backwards and forwards and ambulances flying in to unload casualties into the overcrowded Accident and Emergency Dept. The hospital first opened its doors to patients in 1782 and contemporary drawings show cattle grazing peacefully on the front prospect and open fields all around (see colour photos: fig 1). The various departments such as Outpatients, Pay Bed Wing, the Eye Hospital, Pathology and Radiotherapy metastasised from the courtyard area, not far from where Charles II had raised his standard in 1660.

A timid, underweight secretary took me to the offices; I quickly realised that I was the only candidate invited for interview. I wasn't sure whether this was a good thing or bad.

The General Hospital Nottingham, in the year of its foundation 1782

We sat in the Board Room - a room of dark brown solemnity with a long highly polished table, uncomfortable high backed chairs, and panelled walls decorated with faded sepia photographs of the great benefactors of the past. Sir Charles Seely, William and John Player, Sir Louis Pearson, and Sir Thomas Shipstone, all stern, brooding and generously moustachioed, looked down on me.

50

There were more recent photographs of distinguished physicians and surgeons, Dr Frank Jacob, Mr W F Neil, the two Ransoms, father and son, Mr A R Anderson and Mr R G Hogarth. The room smelt of floor polish and disinfectant. My interrogators were my future chief, Mr J F Sheehan FRCS Ed, Dr Sparks, Chairman of the Medical Committee and Miss Reynolds who with her boss, Mr H M Stanley, the hospital secretary, ran the hospital. Two administrators were enough then!

I was to see much of John (Joe) Sheehan in the next six months and indeed in the next thirty years. He was a tall, broad shouldered, handsome Irishman with a Ronald Coleman moustache and distinguished crinkly grey hair. For such an impressive looking man he spoke quietly, hesitantly and, I thought, somewhat nervously. But I warmed to him. He had read my C.V. carefully and was prepared to talk about the job in detail. At the end of the interview he offered me the post, shook my hand, and thanked me for coming. I was glad to get the job.

I was to learn later that John Sheehan had lived and worked under the influence of the General Hospital since 1933, except for four years' war service in India as a Lt Colonel in the RAMC. After the war, as well as working as a consultant surgeon, he was able to develop his sporting skills as golf captain of Nottinghamshire, a fearless rally driver, a racehorse owner and a greyhound trainer.

Nose to the Grindstone

Within a few hours of starting work in Nottingham I realised that the General Hospital was not just a hundred and twenty miles from University College Hospital London. It was a whole world away! "The General" as it was known in the town was a frantically busy hospital, bursting with energy and with opportunities galore for training and experience. My year there as house surgeon and house physician was to prove the most formative of my life and I was to embark on a terrifyingly steep learning curve. This did not mean necessarily that it was formal training. It was a 24-hour day, seven-days a week clinical apprenticeship.

The wards on which I worked, Anderson and Two Top, were decidedly old fashioned. Anderson ward, the male ward was the floor of a magnificent Victorian round ward building, the Jubilee Wing. The centre of the ward was occupied by a fireplace, in which there was always a coal fire in the colder months. The Sisters, both unmarried, had sitting rooms on the wards and were, for much of the 24 hours of the day, available to deal with the problems that arose even when they were off duty. And, in those days, the Ward Sisters really were in charge of the wards. There was another junior consultant on the firm, who had a handful of beds, a senior registrar, of whom we had just a quarter share of his time and a senior house officer who was my immediate superior and soul mate. This small group completed the medical workforce on the firm.

Ted Oliver, the senior registrar carried an enormous workload. He was an uncomplicated Geordie (Cantab. and Barts) who had to carry out any surgical procedure necessary - and he did, because he was the only senior surgical registrar in the hospital. Later he was appointed Consultant Surgeon to the City Hospital. Sadly he died prematurely as a result of being a heavy smoker. But those earlier years of unremitting grind had taken their toll on his health. The Senior House Officer E W (Eddie) Carr was to become a valued colleague and lifelong friend. He was a slim, slow speaking, hatchet-faced Australian from Sydney with a burning ambition to do well in surgery. Like many Australians he spoke his mind and had an explosive temper when others failed to come up to his high standards. After he had been on the firm for a few weeks, he modestly let slip the fact that he had won gold medals for the individual 400m and the 400m relay in the Commonwealth Games in Auckland in 1952 and had competed in the 1954 Helsinki Olympics.

My job was to admit all the patients coming into the wards, routine list cases and emergencies and to assist in theatre and outpatients. It really was a full time job, on call all the time except for one weekend off in six and one evening off each week. One of the problems was getting a hair cut! In theory there was the problem of getting to the bank but as there was never time to spend money it didn't matter. There were no mobile phones, text messages, or even bleeps. Contact was made by sets of lights, similar to traffic lights, in all the rooms, corridors and wards. I remember my combination to this day - flashing red and green. Fifty years ago they were like the modern CCTV systems; you couldn't get away from them. One evening during dinner, after being relentlessly pursued by them all day, the duty resident anaesthetist bad-temperedly threw his shoe at the lights in our residents' dining room, smashing them completely. Sadly they were repaired by next morning.

Being a swift and technically correct surgeon, Joe Sheehan could get through long and difficult lists with ease. A typical list starting on Monday morning at 8.30 would consist of two partial throidectomies, two gastrectomies, two hernias and varicose veins - all finished by 1.30 pm in time for 2 pm outpatients. It all went slickly, there was even time for coffee whilst Ken Crawford, a mercurial Scottish anaesthetist was preparing the next case.

The firm was "on take" one week in four when we were responsible for the care of all the surgical emergencies that were admitted. It was physically and mentally exhausting. Not the least of the problems was finding beds for the patients as they came in. Beds had to be found because there was no St. Elsewhere in Nottingham. The City hospital in the 50s concentrated mainly on cold surgery. Having seen only one case of acute appendicitis at UCH as a student, I saw three on my first take-in day. The firm SHO and I started the evening emergency list in theatres when the day's routine work ended, usually finishing about midnight. This had its compensations because one of the kitchen staff would always produce bacon and eggs to refuel us before we dropped into bed. If the kitchen staff weren't there, a sympathetic night nurse would produce poached eggs on toast in the ward kitchen. Many a pact for life started on a poached egg!

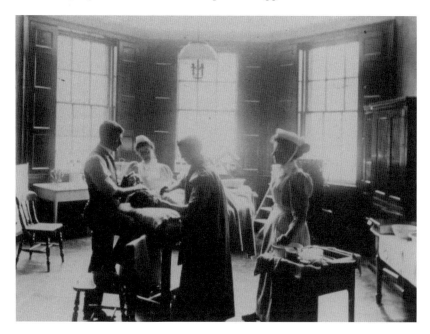

Shipstone Theatre General Hospital
c 1890. It was still being used for surgery in the 1950s

We certainly saw a spectacular range of emergencies. Many were rushed in through Casualty: intestinal obstruction, perforated peptic ulcers, acute pancreatitis and peritonitis to mention just a few of the life threatening emergencies. As a student I was taught to listen carefully to the patient's symptoms. This indeed was usually true and I taught it to generations of my own students in later years.

Sometimes though you couldn't believe everything that you were told. One summer's evening a young schoolboy was admitted claiming that he had been bitten by a snake. On further questioning he hadn't actually seen the snake but felt a sharp pain when he thrust his arm into a hedge bottom to retrieve a cricket ball. There was indeed a puncture wound but no local swelling or generalised upset. Fortunately we took an X-Ray and later that evening were able to extract a 6 inches-long sliver of Perspex that had pierced the skin and slipped up in the subcutaneous space. Some snake!

Some of the stories were even more far fetched. A slightly inebriated middle-aged lady attended Casualty late at night asking if we would remove the end of a cucumber from her vagina. Her story was that she had tripped and fallen in the greengrocer's that afternoon. We asked no further questions.

In spite of long hours, hard work and a poor salary the resident doctors had one enormous benefit denied to the modern junior doctor working a shift system. The doctors at the General had a large house to themselves in the hospital grounds. There we each had a room, with communal lounge, kitchen, and dining room and were looked after by our own housekeeper and a staff of maids. This house, Broxtowe House, was our home. There we lived as a family and enjoyed our life together. On Christmas Eve we had a rumbustuous party which left Broxtowe a complete shambles on Christmas morning. The tyrannical Home Sister nominally in charge of the residency was incandescent and declared that she would summon the House Governor to survey the damage. A working party was hastily arranged amongst the doctors. When the inspecting party arrived the whole place was immaculate with, as crowning glory, a huge open family bible at the senior resident's place!

There was always an excuse for a party, usually boozy and smoochy, but sometimes fairly noisy. From time to time our neighbours in the Ropewalk some 50 yards away complained to the police about the commotion. Some of the young policemen were well known to us from their visits to the ward and casualty. After formally telling us of the complaints they often joined in the fun.

A Slower Tempo

After six months it was time to switch to being a house physician. Normally this meant going through all the rigmarole of applying for advertised jobs elsewhere. Working on the principle that the devil you know is better than the devil you don't know, I moved over, on the nod, to the medical side to work for Dr Bill Whimster. He was a plump, jolly Mr Pickwick sort of a man with a wide grasp of the medical problems facing doctors and their patients in Middle England. He loved chattering to us and to the patients and always did one of his ward rounds on Sunday morning. It was rumoured that his wife encouraged him to do this to get him from under her feet whilst she cooked the Sunday dinner. I often wondered if he realised that his Senior Registrar stayed for the ward round and then drove off to his home in Bridlington, only to return to Nottingham in the early hours of Monday after snatching a few hours with his family.

The tempo of work on the medical side was slower and I was glad to get the chance to consolidate my practical knowledge with some theory. Our therapeutic armamentarium was relatively limited. For example, there was little to be done for coronary thromboses except bed rest, pain relief and other supportive therapies. Malignancies such as those of the bronchus and stomach were only occasionally cured by surgery. Chemotherapy was restricted to a few rare malignancies. Most cancers were regarded as a death sentence More could be done for the infections. Antibiotics, arriving on the scene after WWII, were regarded as miracle cures by the public but their use was limited and we were well aware of the potential problems of drug resistance. Now infection with MRSA threatens every surgical procedure. Little could be done for the common problems of osteo and rheumatoid arthritis and joint surgery was very much in its infancy.

Tuberculosis had been rampant during the first half of the 20th Century and every town throughout the land had its sanatorium. By the late 50s it began to look as though we were going to eliminate the scourge of tuberculosis in the UK. Streptomycin, the first drug to treat it effectively, had been introduced during my early days as a student. Until then the only cure was bed rest in a sanatorium, preferably at high altitude, fresh air, and collapse of the affected lung with an artificial pneumothorax. Many patients slept in the open air on ward balconies. Sadly, events have overtaken us, as they have a habit of doing, and tuberculosis is undergoing a resurgence with the world epidemic of Acquired Immune Deficiency Syndrome (AIDS).

However after a year of being bombarded with clinical experience I felt that I could recognise and deal with most common problems. I was deemed fit by the GMC to become a fully registered medical practitioner. But I was still a very raw clinical apprentice. Legally we were considered sufficiently well trained to look after patients without supervision but our clinical apprenticeship was without formal or structured education. Many of my contemporaries had narrow experience in their pre-registration year. It was possible to spend six months in an ENT surgical post and six months in dermatology as a medical post and to become fully registered without any exposure to more general surgery and medicine. At Nottingham, as with similar non-teaching hospitals, we had far too much responsibility for our level of training and were left on our own to get on with things. Thankfully the experienced sisters who ran the wards were generous, and usually tactful, in their help.

The hours for all of us were long and time off short. Many were expected to spend every minute of the day, every day of the week and every week of their six months' post in the hospitals. There were still domineering, bullying and autocratic bosses who insisted on this. One of my friends working at another hospital, asked for the weekend off to be best man at his brother's wedding.

"Certainly" agreed his chief "but don't bother to report back for work on the Monday because you will be sacked."

This did not mean that the majority of consultants behaved in this autocratic way. Many remembered the hard times that they themselves had, working for several years, between the wars, as resident house physicians and surgeons. Marriage was incompatible with their early careers in hospital. Joe Sheehan told the story of one house surgeon. A very anxious night sister had sent a message by porter late at night to his bedroom (no phones then of course) to tell him that one of his patients had not passed water since early morning. Awakened from his deep and much needed sleep he replied: "Tell sister, neither have I." He did, in fact, get up to relieve the patient as well as himself.

With my own foot firmly on the first rung of the professional ladder I was deemed ready to move again.

Chapter 5

Her Majesty Calls

I count myself lucky that I was not required to serve as a combatant in the Forces. Many of my generation had fathers and mothers, uncles and aunts, older brothers and cousins who served through WWII. Many of them did not return. During our formative years we children all had heard first-hand stories of the horrors of that war. A neighbour in Bushey survived a Japanese Prisoner of War camp in Burma. He described the degradation and torture meted out to British and Australian soldiers, cachectic and weak from chronic starvation. A family friend spoke of the slaughter on the Normandy beaches after D-Day when the blown out brains and skull of a comrade had splattered his face. A medical colleague in the vanguard of British troops entering Belsen recounted vividly his impressions on entering the camp. The stench of death had been overwhelming from two or three miles out. In the camp the corpses were piled in stacks like the sleepers alongside a railtrack, some were rotting others nearly mummified. And the Germans living in nearby villages claimed that they knew nothing!

We, as National Servicemen, were no more than softies in a peacetime army.

I was called up on 3rd September 1956 with a batch of 50 or so other young doctors. We had found ourselves in the Army by a process of exclusion! The RAF had limited postings and the Navy decreed that they would only accept those who would sign on for a three year short service commission. Free railway travel warrants had been issued - but just for one way - and we had been told to report to Aldershot Station where we would be collected. As we assembled in the forecourt of Aldershot Station, I looked round at my companions for the next few weeks. Some were immaculately dressed, smart suits and waistcoats, stiff collars, club ties, confident types with public school accents - typical St Thomas's I thought. Others had already ganged up together, having hailed each other in Glaswegian accents. A Mancunian mafia muttered disconsolately amongst themselves. A Welshman with jet black curly hair, St Mary's Hospital no doubt, was talking rugby with a bullock of a man with a squat neck and crumpled ears, London Hospital front row I guessed. Three longhaired, round shouldered, studious, bespectacled types talked medicine enthusiastically.

"I bet the others think that they are the brainy ones from UCH," I said to myself. But I knew they weren't because I was and I didn't recognise them!

Out of this confused miscellany emerged a familiar face. He extended his hand.

"Trevor Tiplady," he said, "I know you, don't I?" He was right. We had met before, but the place and time eluded me, as with him. He had qualified at King's College Hospital but, like me, could not remember when our paths had crossed. But being Ts (Tiplady and Toghill) we were thrown together for our so-called military training - my first bonus for National Service. He later became a distinguished general practitioner in Wiltshire and we were to see much of each other in the years to come. After fifty years of friendship we still cannot remember how we met.

The lorries sent to meet us were filled. They coughed and spluttered into action and whined off into the Hampshire countryside to the Royal Army Medical Corps (RAMC) Depot at Crookham, where those expected to convert us into proper soldiers awaited our pleasure.

It soon became obvious that there were several categories amongst us. There were those who were determined to hate the Army from Day 1, those who were looking for a new challenge in life and who were anxious to get the most out of their experience and others who resented the intrusion into the course of their professional lives. Some wanted to use the two years as a breathing space to decide what they wanted to do with their careers. I fell into the last group.

We youthful doctors were an awkward and somewhat embarrassing tribe. The Army wanted us for our knowledge and to undertake skilled work, which could not be delegated to unqualified regular soldiers. At the same time it had to instil into us some knowledge of how the Armed Forces were run and offer us some basic training. Without actually saying so, the regulars had to ensure that we would not let down the officer cadre. They had to teach us some discipline but yet at the same time they couldn't discipline us. An uneasy compromise was reached. As one senior NCO explained on our first day

"We have a unique system here, gentlemen. I call you Sir, and you call me Sir. The only difference is that you mean it." Over the next few weeks we learned that he did mean what he said.

For many of us Army life was not unfamiliar. Most public and independent schools had had their Combined Cadet Forces and, with WWII in recent memory, most of us had joined. Our drills on the parade ground converted us from a shambling mongrelist mélange to an untidy marching mob; but at least we moved in the correct direction and could salute anything that saluted us. Some of us felt quite smart with our peaked caps, swagger sticks, shoulder pips and shiny boots. A few found it impossible to march co-ordinating their limbs, always advancing the same arm and leg together. I wonder where the precise location of the neurological lesion is? Another with an apparent dressing dyspraxia always wore his gaiters with the straps on the inside. The Commanding Officer nearly had an apoplectic fit when he saw him incorrectly dressed on our passing out parade.

Much of the training was to familiarise us with military medical documentation and to ensure that we understood the deployment of medical services in the field. The PULHEEMS system had been in use for many years and was shorthand for Physique, Upper limb, Lower limb, Hearing, Eye, Ear, Mental State and Skin. Each component was allocated a number from 1 to 8. 8 was the worst and was equated with rejection on medical grounds. Even in peacetime British Forces were spread far and wide over parts of the globe and it was essential for us to brush up our theoretical knowledge of tropical diseases. So, a spell at the RAMC College at Millbank was essential. Our clinical instructors were excellent, well-informed and able clinicians. A few of the long serving administrative officers there were past their "sell-by dates." Many appeared to have become glued into the capacious leather armchairs in the Officers' Mess. With a whisky alongside, The Times in front of them, and the heads of dead animals glowering down from the brown panelled walls, they were immune to our comings and goings.

"Some of us felt quite smart with peaked caps, swagger sticks, shoulder pips and shiny boots"

Though we were involved with learning how to be medical officers in the Army much was happening in the world around us. After three spells as Foreign Secretary (1935-38, 1940-45 and 1951-55) Anthony Eden had eventually replaced the ageing Winston Churchill as Prime Minister. The longest wait in modern history for the post of Prime Minister had soured the young, elegant, suave and clever politician of the pre-war and wartime years. His health had suffered too. In 1953 he had undergone a gall bladder operation. Rumour had it amongst the medical fraternity that his common bile duct had been ligated by mistake. As a result he had to travel to Boston USA, where they were used to dealing with botched-up surgery for similar bile duct problems. By the time he became Prime Minister he was tetchy, over-sensitive, conceited and indecisive. Under his leadership Britain joined France and Israel in attempting to prevent General Nasser from nationalising the Suez Canal. Suddenly a military confrontation loomed and the Forces were put on the alert. Those of us who had become temporary soldiers were certainly bewildered and confused by what was going on. Around us reservists were being called up and it seemed clear that this was a war that was to be fought by National Servicemen as well as regulars.

We raw, newly recruited medical officers were assembled at the Depot in readiness for transfer to Cyprus and then on to Suez. Our inoculations for overseas duties were quickly brought up to date. The injection techniques of those days were unbelievably dangerous. It was amazing that no diseases were transmitted. We formed a circle with hands on hips and moved in a clockwise direction with an MO on the outside of the ring giving injections and an orderly on the inside vaccinating. I heard of one group of recruits dealt with in this way which went round twice and all had a double dose. The risk of cross infection was high, as, although each had a clean needle, the vaccine was from a huge common syringe. Lightweight tropical kit was issued; tropical shorts weren't particularly glamorous extending to below knee level.

As quickly as it had blown up this unexpected and unpredicted war was over. No one could have called it gunboat diplomacy. The battle, whilst it lasted was fierce. Our colleagues who were actually involved with the fighting told us that the military confrontation was intense and whole tracts of Alexandria had been flattened by heavy bombardment. My long-felt cynicism for politicians was strengthened when we heard on the news that, "the damage to civilian property was minimal."

So my chance of fighting for the old country had gone. I wasn't sorry as Britain was acting very much against world opinion. The United Nations had intervened in this fiasco and Anthony Eden was left with egg on his face. From then on he was a broken man. He continued to have recurrent episodes of ascending cholangitis following his earlier surgery and remained in poor health. He resigned in 1957 and was replaced by Harold Macmillan.

A Peacetime Doctor in the Army

"Thank God that is over" remarked one regular officer from the RAMC about the Suez crisis- "Now we can get back to some proper soldiering." Perhaps this was how Army life was viewed by some.

We new recruits found ourselves posted to all parts of the globe. I never really worked out the logic of these postings though there were clues. One of my ex-UCH colleagues had, at an early stage, demonstrated his contempt for everything in khaki, including the commanding officer. He was rewarded with a posting to Aden, not the most salubrious of places. There he stewed and festered for two unhappy years. I met him on his demobilisation when he confessed that he had not passed a solid stool in the whole of his two years there!

I made a serious mistake when we were interviewed for our postings. I fancied East Africa but there were limited opportunities. Foolishly I had entered under "Additional Points" the fact that I had played cricket for United Hospitals and had captained my Medical School.

"Ah," exclaimed the Jolly Hockey Sticks Colonel, "just the man to bolster the RAMC team next season. You'll get all the sport you want as MO in-charge at Mons Officer Cadet School in Aldershot." My heart sank. That was it, no thought of my professional qualifications - just good on the sports field. Mons was to prove a mixed blessing!

It was clear when I arrived there that this was no run of the mill posting. Firstly, Mons valued their MO and were going to look after him; secondly this posting seemed to be a prestigious one and thirdly I would be living life on a social scale well above that which was familiar to me. Mons was the School at which National Servicemen, who had been identified as potential officers, were trained and commissioned as 2nd Lieutenants. A taste of what was to come was when I arrived by taxi on my first day. The Mess Officer who doubled up as Sports Officer greeted me. I noted the rhinophymic nose, bristling military moustache and whiff of alcohol on his breath.

"Delighted to see you," he exclaimed. "We'll send a driver to collect your kit from the Station." I had to explain that the cases I carried contained all that I had in the world including my Army uniform. I later learned that many of the officers brought everything except the kitchen sink, including several sets of uniforms, dogs, and horses. My heart sank on looking round the Officers' Mess; the Mess Bills would be enormous.

Mons OCS was responsible for training the cavalry and artillery Officer Cadets whereas the other OCS at Eaton Hall, near Chester, dealt with the PBI (poor bloody infantry) cadets. This meant that, broadly speaking, there were two groups of officer instructors at Mons: the highly professional and intelligent gunners (the artillery) and the well to do cavalry officers almost exclusively from privileged regiments. Some of these cavalry officers were a bit dim. They came mostly from wealthy families and used a spell in the army as a comfortable way of filling in time before marrying, running their estates, or inheriting their titles. After graduating from Sandhurst they had moved on to the family regiment which ensured that they would live as comfortable a life as possible in spite of the Army. Some left Mons on a Thursday evening and returned late Monday, in time for Mess Dinner when their braying laughter reverberated through the building. War, if it came along was a decidedly unwelcome intrusion to them. The remaining officers made up the administrative staff - the padres, education officers, catering, mechanical and electrical engineers. I was one of these, known to everyone as Doc.

In contrast the life of the Officer Cadets was tough. The course was both physically and mentally demanding and some were disappointed to be RTU-ed (Returned to Unit) without their commissions. Those who completed the course and passed out from Mons as 2nd Lieutenants were of the highest quality. This was not surprising, as they were the cream of British National servicemen. Before I arrived three had died from heat stroke during a forced march. As a result fitness training had been tempered and discipline somewhat moderated.

Much of their training was supervised by the RSM and senior NCOs from a wide range of regiments who were of high quality. The RSM was a much-revered figure by both Cadets and Officers. He had followed in the mould of such legendary characters as RSM Brittain. When Brittain was RSM at Sandhurst his voice was heard bawling at Officer Cadet Hussein (King Hussein of Jordan)

"Mr Hussein, Sir, you are quite the idlest King I have ever drilled on this parade ground."

My job at Mons was termed "General Duties Medical Officer." The duties were not onerous. I was required to conduct a sick parade each morning for the cadets and camp staff at 8 am, to deal with accidents and injuries, to arrange inoculations and vaccinations and to give lectures on hygiene topics including sexually transmitted diseases. The local MOs ran a rota for evening and night work but the Cambridge Military Hospital was nearby in Aldershot and it dealt with anything other than the most basic problems. Later in my stay at Mons I was appointed an additional surgical officer at the Cambridge and spent my afternoons learning some basic orthopaedics.

I quickly found myself playing rugger and cricket for Mons and, on the strength of a reduction of a dislocated shoulder on the field, became an expert on sports injuries. As expected I found my way into the RAMC cricket team but didn't do my career much good by running out my Colonel in the second over on an easy wicket, during the annual match against the chaplains. My fellow officers at Mons were, on the whole, kind, tolerant and friendly and taught me to shoot and how to take part in fire drill on the artillery ranges in Wales. The monotony of Aldershot was broken by spells accompanying the Officer Cadets on training in Germany. We were then with the British Army of Occupation of the Rhine (BAOR). As a treat (unofficially) they showed me how to drive a tank. When you are inside a tank yourself you realise the murderous potential of a lump of shrapnel hurtling round inside the turret.

As an MO, you see how unforeseen incidents can become disastrous fatalities within seconds. The first was at a sewage works near my medical centre. One of the workmen stepped over a shaft rotating a few inches above the ground. The corner of his raincoat touched the shaft and within moments had wound itself round the shaft dragging his body under and around it. Before any help could be summoned his trunk had been flattened as under a steamroller. He was dead when I arrived moments later. The second was when an army truck backed over a large cardboard box in the road outside married quarters. Unknown to the driver a child was hiding inside.

I found myself in serious trouble over a chance remark to a new recruit, not an officer cadet I hasten to say, who was attending for a routine medical. I noticed that one arm was significantly shorter than the other.

"However did they let you into the Army with a short arm?" I exclaimed. I thought nothing more of it until a few weeks later I had an irate summons to my Assistant Director of Medical Services who was having to deal with a Ministerial Enquiry! Apparently the lad's father had written to his MP reporting my remarks and a question was to be asked in the House.

"For God's sake think before you make remarks like that in the future," he blustered. I heard no more of it. Shortly afterwards every MO in the UK received a memo reminding them not to convey potentially sensitive information to soldiers without permission - even if it might be true!

What to do next?

By 1958 Britons were able to settle into an uneasy peacetime existence with a more comfortable life style. True the Cold War was a reality with the Eastern Bloc, an unknown quantity dominated by Russia. I had been able to visit Europe and go to the World Fair in Brussels where we all gazed in awe at the Sputnik, the first man carrying satellite. It focussed minds on how the social inequalities of a Communist State could run in parallel with their highly developed scientific technology.

Though claimed to be the envy of the world the NHS was struggling. The initial argument that universal free preventative health care might reduce the need for expensive treatment was badly flawed. The demands on the service were growing faster than what was available. Drugs and technical advances were proving extremely expensive. The fabric of our hospitals was deteriorating and little new was being built. We were short of nurses, we were short of doctors and the service was short of money.

It was against this background that I had to decide my own future in the profession. Many friends and colleagues looked to greener pastures on the other side of the fence. The fence, on this occasion, was the Atlantic. Canada was the favoured option where salaries were higher and the life style better. And it was still part of the old British Empire. The USA was too brash, too commercial and too vulgar for many. Many saw an attractive future in South Africa where its pleasant climate, sporting environment and a comfortable life had much to commend it. The spectre of apartheid was still in the shadows. Looking at the lists at our reunions 50 years later, well over a third of those young men and women who joined as medical students with us in 1950 had emigrated, never to return to the old country. Being an only son, I felt that I had family responsibilities and elected to stay in England.

I favoured going into general practice somewhere in middle England. So with my National Service out of the way, I made a positive decision to look first for an obstetrics post and then to enter General Practice.

Chapter 6

Events Overtake Me

Bawling Babies and Pregnant Mums

If you cross York Road from what used to be the headquarters of London County Council you will find a neglected old building with a surprisingly impressive portico. The engraved stone over the door proudly announces "The General Lying-In Hospital." Sadly it has fallen from grace but from 1830, when it opened and for much of the 20th Century, it served as an independent maternity hospital for the poor of Lambeth and the surrounding area. It was concerned with the welfare of women and the frequently fatal conditions of childbirth in the urban slums. It was also well known for its liberal treatment in giving shelter to unmarried mothers.

After the inception of the NHS it was taken under the wing of St Thomas's Hospital which used it as an additional obstetric unit until 1971. It was then deemed unsafe to practice obstetrics as an isolated unit without supporting services. Since early 2003, when it was renovated, it has housed the Trust's Training and Development and Procurement Departments.

It was to the General Lying-in Hospital that I came in 1958 to learn some obstetrics prior to entering general practice. That was the plan at least. At that time much home midwifery was carried out by family doctors and a good grounding in the speciality was regarded as a material advantage. Junior hospital posts in obstetrics were difficult to come by and preference was given to those who wished to enter obstetrics and gynaecology for a career. Though attached to St Thomas's, the General Lying-in Hospital liked to exert its independence and tended to appoint housemen from outside, particularly those who had completed National Service. I learned later that I had got the job there because my colonel in the RAMC had given me a good reference, emphasising that I was a good cricketer. I'm not sure that those skills would be helpful in the York Road. Once more I was being appointed to a post on false pretences!

The two housemen at the General Lying-in Hospital were answerable to four consultants and overseen by the friendly and helpful obstetric registrar from St Thomas's, Peter Huntingford. He was later to become a distinguished professor at St Mary's Hospital, London and advisor to the S E Asia World Health Organisation. We residents were quaintly named obstetric house physicians rather than house surgeons, as would be the case everywhere else. This was, I imagine, to emphasise that at the Lying- In the doctors supervised the medical care of the mums and the midwives concentrated on natural childbirth. We house physicians were the only two males in an establishment of fifty or sixty women - sisters, midwives, trainee midwives and nurses. "Two rams in a flock of eager, willing sheep," as the outspoken senior surgeon put it.

In many ways this determined little hospital was steeped in the traditions of British midwifery and every effort was made to support the mothers in labour and encourage them to deliver "*per via naturalis.*" This did not mean that the obstetrics was old fashioned but the hospital regarded the delivery of babies primarily as a midwife's job. The doctors were there to deal with complications. There were some interesting relics. In the basement there was still a "birthing chair" i.e. a large wooden arm chair with a hole in the seat through which the sitting mother delivered her baby; the midwife conducted the delivery looking upwards from below the seat. I have to admit that I never saw this piece of archaic apparatus used! In the cellars there were temperature charts from the early 1900s showing hectic puerperal fevers, with arrows at the height of the fevers, labelled "Visitors." Clearly the excitement produced by visitors was regarded as being more pyrogenic than infection with the Streptococcus!

We house physicians actually lived most of our lives on the wards. My bedroom was next to a nursery full of bawling babies - not conducive to sleep when you had been on duty the previous day and night. We did alternate nights and alternate weekends for the whole of the six months. This was of course in addition to the day job of clinics, ward rounds and writing discharge summaries. Most nights on duty involved at least one call for stitching, forceps delivery or assessment of progress of labour. The monitoring of childbirth was mainly by eyes, hands and stethoscope; the only other help was the foetal heart rate chart. How different it is now when everything that is measurable is monitored.

We learned quickly the run of the mill routines and also how to deal with the commoner complications - the management of antepartum haemorrhage, low forceps deliveries, suturing, breech delivery and treatment of retained placenta. There was always help available within minutes, usually Peter Huntingford from the main hospital, but at times it was scary. One knew how quickly a baby's life might be lost.

Living in such an environment was highly detrimental to any social life. If one took a nurse out for the evening, the whole hospital knew about it next morning. If one invited a girl friend to one's room, sister in the adjacent office or baby ward, would know and would invariably find an excuse to knock on the door with an unnecessary query.

It was not yet the swinging sixties in London. but the war was receding into the background and life was a good deal more comfortable for ordinary families. Harold Macmillan's Conservative Party had been returned with a large majority. He was then "Supermac". Restaurants were beginning to flourish and it was possible, for even an impecunious houseman, to dine out at a smart venue. Albert's in Beek Street was my favourite at the time. We could gawk at all the tennis stars who were regular customers there. The production of a signed photograph to decorate the wall would pay the price of their meals.

At last Londoners were beginning to enjoy themselves. Cliff Richards had a zingy best seller with "Livin' Doll" and from the States "Some like it Hot" was a box office hit. Duty free wine and spirits were allowed for travellers abroad and the £500 Mini was launched.

A substitute form of entertainment, which aggravated my already growing cynicism for politics, was to walk over to the House of Commons in the evenings to listen to and watch the debates. I soon came to recognise the various characters on both sides of the House. It has to be remembered that there were no television cameras in the Chamber then. Political figures were less easily recognised than they are today. At my first visit I was utterly astonished by the scene. Twenty or thirty MPs lounged around; talking amongst themselves, surrounded by discarded papers and apparently paying no attention to the Member who was earnestly addressing them. When the division bell rang the whole place burst into activity with the great, the not so great, and the good and the not so good scrambling into place ready to vote. In spite of his immense experience as a politician, Harold Macmillan always struck me as being something of a dilettante with his coterie of colleagues; no more than members of an exclusive club in a materialistic world. Some years later, my landlord, a very senior civil servant, from whom I rented an attic flat in his lovely house in Hampstead, told me about the PM's relaxed style. One morning he was asked to take some papers for checking up to the private flat in No. 10. "But surely the PM is too busy to do that now", protested my friend. "Of course not," the Private Secretary replied. "He's only doing the crossword. He does it every morning." Compare this with the frenetic activity of recent Prime Ministers!

A few years later Harold Macmillan's "Supermac" image was to collapse after the "Night of the Long Knives" when he sacked seven Cabinet members after a huge Tory voting collapse in a by-election. Later he suffered the embarrassment of the Profumo scandal. The press at the time kept a discrete silence about the Prime Minister's private life. His wife Lady Dorothy had been two-timing with Lord Boothby for years. Peccadilloes in political circles are nothing new!

Like his predecessor, Anthony Eden, Harold Macmillan was not well served by his medical advisors. When he developed acute retention of urine in later years, his personal physician advised him to retire on health grounds, which he did. In fact his retention of urine was due to benign prostatic hypertrophy and his renal function was excellent. He could have returned to work in six weeks time, even in a few days using today's techniques.

But for me time was passing. With some useful obstetrical and paediatric experience under my belt I moved back to Nottingham to a Senior House Officer Post in Medicine, preparatory to going into general practice in the Midlands.

It seemed a good idea at the time. I planned to spend a year at a busy hospital that I knew, learning some more medicine, whilst I kept my eyes open for a rural practice in the Midlands. The expected outcome for that year did not materialise. I was to come under the influence of a man who was to become my second hero, John Douglas Proctor. He was my chief for a year and proved to be the best physician I ever met. After a year with him I knew that I would not be happy with anything less than a consultant post in medicine.

John Proctor was then in his 50s, silver-haired, alert, quick moving, a charming smile of greeting but with hooded questioning eyes. He had been appointed a consultant physician in Nottingham in 1946 after being house physician and later assistant on the Medical Unit at University College Hospital to Professor T.R.Elliot. For part of his time at UCH Max Rosenhein, later Professor of Medicine and my other hero, was his colleague on the Medical Unit.

It was at Nottingham General Hospital that John Proctor honed his skills as a superb diagnostician and all round physician. These attributes stemmed from his observations on the natural history of disease, which he studied in his large and carefully followed-up clinical practice. He always maintained that his outpatient clinic was his own textbook of medicine. He had an encyclopaedic memory and his notes, written in inimitable style, were for others; he rarely needed them himself.

His letters about patients to their doctors would scarcely be acceptable in these days of political correctness; but they made entertaining reading and conveyed the spirit of the occasion. "This huge bull of a man charged into the clinic, red-faced and snorting foetid breath at everyone." This was the start of one letter about an irascible patient with hypertension. His consultations were not limited to the outpatient clinic or hospital bed. One letter to a GP described a chance meeting with a patient on the canal path on a Sunday afternoon walk. " I asked him how he was," said JDP writing in the letter. "I can't stay to talk, Dr Proctor," the patient replied, "my ulcerative colitis is playing up no end. I need to find a toilet." "I let him go on his way" continued JDP in his letter " but took the opportunity to suggest a modification of his treatment until he came up to the clinic again."

We are now charged by our political masters to see more patients promptly and yet give them longer consultations. I have never been able to square this particular circle. John Proctor's punctuality and time keeping were not his strongest suits. He always started early but became progressively further behind as the day wore on. Everyone had his undivided attention. Every Tuesday he was in outpatients both morning and afternoon - Black Tuesdays we called them. The problem was that the clinics were so large. He wanted to see everyone and everyone wanted to see him. By 2.15 pm he had usually finished the morning clinic and dashed across to the main hospital for a 10 minute lunch. By then the 2 pm afternoon patients were already queuing. It was often 7.30 pm before he had finished, always still bursting with energy. I had a migraine by teatime!

Dr J D Proctor –
my second hero

And then there were still the letters to be dictated. His devoted secretary Liz would be waiting (she became my private secretary many years later). Secretaries stayed late in those days. On one occasion, while he was dictating his letters, the cleaner found an old lady asleep in a cubicle, still waiting for him to examine her. No problem. He completed his examination, put the lady in his Austin Princess, drove her home to Ilkeston (10 miles away), and came back. Liz was still there. So he finished his letters.

Eccentric- yes. Unconventional - yes. Workaholic- yes. But as a boss we all adored him. He was so enthusiastic, always supportive and had a marvellous nose for a diagnosis. There were times when we made serious errors or missed important points. He was never cross, but the hooded eyes would narrow and he would whistle faintly through his teeth. Of course he wasn't perfect himself - unpunctual and maddeningly unpredictable. Patients who insisted on using loose quasi-medical terms easily exasperated him. Flatulence was one term that always irritated him. "Up or down" he would say, "Do you belch or fart?"

Developing a Nose for a Diagnosis

This was the background to my life for more than a year, seeing lots of patients and developing, like the boss, a nose for a diagnosis. There were three medical firms at the General Hospital each taking-in emergencies, which formed the bulk of our admissions, in rotation. These emergencies were mostly strokes, heart attacks, gastro-intestinal bleeding, asthma, chest infections and a large number of cases of self-poisoning. The work was all "clinically based." By that I mean that there was very limited access to investigations which now would be regarded as routine. The technician on duty, who had to be phoned out of hours to come in from his/her home, performed all the pathological tests by hand. These included haematology, biochemistry and microbiology. It meant that investigations were, of necessity, limited. The labs had no autoanalysers, which now provide almost immediately a battery of tests for each patient. It was the same for imaging except for routine chest and abdominal films and trauma. The management of diabetic coma was a nightmare as it was a full time job for the technician keeping pace with the requirements of the doctor on duty.

W G Player Ward at the General Hospital Nottingham in the 1930s.
This was Dr Procter's Ward in the 1950s and my ward
when I first became a consultant in the late 1960s

Looking back there was little that could be offered therapeutically for many common conditions. For example, everyday on take-in we would admit at least one or two patients with coronary thromboses. For these there was little to be done apart from pain relief and the management of associated complications such as arrythmias; there were no "clot-busting" drugs, no coronary angiograms, no stents and no bypass operations

One particular nightmare was finding enough beds for the emergency admissions. I remember, as admissions officer, sitting for hours on the end of a phone, ringing around trying to find a bed for a sick patient. Our masters at the Department of Health maintained that it was just a matter of organisation! ˝

The next hurdle

After this year my decision was made to join the scramble for a consultant physician post. In theory there were three simple hurdles. First, to secure a recognised registrar post for two or three years. Second, to pass the specialist examination Membership of the Royal College of Physicians (MRCP London or Edinburgh). And third, to be appointed to a senior registrar post for a tenure of four years. Then, 7 or 8 years after qualification, one should be in contention for a consultant post.

Unfortunately it wasn't as simple as all that. The promotion structure was seriously flawed. There were plenty of registrar posts available but to get onto the promotion ladder it was virtually essential to work at a teaching hospital, to do some research and to publish papers. Then, as now, the majority of "junior" posts in NHS hospitals were filled by doctors who had qualified outside the UK. Most were from the Indian Sub-Continent and they filled many of the posts in non-teaching hospitals. Indeed, many hospitals in the midlands and the north were staffed almost entirely at a junior level by overseas graduates. These overseas doctors were no more than workhorses with little training and poor expectations of promotion. Successive Ministers of Health, politicians and the Department of Health turned a Nelson's blind eye to this problem and, even today, our politicians seem to find no ethical problems in siphoning away badly needed doctors from underdeveloped countries to prop up our ailing health service.

Getting the MRCP examination was a difficult but acceptable hurdle to be jumped. The bottleneck was at the senior registrar level. Often ten or more candidates with an MRCP and a good registrarship under their belts would be competing for the one senior registrar post. Again, in theory, the numbers of these posts were tailored to match the numbers of consultants retiring or dying. In practice this was not the case and it was commonplace to hear of time-expired senior registrars, i.e. those who were past the four -year term, to be waiting 6 or 8 years for a consultant post. Many were "junior" doctors well into their 40s. This was particularly the case for senior registrars in service posts. Those appointed to academic institutes, such as the Hammersmith Hospital, had limited service loads and hence were able to undertake research to enable them to publish. As a junior doctor I was aware of these hurdles and decided to test the course.

Looking Down a Microscope in Sheffield

It is always said that to become a good physician you need to have grounding in clinical pathology i.e. microbiology, clinical chemistry, cytology and haematology. To these disciplines must now be added molecular biology. The larger hospitals, particularly the teaching hospitals, usually employed junior doctors as resident pathologists to learn some basic clinical pathology, to link with the junior clinical staff and to undertake simple emergency procedures themselves. The work was not particularly onerous and traditionally young physicians took such posts for a year or two to broaden their horizons and to study for higher diplomas such as the MRCP.

This was the advice that I obtained from my seniors. My boss John Proctor had put in a word for me with Max Rosenheim at UCH who intimated that my training so far, plus the MRCP Diploma, would place me in a favourable position for a registrar post at my old teaching hospital.

Sheffield was the Regional Centre for Trent, later to be divided into three by the development of two other teaching centres at Nottingham and Leicester Teaching Hospitals. Resident Clinical Pathology posts were not all that popular and before long I found myself working at Sheffield Royal Infirmary, a hospital with great northern traditions.

As a Londoner I took a long time to settle into this Victorian town of grimy self- importance and for what seemed months, mainly because it was for months, I moped round feeling a bit sorry for myself. For me Sheffield was a northern town. The weather was undoubtedly worse than in the midlands and for the first few weeks it was either misty or drizzling. When it wasn't misty or drizzling it was raining hard. The redbrick public buildings were smoke-stained and shabby. Grey, dismal slabs of high rise flats were appearing to replace the old decaying urban housing built in the City's industrial past. As a young man on the City Council, Roy Hattersley, (later Lord Hattersley), regarded these as his brainchild; this style of replacement housing was his vision for the future. In later years when they had become the new slums of the 80s and 90s, crime ridden and crumbling, he admitted that they were a mistake. Even though high rise flats seemed to work elsewhere in the world, they didn't work in Sheffield. Many of these hideous flats have already been pulled down and now when I visit Sheffield again I scarcely recognise the place.

Sheffield was then the heartland of the British steel industry. No one would have foreseen then its imminent decline with cheaper steel bought in from abroad. The huge furnaces and chimneys belched out flames and soot night and day with only a brief respite when they shut down in the summer holiday fortnight - wakes fortnight. One hazy day, with the sun struggling to break through, I walked across the asphalt at the Royal Infirmary entrance. There was a soft crunching sound under the leather soles of my shoes. A friendly porter was passing "What's the gravelly feel underfoot?" I queried. "Muck," he replied "muck from the chimneys. We always get it when it's fine and t'wind's in the right direction." Having heard my southern accent and sensing my naivety about peculiarities of everyday life in South Yorkshire, he added, "Even the sparrows cough here!"

A downward trend in Sheffield continued when I became ill. In many ways it was my own fault as I had been careless in handling some cerebrospinal fluid from a baby with a low-grade meningititis. I pricked my finger with a contaminated Pasteur pipette but didn't think too much of it at the time. Now it would have meant extensive tests and screening. It was different then and no one worried too much. The baby was shown to have Listerosis and happily recovered. Several days later I developed a glandular fever type illness with fever, malaise and enlarged glands. After a fortnight's illness I recovered too. In spite of the earlier finger prick no specific diagnosis was established. But it taught me a lesson to be more cautious handling potentially dangerous material.

But then life began to pick up again. After boring spells in chemical pathology and microbiology I moved to the Department of Haematology. It was housed in shabby single storey huts on the edge of the hospital complex but I liked the people there and the work was more clinical, in tune with what I had been used to. I had discovered in the few months in Sheffield that I missed the blood and thunder of the emergency wards and the rush of adrenaline that came with every new crisis. The boss was Eddie Blackburn, born and bred in Yorkshire and proud of it. He was really a laboratory haematologist but fancied himself as a physician and was always reminding us of it. His opinion was much in demand by the local GPs and he was frequently asked to see patients in their homes. Sometimes his use of words was not all it should be and he would announce in his broad Yorkshire accent that he had been "sorting out patients on the way in this morning" as he hurried into the lab. We knew that these were domicilliary visits but the lab technicians were often puzzled by what he meant. Nevertheless he was a good teacher and looked after his junior staff well. Everyone who had ever worked in the Department always got a letter from him every Christmas bringing us all up to date with developments. Nothing made him happier than to learn of the success of his lads or lasses.

Harold Swan, his colleague, an Edinburgh Scot, was the complete antithesis. Tall, slim and upright with the pallid complexion of a dyspeptic northerner, he was a committed microscope haematologist. To him was given the

73

doubtful pleasure of teaching me laboratory haematology. We would sit together at the bench whilst he explained the morphological characteristics of megaloblasts, promyeloctes, plasma cells and glandular fever cells. I didn't find it easy and I am sure that privately Harold thought that I was mildly colour blind and very stupid. But he was tolerant and apart from a few "Tut, tuts!" we got on fairly well.

It was decided at an early stage that I would go up to Edinburgh to take the Edinburgh MRCP as this was regarded as being easier than the London MRCP. The difference was that you had, at that time, to nominate a special subject for the exam. Naturally, in my case this would be haematology, in which the interpretation of 20 slides was an essential component. Both Harold and I knew that this would be my Achilles Heel.

I remember little of the exam itself except the wretched slide session. There seemed to be dozens of candidates, many from distant outposts of what used to be the Great British Empire. All the white candidates I spoke to were asked "School?" "University?" And "Where are you working now?" It struck me at the time as being quite irrelevant but I imagine now would be regarded as being wildly politically incorrect. I suppose that the examiners wanted to be friendly. The dreaded slides came at the end of the examination. We moved from one microscope to the next after every 2 or 3 minutes in a dimly lit room. I guessed at a few but must have done better than I thought as, at the end of the examination, I learned that I had passed. I drove home in high spirits stopping for fish and chips on the way.

Going into the lab next morning Harold Swan looked up from his microscope. "How did you get on?" he asked. "I passed," I said proudly. "You do surprise me" he replied and, head down, busied himself with the task in hand.

This was the turning point in my pathological career. I had learned some clinical pathology, I knew what I was looking at down the microscope and I could cope with patients with haematological problems. Most of all I had in my possession the Edinburgh MRCP. I started to enjoy myself again. My particular friend was Neville Lambton, an SHO in medicine, who had qualified in Leeds. Neville was always elegantly groomed with impeccable manners, though he could be pompous at times. He could certainly turn on a splendid character assassination of any of the consultant staff when he put his mind to it. Initially we had both been regarded as unwelcome intruders into what was termed by some at the time, the Democratic Republic of South Yorkshire. But after a protracted trial, the Sheffield medical world had accepted us.

Chapter 7

A Lighter Side of Life in the 50s and 60s

The swinging 60s brought with them a more relaxed and affluent society.

"You've never had it so good!" boasted Harold Macmillan the Prime Minister. This was true. Many of the teenagers of the sixties had been born after the end of WWII. The dismal austerity of the 40s and 50s was slipping into the past. My own generation, so-called "Children of the War", were by now settling down to married life. And indeed for the majority it was conventional married life. Living with a partner of the opposite sex was considered risqué and was generally referred to as "living in sin." By contrast same sex partnerships were accepted without much comment. Nevertheless the pattern of family life was changing and the demands for a home with central heating, fitted carpets, television, and refrigerator made it essential for many married women to go out to work. Work was easy to come by and the bosses soon learned that they could employ women to do men's work just as efficiently and at a lower wage. With mums and dads both working it was often a problem getting children off to school in the mornings and those same children came back to an empty house at teatime.

But undoubtedly life was better in most respects. Even the most basic parameters showed that. The expectation of life for women in the 1950s was only 71 years. We did not know then that by the end of the century their daughters and granddaughters could expect to live to an average age of 80. For men the figures were not so good but the expectation of life would rise from 66 in the 1950s to 74.4 by the end of the century. Improved medication and surgery, vaccinations, better food and housing and improved public health measures were all to contribute. We expected to continue to see the ravages of smoking related deaths but no one would have imagined the new epidemics of HIV infection, obesity, and drug and alcohol dependence. One medical development, which was to have far reaching consequences, was the licensing in 1961 of oral contraceptives.

So what was happening in our everyday lives as we moved on from the late 50s to the early 60s. The young were enjoying themselves. A new sound had emerged. In 1960 the Beatles gave their first public performance in Hamburg, West Germany and were appearing regularly in the Cavern Club in Liverpool. Two years later they were taking the world by storm, with their own inimitable style of music. A few years earlier *This was the Week That Was* had exploded onto our lives through the medium of television. David Frost, Roy Kinnear, William Rushden and Lance Percival attacked the Establishment mercilessly in a series of topical programmes. Public figures were held up to ridicule. From the clipped accents, twin sets and pearl necklaces of the pre-war theatre we were seeing kitchen sink dramas on stage and we were reading novels of working day life like Alan Sillitoe's "Saturday night and Sunday Morning."

J F Kennedy was elected President of the United States in 1960 and Yuri Gagarin was launched into space in 1961.

In my own life, I grasped the new opportunities for travel which opened up. My very first trip abroad had been in 1949 after the end of the war. A mixed group of teenagers from St Peter's Youth Club in Bushey Heath went Youth Hostelling in the Low Countries. Looking back there were no worries about accommodation, racism or aggression even when we ventured into Germany for a few days. Our parents seemed happy to let us go without adult or more senior supervision. We were not aware of paedophiles preying on youngsters; indeed I'm sure that we didn't know the meaning of the word. Child abuse and sexual assaults on children must have occurred in England in the post -war years but in our circles, mainly working class, we rarely heard of them.

The Youth Hostels Association played a significant role in the lives of teenagers and young adults at that time. No one had cars so you walked or cycled from one hostel to the next. Accommodation and food was basic but cheap and it was always easy to get in. Arriving in Ostend on our first afternoon, having just vomited up my sandwiches during the choppy ferry crossing, we were nervous about the nature of the stringy meat with our evening meal in the first Youth Hostel. "Cheval!" declared the manager proudly. He rather implied that it was a luxury but we guessed that we were getting some leftovers!

We had chosen the Low Countries simply because they were near and flat. We were pleased to find the Hostels welcoming and wholesome even if the food left something to be desired. One of the few pieces of advice that we had been given before leaving home was to pin the Union Jack on our saddlebags. In those days the British were welcome everywhere and certainly the flags opened doors in every home and building. Waiting at a railway crossing a shopkeeper ran across the road to give us some bars of chocolate "For what you did for us in the war," she said pressing them into our hands. . The family of a Dutch couple we met whilst cycling invited us to stay in their house for two nights "We loved to hear your bombers droning over us in 1944 and 1945 on their bombing missions," she told us. What a change now. Fifty years on and our football yobs are loathed, despised and feared by the continentals.

We saw much of the Netherlands then; a tidy, welcoming, self-confident country, which had dragged itself out of the chaos and misery of WW11 and which, was now presenting itself as a liberalising influence. The London Olympics took place during the summer of 1948 and we joined Holland holding its breath whilst its heroine Fanny Blankers-Koen, an Amsterdam housewife, won the 80 metres hurdles, the 100 and 200 metres sprints and was a member of the winning

4x 100-metre relay event. This little country of tulips and windmills had something new to celebrate.

It was also transforming itself from a predominantly agricultural economy to an industrial one. At that time we saw the reclamation of vast stretches of marshlands and lagoons by the construction of sea walls and dykes, the pumping out of the water and the cutting of new canals. The polders, as the re-claimed areas were called, were originally intended for agricultural land to rear dairy cattle and to grow crops. But with its increasingly high population density, these functions were overtaken by the need for more housing for an increasingly industrialised society. Our travels took us through tidy towns with handkerchief sized gardens full of flowers and vegetables. Though many of the houses were showing evidence of wartime neglect, their doorsteps were scrubbed white and diligent housewives shone the windows until they were crystal clear.

At the beginning of the 21st Century this fine little country's valiant attempt to show the world how to be freethinking, emancipated and liberal has miscued. The once gracious and picturesque city of Amsterdam has the walls of its buildings vulgarised by graffiti, its pavements littered with dog faeces and its squares cluttered with squadrons of drug addicts. High profile politicians have been assassinated for expressing their views for what always was regarded as the civilised right of freedom of speech. We learn now that the indigenous Dutchmen and women are voting with their feet and that for the first time ever emigration has exceeded immigration. The Dutch see Australia, New Zealand and South Africa as the new Utopias.

We also saw something of Belgium on this trip though what we saw then was singularly unmemorable. Belgium, as it has been on every visit that I have made subsequently over the years, was rebuilding its roads and public buildings. With the increasing international importance of Brussels as the headquarters of the European Union and of the North Atlantic Treaty Organisation, building programmes have burgeoned and Brussels itself is very much a cosmopolitan and international city. In 1958 it was still little Belgium famous for its chocolate and the *mannequin pis,* a tiny statue of a cheeky boy piddling into a fountain. Such a statue was risqué then!

With every further trip I have enjoyed Belgium more and more. In 1957 I flew over for the World Exhibition, my first real experience of being a tourist. Staying in a seedy and gloomy hotel, reeking of French cigarettes. I met a high powered mathematician from Nottingham University, Joe Watson, and the two of us toured round day after day gawping at the Sputnik, the Atomium and the national displays.

The next overseas trip, two or three years later, was to sunny Spain. In the 50s and 60s the Costa Brava and Majorca were fashionable destinations. Guaranteed sun, cheap food and wine were undeniable attractions for the Brits for whom the traditional bed and breakfast seaside holiday in bracing Skegness was beginning to pall. And the travel agents could tempt them with attractive package deals.

For pallid, tired, sleep deprived, unattached young doctors, who could go away on holiday outside school holiday time, the Costa Brava in 1959-60 was not to be missed. A group of 8 of us from the General Hospital, Nottingham decided, almost on impulse, to give it a go. There was one married couple, one pair who were what would be called now an item, a dentist and three unattached residents including myself. There were three cars between us, we rustled together some ex-army tents, Khaki shorts, sleeping bags and cooking equipment and set off. My buddy was Jack McGee, a phlegmatic Canadian orthopaedic Senior House Officer. His father was a lumberjack in Vancouver and Jack was as tough as they come - though he was to learn as the trip progressed that even he was vulnerable. Brimming with eager optimism but with the impetuosity of youth, we had made no plans except that we would drive across France to the Mediterranean coast. One of the reasons why we departed in such a hurry was because we did not want the hospital authorities to realise that a sizeable component of their junior staff would be away at the same time!

As it was early season we drove straight on to a ferry and we were away. We did at least have some maps and found our way, mainly on highways and byways through Reims, Dijon, Mâcon, St Étienn and Carcasonne. Our second, third or fourth hand tents weren't universally admired but "le camping" was gaining popularity in France then and makeshift sites (we camped in a football stadium once) were easy to come by. The problem was that we had run into one of the most ferocious heatwaves in living memory. From early morning to sunset the sun burned down relentlessly. As indoor workers who scarcely ever enjoyed direct sunlight in the English midlands we basked in the unaccustomed heat. No air conditioning in cars then! Jack was a fitness fanatic and whenever we stopped he was off jogging whilst the weaker members of the party collapsed in the nearest shade.

After the furnace of southern France we welcomed the slightly cooler Mediterranean coast at San Feliu de Guixols, no doubt like Columbus sighting land. By then the iron man was not too well. Jack was complaining of headache, faintness and dizziness and within an hour started talking gibberish. At least his description of the surgical approach he would adopt when pinning the right femur of the Prime Minister on whom he was going to operate the next morning, indicated to most of us that he was confused. As the only physician in the party I was put in charge. My initial thoughts were of meningitis but there was no neck stiffness or photophobia. His pulse was fast and weak, skin hot and dry, and limbs floppy. Could this be heat stroke? We put our heads together and decided to cool him down. The sea was nearby and we stretched out a confused but non-protesting Jack in the ebbing evening tide. In retrospect it was a risky course of action though even in hospital, cooling is the most effective measure. We took it in turns to watch over him and by late evening he was stronger and no longer rambling. A night's sleep and more immersion next morning and he was back to his ebullient self albeit a wiser man. I had seen my first case of heat stroke!

After this minor mishap our travels further down the coast went well. The heat wave ended in a torrential storm, with lightning striking nearby pine trees and the rain flooding our simple tents. It quickly became hot again and Jack slept under the stars at night and in the shade during the day. Even he realised that he had had a close shave. We returned to England restored to health but wiser.

As the 60s ended I realised that I had a career to sort out. I'm not sure what part I was of the swinging 50s and 60s but there are good memories.

Chapter 8

A More Senior "Junior Doctor" in London

Back to my Alma Mater in London

I had no wish to spend my professional life in the metropolis. By the sixties London was getting dirtier, more crowded and cosmopolitan, and singularly expensive. Nevertheless I could not escape the conclusion that the quickest way to get a consultant job in the provinces, which was what I wanted, was to do a further spell of training in London. At that time the London Teaching Hospitals were the "crème de la crème", believed to offer the best training in the world. I was to learn later that this was not necessarily true!

The great and the good in the profession advised about appointments of consultants in the NHS. They made pious statements about young men having an appropriate mix of academic medicine (using the term medicine in its widest sense) and "heat and burden of the day" medicine. The former usually equated with work and research in a teaching hospital and the latter with getting your hands dirty in a busy District General Hospital. The truth was that the great and the good in the profession were usually men or women who held University Chairs or who were officers of the Royal Colleges. They sat on all the important committees but their feet were rarely soiled with the mud of the real world. For many of them research and publications were undoubtedly more important on a Curriculum Vitae (CV) than large numbers of patients seen and properly cared for. It might be added that if you could get the BTA (Been To America) diploma this would hasten one's scramble up the promotion ladder.

Being aware of all this, and feeling rather guilty about my personal career reasons for returning to London, I found my way back to UCH as a medical registrar. I placated my conscience by telling myself that I had borne the "heat and burden of the day" by doing busy jobs in Nottingham and Sheffield and that I had done some general practice in the Army. So, conceitedly, I felt that I had enough general experience for the time being.

One of the problems about moving to London then (and now) was finding suitable accommodation. A registrar's modest salary made the choice limited. UCH could provide nowhere for a single doctor to stay even though he or she might have to be on call on alternate nights. There was no alternative but to scan through the advertisements in the evening papers or to pick up news on the grapevine. In the 1960s the term Rachmanism was finding its way into our vocabulary, following the exploitation of cheap property by an unscrupulous landlord. He was only the first amongst many and it seemed to me that owning property to let in London was a licence to print money. Times haven't changed. It still is!

For a start I found myself a room in a flat in Belsize Park. The area had undoubtedly seen better days and when I moved there it was bed-sitter land filled with a mix of students, resting actors, solicitors' clerks, shop assistants, secretaries, semi-professional filles de joie, left wing politicians, university lecturers and journalists. My landlord was a wealthy elderly Indian gentleman married to a middle aged English lady. Unkindly, I believed it to be a marriage of convenience. She was thin, haggard, hennaed and bangled, with her skin atrophied and wrinkled from over exposure to the sun and heavy smoking. She always had a smouldering cigarette balanced on her lower lip with the wisp of smoke curling upward tinting her nose and forehead yellow with the nicotine.

My ground floor room was spacious but bitterly cold and I shared a kitchen and bathroom with the family and another lodger, a young newly divorced business lady. It soon became apparent that the bed-sitter had many disadvantages. Time was allocated for bathroom and kitchen use and the minute electric fire in my room scarcely raised the temperature above freezing point during the viciously cold months of that winter. My stingy landlady soon made it obvious that using the fire for more than two hours each evening was flagrantly extravagant. Thrown together in these disagreeable circumstances my not unattractive fellow lodger was soon suggesting that we might look together for alternative accommodation. This clearly had many advantages but I was uncertain of the consequences. So I left Belsize Park before I was precipitated into a complex relationship that I could not control.

In this world you have to be in the right place at the right time. Walking into an Estate Agent's on Haverstock Hill, anxious to find somewhere quickly, a gushing and impeccably dressed lady assistant engulfed me. In her newly acquired Hampstead Heath accent she told me that, only half an hour previously, a pleasant lady had walked in anxious to let the attic flat in her substantial house at a very reasonable rent. Within the hour I had seen the flat in nearby Belsize Lane, approved and settled the deal. The attic flat was up a narrow flight of stairs from the rest of the house and was self-contained.

That evening I met the owner who invited me down for a drink. He was a high-powered civil servant in the Cabinet Office, stentorian, authoritative but with a persistent smoker's cough. He was clearly familiar with the corridors of power and questioned me probingly about my career prospects. Satisfied that I was who I said I was, he then astonished me by reducing the rent! I learned later that the income from the attic flat paid for the youngest member of the family to go to a local private school but that those who had responded to a previous advertisement were, in my new landlord's words, thoroughly unsuitable. I was glad to be settled there because by now I was a confirmed bachelor and able to cook every dish that was offered from a tin. It has to be remembered that these were the days before microwaves and prepared meals from supermarkets. The only downside to these agreeable digs was that with his first cigarette of the day the landlord coughed his heart out "to clear his lungs", shaking the whole house. Careerwise he later became an ambassador but died relatively young - no doubt from a smoking related death.

Medicine- from an Art to a Science

But of course the primary reason for being in London again was to continue training as a physician. Medicine was moving rapidly from an art in the 1930s, 40s and 50s to a scientific discipline in the 60s. Though we did not use the term then, we were beginning to practice evidence based medicine. One of the essentials for us trainees was to work in as many specialities as possible. This meant rotating round various firms in different hospitals to get wider experience and to learn an increasingly large number of practical procedures. One of the problems was that many of our bosses had no great personal experience of new practical techniques. Consequently the registrars had to seek out experts elsewhere, watch them perform and then to set about honing those skills on unsuspecting patients at their own hospitals. Already the distinction between what was surgical, what was medical and what was radiological was becoming blurred.

Physicians were taking biopsies from every organ: liver, kidneys, stomach, gut, the bronchi and lungs. The cardiologists were perfecting cardiac catheterisation. Pressures could be recorded in all chambers of the heart and injections of radio-opaque dyes outlined the valves and the vessels. But perhaps the most exciting advance to me as a clinical haematologist/gastroenterologist was the introduction of fibre-optic endoscopy. This was already enabling us to view the oesophagus, stomach, and duodenum and, in later years, the whole of the large bowel.

At the time I was particularly concerned in perfecting small intestinal biopsy. The ingenious Crosby capsule made it possible to take tiny samples from the lining of the small intestine. The capsule consisted of a hollow metal sphere 1 cm in diameter with a tiny porthole in the side. It was attached to a fine hollow tube and was swallowed. When it reached the right place in the small intestine one sucked air from the capsule via the tube. A tiny knuckle of gut wall lining was pulled into the porthole thus creating a partial vacuum. This knuckle of gut wall was then sliced off inside the capsule with a spring-loaded blade. The capsule was then pulled back out of the mouth with (hopefully) the small gut biopsy inside. It sounds complicated and it was!

The earlier capsules were desperately fiddly to prime and my fingers were always too fat and clumsy. It was always a nightmare trying to get the capsule primed properly and getting the patient to swallow it. Then there was always a long wait until we were sure on X-ray screening that it had reached the right place in the gut. The greatest frustration to oneself and the patient was to pull the capsule up and find that it hadn't fired or had fired and not taken a biopsy. We practised on ourselves and as a human guinea pig I remember the dreadful retching as I tried to get the thing down. Nevertheless it represented an enormous advance in the management of coeliac disease. Nowadays we take biopsies using a fibreoptic endoscope and the whole procedure takes 10 minutes!

The Old Workhouse at St Pancras and the New Workplace in Gower Street

UCH couldn't provide all the jobs and experience that we wanted and spells at the Whittington Hospital, Highgate and St Pancras Hospital were on the rotation. I started with the St Pancras rotation and split my time between looking after patients in the professorial medical beds under John Dickinson's care (later Professor Dickinson) and on Lord Amulree's Geriatric Unit.

Geriatrics was then very much a Cinderella speciality - under funded, looked down on by the supercilious consultants of the Harley Street brigade, and unpopular with junior staff for training. University College Hospital, as a result of the National Health Service Act, had incorporated St Pancras Hospital in 1948. It was originally the old workhouse - and indeed, viewed from the outside, it still looked like it. The Victorian red brick of the buildings was discoloured with decades of smoke from the chimneys of dismal terraced houses and tenements around, and from the old steam trains from St Pancras Station nearby. By the 1950s when I was there as a student and registrar it had been extended and redesigned to include medical and surgical wards, an acute mental observation block and a large geriatric unit.

The inadequacies of long term care of the very old had been brought starkly into perspective with the inception of the National Health Service in 1947. Until then the very old, who were unable to cope for themselves, either lived with their families or were taken into institutional care. As Alan Bennett pointed out in his "Untold Stories" - "They are not dying; they are just incapable of living, though capable of being long-lived nevertheless." For those who were well off there were nursing homes or charitable institutions but for many poor and needy without family support, it meant long term care in a Council Home. For those living in North London this was the St. Pancras Workhouse. With the social changes after World War II and families spread far and wide children were reluctant to care for their elderly parents. An elderly mother who had lived the whole of her life in the Kings Cross area might have a son in Edinburgh, another in Wales and a daughter in Australia. The relatives living nearby often resented having to take complete responsibility for their parents.

Advances in health care meant that people were living longer, though not necessarily in better health. There is no doubt that many Local Authority Homes and Privately Owned Nursing Homes were the last refuge of the destitute. Those residents able to leave their beds sat in circles in cheerless lounges, hunched up,

83

brooding, silent and unhearing, staring unseeingly at the permanently-on television set in the corner. The bedrooms stank of stale urine, unwashed bodies and dirty bedding. The bedfast lay curled up in a foetal posture with contractures and bedsores. Mercifully not everywhere presented this dismal picture and there were many units with devoted staff who struggled to maintain better standards.

The shocking fate of many neglected elderly folk in institutional care was highlighted later by the pungent criticisms in a book "Sans Everything" written by Barbara Robb, published in 1967. It was the sequel to a letter published by her and other important dignitaries in the Times on 10th November 1965 about the plight of old people in hospital. It protested about the evil practice in certain hospitals, including general and mental hospitals, of stripping geriatric patients of their spectacles, dentures, hearing aids and other civilised necessities. They were left to vegetate in idleness and loneliness. Rosemary, soon to be my wife recalls, during her training, seeing nurses sorting through a washing bowl full of dentures pondering over the ownership of the various sets. "Sans Everything" related the grim details of so many aspects of geriatric care that it brought the plight of the elderly to the forefront of the political agenda.

Happily the patients in the long-term beds at St Pancras were better cared for than most. The kindly, benign, but badly stuttering physician, Lord Amulree, supervised them. As I have mentioned before his earlier experience during the War in the Department of Health fitted him well for the task and he was one of the first to recognise the burgeoning needs of the elderly. Known to everyone on the staff of St. Pancras as "The Lord" he worked hard to publicise better health care for the elderly and was instrumental in improving their lot. He spoke regularly in the House of Lords about the problems of the aged and carried a deal of influence amongst politicians in the Department of Health. At "the coal face" on the wards he was diligent with his work and was on good terms with his patients who were tickled pink to call their doctor "M'Lord." He didn't even mind, as I remember once, a patient coughing spit onto his brand new suede shoes. The sisters were devoted to him and to their work, as were the teams of caring nurses and rehabilitatory physiotherapists.

Nevertheless those wards were vast echoing caverns almost the size of aircraft hangers with four rows of beds along their length. There was little privacy or personal space, just a bed, a locker and a geriatric chair. At night the wards were noisy with snores, grunts, farts and shouts. It always astonished us that those who made so much noise at night could doze and sleep so peacefully during the day! Many were confused and demented but were able, to the amazement of their friends and relatives, to recount episodes from their distant past with unerring accuracy. Often the past and present were entangled inextricably.

For the young doctor in training, the care of the elderly introduced a new concept which hadn't been emphasised in training or been fully appreciated in the blood and thunder of acute medicine and surgery. We learned to keep an open mind when an elderly patient was admitted who seemed muddled. So often before, our minds had snapped shut when confronted with this problem, the main thought being how to prevent a bed being blocked. Yet life or death outcomes depended on a correct appraisal. It did not take long to realise how quickly elderly patients became confused as the result of a move, concurrent illness or new drugs.

There were special diagnostic difficulties with the elderly, partly because of the multiplicity of co-existing acute or chronic illnesses. Acute illnesses such as stroke, heart attacks or chest infections might present atypically as falls, incontinence, immobility and confusion. I owed much at this time to my senior registrar, Arnold Rosin. He taught me, a brash young man, used to dealing with the life and death dramas of acute medicine, that there was a gentler and more caring side to life in geriatrics. Arnold was a serious Glaswegian who was deeply religious. Because of his Jewish faith he would reject transport and walk from his home in Golders Green over Hampstead Heath into the hospital when called in on the Sabbath. Being unattached at the time I told him that I was quite happy to take all the calls then but he was adamant about sharing work equally.

Now in the 21st Century, the management of the elderly has improved immensely. This does not mean that it is completely satisfactory. Whereas the elderly were, in the early days of the National Health Service, defined as those over the age of 65, most in the Geriatric Wards are over 80 and are, by and large, women. Their hospital wards are brighter, cubicalised, with spacious day rooms and adequate supervisory staff. The problems arise when they reach the time for discharge but are not able to live independently. The Government and the Health Administrators are obsessed with so-called Community Care. The theory is that these elderly folk are supported at home by nursing and other services. This, of course, is to save money on institutional care. Everyone dealing with this sort of problem knows that, for the majority, community care means someone popping in for ten minutes twice a day to make a cup of tea.

The current financial injustice in England and Wales, but not in Scotland, insists that those with savings have to pay for their care in long term nursing home accommodation, whereas those who have nothing go free. This penalises those who have sought to safeguard their futures. Mercifully there are many worthy charitable organisations, such as Abbeyfield which seek to offer comfortable care and companionship during the long evening of lives blighted by mental or physical illness.

Back to Gower St

When I moved back to the main hospital in Gower Street I was fortunate to be attached to physicians who had powerful influences on my career. During those years the medical side of University College Hospital had reached preeminence amongst other hospitals in the land. This was because it numbered on its staff distinguished men who were expert clinical investigators and teachers. Towering above all others, though not physically, was Max Rosenheim, soon to become President of the Royal College of Physicians and later Lord Rosenheim. But around him there were such figures as Charles Dent, John Dickenson, Eric Pochin, John Stokes and Tom Prankerd all of whom made the place buzz and provided an exciting environment in which to work.

I quickly realised that although my registrar colleagues were agreeable, well informed and lively, some of their elbows were remarkably sharp. The reason for this was clear. We were all in competition for more senior jobs in a well-defined hierarchy. We had to knuckle down to the work and to show ourselves to best advantage to our seniors who, eventually would be the ones to move us onwards and upwards. On Saturday mornings three or four registrars had to present difficult or unusual cases and give commentaries to the "Circus." This was a compulsory gathering of most of the medical staff, both senior and junior, who watched and listened carefully to the presentations. The medical discussions were at the highest level but there was also a covert agenda. On the game board of the morning lottery would the speakers be clambering up a ladder or slithering down a snake? Max presided, often appearing to doze off but apparently waking at the end of the presentation with a start to ask a searching question. The great and the good, i.e. the consultant staff went away having enjoyed the cut and thrust of the discussion and either pleased or disappointed with their registrar's performance.

To the Matterhorn to meet an English Rose

There were always holidays to look forward to. I had never been skiing but in the winter of 1962/3 a friend, fellow registrar, Denis Guttmann, asked me to go winter sporting with him to Zermatt. It was, and still is, a fashionable skiing resort dominated by the brooding Matterhorn, famously climbed by Edward Whimper in 1865; four members of his party of seven were killed when a rope broke during their descent. Dennis was a bright young man, a double first from Oxford with a famous father, Sir Ludwig Guttmann, who had established the paraplegic unit at Stoke Mandeville. Dennis had seen service in the RAF and was a member of their Winter Sports Association which organised skiing holidays at unbelievably low cost. The fact that I hadn't been in the RAF didn't seem to matter; service in the Army was adequate! It all seemed an opportunity too good to resist.

Looking back I realised how casual I was. I made absolutely no preparations until the evening before we left. I had no weatherproof anorak, no skiing gloves, no goggles, no ski pants, no sun cream and no injury insurance! The only advice I had been given was to take some long johns to wear under my ski trousers, which were in fact an old pair of slacks. Fortunately we were able to hire boots and skis to get going but my first morning on the slopes left me wet, shivering and miserable. Some quick, but expensive, shopping was required.

Whilst hiring our ski boots at the local sports shop I had found myself sitting next to a healthy looking, strong-limbed, bobbish, friendly English girl who was plainly embarrassed at having to ask for boots that were at least a size bigger than mine. I recognised her as being with the RAF Winter Sports Association party and mentally classified her as being an occupational therapist in the services.

An English Rose with the Matterhorn in the background. 1963

Fully kitted out, I felt more the part on the slopes, though I had to admit to myself (and others) that I was not a natural skier. The suave Swiss instructor did not actually say that I was useless but I was regularly reminded to "Bend your knees, you are big man and will fall heavily." I felt that my hefty frame was better suited to the rugby field than to the skiing slopes. The male novices could have done with more instruction but our handsome instructor had eyes that were more frequently focussed on the body movements of the ladies. Most of the RAF party were more experienced skiers than I was and they disappeared high into the mountains whilst I spent extra time on the nursery slopes.

Being red-blooded, unattached young men, the propinquity of so many athletic, attractive and nubile young women boosted our testosterone levels. The evenings were dominated by après ski activities. Dennis was determined to find some female companionship early on and took me on a tour of the bars. In one bar we spotted my earlier acquaintance from the ski shop wearing a roll-necked white sweater. She was sharing an empty table with a petite dark haired girl also from the RAF party. Dennis quickly made up his mind. "Right," he said "I'll take the brunette, you take her friend with the white sweater!" There wasn't much choice but I was more than happy; the friend had a welcoming smile and peaches and cream complexion. I learned that she was a physiotherapist not an occupational therapist as I had originally diagnosed. Her name was Rosemary. Little did I know then that this was the girl who was to become my wife! It was the best piece of luck I ever had.

Dennis's short-term relationship did not flourish but mine did. We went to fondue parties, chatted and smooched on the dance floor. After two or three days Rosemary failed to turn up at our evening parties. What had happened? Had I offended her? I tactfully enquired of her roommate Sue. No, she was alright but had suffered a prostrating bout of vomiting and diarrhoea after downing two large glasses of pure Swiss cold water. Over the next two or three days we began to hear of other tourists who had been similarly afflicted. Rumours began to circulate; there were twenty or thirty in the local hospital with headaches, fever and gastro-intestinal symptoms that the authorities called 'flu. Obviously this was not 'flu and two or three doctors in the RAF party, including me, were sent out to investigate. By now there was an information blackout by the Swiss, anxious to preserve the reputation of Zermatt as a healthy mountain resort. After a further day or two the truth was out. There was an outbreak of typhoid in the town.

The reporters appeared from nowhere and we read banner headlines in the English Press- "Zermatt, where a kiss can mean death." Fortunately the epidemic was soon brought under control; a sewage pipe above the town had been leaking into the town's water supply. Rosemary didn't have typhoid and was soon again on the slopes, now empty save a few mad English who weren't afraid to enjoy the rest of their holidays but who took care to limit their drinking to alcohol and sterilised water. Apart from the 'flu it had been a great holiday and some of us exchanged addresses and phone numbers. More about that to follow.

Isotopes, Big Spleens and Scanners

My haematological experience from Sheffield gave me another lucky break at this time because, back at UCH I was able to take up a British Empire Cancer Campaign Fellowship to work with Tom Prankerd, the Professor of Clinical Haematology. The task I was given was to try to evaluate the role of splenic enlargement in the malignant lymphomas and the leukaemias. The tool that I was to use for this was the isotope 51Cr that could be attached to red cells as a radioactive label. The idea was to label a sample of patient's red cells with 51Cr, to reinject them and follow their fate in the body as they were destroyed. This could be done *in vivo* by scanning over various organs such as the spleen and liver and determining if the blood was being destroyed prematurely to produce anaemia. My field of interest encompassed the leukaemias, the lymphomas and some complex anaemias. This research was dovetailed in with some clinical work so that I could keep my hand in as a practising physician.

Tom Prankerd was an opportunist who fired off exciting ideas for one to follow up. And at the same time he didn't interfere too much in the detailed experimentation. At that time many patients in teaching hospitals underwent investigations that were not entirely necessary for the management of their diseases without their being fully informed of all the implications and risks. Many patients were pleased to take part and they took the view that this was a way in which they could help others with similar problems. What they were not told was that the investigations were part of research programmes undertaken by research clinicians who were sometimes more interested in advancing their careers.

Concurrently patient groups, medical activists and doctors began to question the ethics of what was loosely termed "medical research." One such activist was Maurice Papworth, a physician to two or three North London Hospital Psychiatric Hospitals. He had acquired, over many years, a national reputation coaching doctors for the MRCP examination and was rumoured to earn a comfortable income from this. He spoke and wrote publicly about his concerns about medical research and became a thorn in the side of the Royal Colleges, the Medical Schools and the medical establishment. Many regarded him as a crank. He never disguised his contempt for unethical academic researchers and in 1967 published a book entitled "Human Guinea Pigs" in which he named and shamed dozens of doctors whom he thought were performing unethical work. Much of what he wrote was unquestionably true and "Human Guinea Pigs" ignited fierce debate on the radio, television and in Parliament. It forced everyone in medical research to re-examine their own positions and led to the formation of ethical committees in hospitals and formal legislation.

Full recognition of Maurice Papworth's worthy crusade did not come until late in his life. A caucus at the Royal College of Physicians had successfully blocked his elevation to their Fellowship until his old age. Eventually when sanity prevailed and he was awarded the Fellowship he received a standing ovation - a most unusual departure from the dignity of such functions.

It was in this climate that I entered research, undertaking investigations that were primarily for the benefit of patients, though undoubtedly we did attempt to gain additional information that was academic as well as clinical. And I learned a lot as well that was to be of use under sometimes surprising circumstances later in my career - statistics, epidemiology, calculus, the use of isotopes and scanning.

Research never quite leads along predicted paths. In my case I was forever drifting off at tangents. But it did allow me to write a formal thesis entitled "Red Cell Pooling in the Spleen" which was accepted by the University of London in 1965 for the Degree of Doctor of Medicine.

From Ski Boots to Marriage and Muswell Hill

Before we left Zermatt I made sure that I had 'Ski-Boots' address in my pocket for future reference. I had learned that she had trained as a physiotherapist at Guy's and was currently working at St Hellier Hospital, Carshalton. She lived in Purley with her parents and had an older sister, Angela, who was married with a family in New Zealand. We started to see more of each other although I have to admit that it was scarcely a whirlwind romance.

There was a significant hurdle that had to be overcome. Though I had the Edinburgh MRCP it was made clear to me that I needed the London MRCP to make myself a more saleable proposition for a consultant post in England. The Edinburgh exam was officially on a par with that of London but was, undoubtedly easier. I had taken the London MRCP whilst in Sheffield but failed at the last hurdle, the final viva. Having reached this stage no one was supposed to fail - but I managed to! It wasn't until my third attempt two years later that I was able to scrape through. On the way through the various parts of the exam I lost my faith in the stupid and seemingly inflexible examiners who seemed to ask questions to which they had their own personal answers. I mentioned Maurice Papworth's success as a coach for the London MRCP earlier. Some of his success was in knowing the questions that some of the examiners asked and the answers that they expected. Those answers were not necessarily the correct ones in the current state of knowledge! Little did I know that twenty years on I would be sitting on the other side of the table as one of those stupid examiners myself.

With the studying and exams behind me there was more time for socialising. Rosemary and I became an item. Her father and old friends always called her Rose - so she became Rose to me too. Eventually she took me home to be inspected by her parents who lived in a pleasant part of leafy Surrey opposite the cricket ground at Purley. Her father, Alfred Cash, was a solicitor and senior partner in an old established firm of Parliamentary Agents, Vizards of Lincoln's

Inn. Her mother was bright and lively and always immaculately turned out. She was an excellent cook and gave me steak and kidney pie on the first time I went to dinner. Anxious to make a good impression I claimed that it was one of my favourites! Thereafter it was cooked for me whenever I went.

Educated at Haileybury, Alfred had served in the legal branch of the RAF during the war before joining Vizards as a young solicitor. It was not until he was in advanced old age that he told us that his job in the RAF was to collate the daily information about air losses and take them in to a progressively more bad-tempered and deaf Winston Churchill in the underground Cabinet Rooms in Whitehall. Many would have dined out on that story for years.

An unpredictable young doctor with irregular habits and hours did not fit in too well with the Cash household where the clock regulated life. Like thousands of other City workers Alfred left on the same train each day from Purley Station in the Reginald Perrin uniform re-created by David Nobbs - bowler hat, stiff white collar, umbrella and brief case. Given on-time trains he returned at 7.05pm each evening. Life was much more orderly for everyone then.

We were married in traditional style on 25th April 1964 at St Mary's Church, Beddington where Rose's parents had been married 30 years earlier and had a splendid reception in a marquee on the lawn. All went well except that an over-enthusiastic photographer, anxious to record the event comprehensively followed Rose up into her bedroom to record the shedding of the wedding dress before the donning of the going away outfit! After a celebratory dinner at the Gay Hussar we left for honeymoon in a beautifully sunny Ibiza. It was then quiet, tranquil and unspoiled, not the ridden drug sex haven of the turn of the century.

We returned to live in a one bedroomed flat that I had found in Muswell Hill. It was in an undistinguished block on a corner on Colney Hatch Lane. We were on the ground floor and the buses and heavy transporters changed gear just as they were going past our bedroom window. But apart from that and the fact that hoards of cockroaches scuttled out of the kitchen at night when one put the light on, it was comfortable and reasonably clean.

Our major problem was that our neighbour, Miss Shrubsall, was a lonely retired spinster who was desperate for company. We were sure that she lay in wait behind her front door like a primed mousetrap to capture us as we arrived back home in the evening. Excuses such as urgent phone calls, guests coming later, cooking boiling over, failed to shake her off. We were living in Muswell Hill at the time of Sir Winston Churchill's funeral. She had a television and we hadn't and were consequently invited in to view the event. The live television coverage of his funeral attracted a record worldwide coverage. Certainly life in the UK stopped for the day. After the hours of viewing I was emotionally drained, not by the historic events that we had been privileged to see happening, but by her unstoppable monologue concerning the events of her life. It was sad that such a trivial association should have overwhelmed such a memorable event.

Our
Wedding Day

The Muswell Hill of the post war years was a shabby but proud community of nondescript dwellings intersected by busy roads. At that time it was beginning to lose its identity. Sadly it wasn't sufficiently run down to be rebuilt and it hadn't enough potential to attract middle class buyers for its houses. They were bought up by landlords who had made easy money in the fifties and who saw the potential of renting out their properties or converting them to flats. As a result Muswell Hill was slithering into the scruffy, homogenous conformity which was overtaking so many North London suburbs.

Nowhere was this more obvious than in the High Street shops. The old family greengrocers, confectioners, drapers, shoe shops, butchers, fish shops and stationers were being infiltrated by curry houses, Chinese takeaways, Afro-Caribbean hair-stylists, gift shops, betting shops and the offices of third rate solicitors and estate agents. To be fair this process was being repeated in many of the North London suburbs hastened by the ubiquitous growth of self-service stores heralding the invasion of the supermarkets from the United States a few years later. Now much of England and Wales have followed the trend of the 60s set by the big cities. The Currys, Dixons, Next, PC World, Superdrug, and Wilkinson's have suppressed the individuality of the High Streets up and down the country.

Nevertheless Muswell Hill was our home for a year though I began to realise that I needed to be moving on. Max Rosenheim had given me a nod and a wink that I would be a favoured candidate for the Resident Assistant Physician Post (RAP) at UCH when the current holder of the post found a consultant post. But no one seemed to want him. I wasn't all that keen as the RAP job, though prestigious, was something of a dogsbody post - deputising for the older consultants when they were away and living in a flat in the hospital for much of the time. So I started looking elsewhere.

My first experience of the job market was something of an eye-opener. A senior registrar job at Barts was advertised and I duly applied. The received wisdom was to make a formal visit to the potential chief. I duly rang his secretary and was rather surprised to be given an appointment at his Harley Street consulting rooms rather than the hospital. On being ushered into his presence a few days later he asked, "Well, tell me what the problem is?" I was puzzled - and so was he. He had imagined that I was a patient. After a few embarrassing moments he made it clear to me that I needn't have bothered seeing him as it was already decided that his present registrar was to be appointed to the post. This seemed distinctly odd as the post had been generally advertised as this was the legal requirement. In my innocence I thought no more of it and politely wrote to the Bart's Hospital secretary that I had been told the job had been already allocated to his registrar. I then went off on a summer holiday.

I learnt later that I had put the cat amongst the pigeons at Barts. A messenger had been dispatched from Barts to UCH with a personal letter to me assuring me that I must have misunderstood what the physician said and that they would be pleased for me to resubmit my application. I had certainly not misunderstood the physician concerned but it would have been an impossible situation to go on with it. The British Medical Association told me on the phone that to fix jobs so blatantly was not only highly irregular but also quite illegal and that if I wished to take action they would support me strongly. I did nothing more but I became aware that open competition for some posts in the NHS was no more than lip service. My wily boss at UCH at the time told me that I was better out of it as the person in question was a well-known alcoholic!

There then followed a disappointing time pursuing posts unsuccessfully elsewhere. Eventually I gained a senior registrar post at Kings College Hospital and another move materialised.

Most senior registrar jobs in the NHS were arranged with a teaching hospital component at the base, with spells at other hospitals (linked to the base hospital) which were regarded as offering an appropriate range of training. The truth was that you went to the other hospitals which wanted an extra pair of hands! In my case it was decreed that I should spend the first year of my rotation at Brighton and then return to Kings for the next three years. Domestically this suited us well as it meant that after a year at Brighton we could move to more permanent accommodation in London. So, we uprooted ourselves from the flat at Muswell Hill with its hoards of scuttling cockroaches and moved into a hospital flat at Brighton General Hospital.

The flat was the dingy top floor flat of the old medical superintendent's house. It had seen better days. Near the racecourse, at the top of the hill leading to the old Poor Law Hospital it was the first stop for the damp winter gales across the English Channel. Window and doorframes did not fit too snugly and with inadequate heating it was pretty draughty. Still it was a roof over our heads and it was home. I doubt if any junior doctor would have put up with such poor accommodation these days.

There was much to be enjoyed in Brighton, particularly in the winter when the holiday tourists had gone home. We acquired a dog, a lively Dalmatian bitch called Pepper, who kept us fit exercising her on the Downs. We had to keep her away from the golf courses and from children's playgrounds as she would inevitably chew the balls up and I would have to replace them. But it was good to be living in a provincial town with its own library, theatre and cinemas. We met lots of new friends and Rose began working as a physiotherapist again.

An older lady in the physiotherapy team at Brighton General Hospital, Gwen Evershed, had a doctor daughter, Judith, married to another doctor, David Banks. By chance we were to meet up with them again at Kings College Hospital. We could not forecast then that our paths would run in parallel in the years to come and that they would become our dearest friends and holiday companions.

But though the social life in Brighton was agreeable, the professional training aspect left much to be desired. In fact, it demonstrated many of the worst aspects that had soured the training regimes of young specialists in the NHS since its inception.

I knew that one of my jobs as a senior registrar would be to deputise for senior colleagues who were away. On my first morning I learned that I had to take the outpatient clinic of the local cardiologist who had become ill. He could not help this, but the illness ran on for several weeks during which no effort seemed to be made by management to find a locum. I was suddenly the consultant cardiologist even though I had had no significant training in this speciality. What was particularly galling was that if I referred a patient for specialist advice to, say, a neurologist, I was sometimes sitting in the neurological clinic deputising there too!

This was a time when junior staff posts in peripheral hospitals were difficult to fill. Overseas graduates were drafted into posts without adequate assessment of their linguistic or professional abilities. One Greek houseman at Brighton spoke English so badly that others had to answer the phone for him when GPs rang up requesting admissions. One particularly dreadful disaster occurred when he had to deal with a pneumothorax (a spontaneously punctured lung) on the left side and finished up collapsing the right lung by mistake in his attempts at curing it. This left the patient with two deflated lungs. I had to move fast to deal with it. Mercifully the patient survived without any residual problem.

I am in no doubt that similar examples of negligence, or just ignorance, resulted from inadequately trained or inexperienced doctors being recruited to fill posts in the Health Service by successive governments anxious to run the NHS "cheap as chips." In later years I felt bitter about Margaret Thatcher who talked about a "slimmed down NHS." There are times when slimming down merges to cachexia. Even later, at the end of the century, Tony Blair told a meeting of doctors at St Thomas's "What we want is more doctors, more nurses and more hospitals." "We've been telling you that for years, " called out one consultant wearily. Sadly it has taken the politicians, of all parties, 50 years to realise that we have been running a Health Service on the cheap compared with most developed countries.

A Curate's Egg at Kings College Hospital

After a year in Brighton I rotated to King's College Hospital where, in theory, I would spend the next three years. We moved to a newly built Town House in Bromley with as large a mortgage as we could afford. Town Houses were fashionable at that time in London, particularly for those who would be moving on within a few years. On reflection they sounded grand but in effect they represented an attempt to provide the builders and speculators with as large a profit as possible for a site which was as often as not a clearance area for old buildings. Ours was like thousands of others, one of a row of three storey terraced dwellings with a garage forming part of the bottom floor. The common feature was that they were all thin houses! Standing in the living room with hands outstretched one could almost touch the adjacent walls of the neighbours' houses. We obtained our mortgage on the promise of a rise in salary recommended by the Independent Salaries Medical Review panel. Mr Wilson, the then Prime Minister, decided to revoke this, which didn't improve my respect for politicians. It has worsened over the years! Nevertheless we managed to scrape some more money together and bought our first house.

95

In fact I spent less than two years at King's. They were like the curate's egg - good in parts. The good parts were at the beginning and the end. The good beginning was the birth, not without obstetrical concerns, of our first daughter Claire. She has given us much joy over the years and has been the source of much pride. The good ending was that I was able to launch myself off on a consultant career with an appointment at Nottingham.

Kings College Hospital was, on the medical side at least, never at ease with itself. When I arrived David Leake, a lugubrious time expired senior medical registrar, sadly despaired of me "I don't know why you've come here. No one has been appointed a consultant from our ranks for years." He emigrated to Canada. The senior medical staff were seemingly all at loggerheads. The Professor of Medicine, a Geordie, was largely ignored. He was supposed to be an expert on medical education but the medical students always told me that no one could understand him or his teaching. He ploughed his own furrow.

I was attached to the Sam Oram/Roger Williams firm. It was an understatement to say that they didn't get on. Because I had gastro-enterological interests I was attached to the Williams half of the unit (quite rightly in my view). Because Sam Oram was the senior of the pair he expected to have two senior registrars attached to him; it was something of a status symbol. As a result I found myself as the buffer between the two taking all the flack when there was a disagreement - which was a lot of the time. Sam, a Londoner of humble background but a real power at Kings, was the senior physician. He didn't take to me and I didn't take to him! Roger, the latest addition to the consultant staff was an opportunist who was determined to establish a Liver Unit second to none in the UK. He quickly recruited a large team and within months of his arrival had a burgeoning research programme. Publications in the medical journals and research papers at clinical meetings became a way of life.

It was a new way of practising medicine for me and although I learned a lot I could not help feeling that everything revolved around the research programme. Nevertheless I found myself with three delightful, hardworking and loyal companions who were research fellows. Paul Smith, a bespectacled, gregarious Thomas's graduate was one of the most extroverted and ebullient doctors I have ever known. He kept us sane with his never-ending fund of stories and experiences, some true, others fanciful. In later life he became a physician in Cardiff. Laurie Blendiss, a very bright Middlesex man worked conscientiously but astonished us all by going off to Israel at the time of the 6-day war. He later became Professor of Medicine at Toronto. The most serious intellectual of the group was Richard Thompson, later Sir Richard, who became a physician at St Thomas's and the Queen's personal physician. I was unquestionably the most pedestrian of the group.

But by my mid-thirties I was anxious to move on. I didn't want to be a junior doctor for ever! By chance the first suitable vacancy to appear was at

Nottingham where I had worked before. I applied and got the job; my first attempt at promotion to consultant status. I remember little of the interview but all six candidates were summoned for 2 pm. By 4.30 pm I was getting fed up with the waiting. Being a "T", I was last in the alphabetical order. When I was eventually called the Chairman said breezily "Sorry to keep you waiting so long, I hope it won't be so bad next time." "I sincerely hope there won't be a next time," I said grumpily. The panel laughed, the ice was broken - and happily there wasn't another time.

I took some ribbing on my return to Kings. "Going to work in the mines?" they asked. I was indeed, but I was the first to be promoted from Kings for many years.

Part 2 A Professional Life

Chapter 9

New Furrows to Plough

1968 - a Turning Point

Some years are turning points in one's lifetime. 1968 was such a year for me. We left London and moved to Nottingham, where I was to work for much of my professional life.

1968 was marked by major events on the world scene. As the tragic Vietnam War continued, anti-war protests erupted across the world. Inexorably the tide was beginning to turn and the war was beginning to wind down. Peace talks were initiated and President Johnson ordered the bombing to stop. We in Britain watched from the sidelines.

Race relations were at a low ebb. The assassination of the civil-rights campaigner, Martin Luther King sparked race riots across the USA. Enoch Powell made his "River of Blood" speech about potential racial problems and, although the Conservative Party was quick to distance itself from what were interpreted as highly inflammatory comments, many living in our inner cities were aware of smouldering discontents. The clenched fists by US "Black Power" athletes soured the Mexico Olympics. South Africa refused to accept a coloured player, Basil D'Oliviera, as a member of the MCC touring side.

History has a habit of repeating itself in assorted guises. Now in 2006, with the Americans, we are seeking to extricate ourselves honourably from a war in Iraq, seen by many of us on both sides of the Atlantic as a colossal mistake. Terrorism has now exploded everywhere on a massive scale in the façade of an Islamic crusade. A new Iranian President threatens to destroy Israel. There are riots between Blacks and Asians in Birmingham, UK.

But the major event for my small family was to find a home in the Midlands, where there was a new job and, hopefully, a circle of new friends awaiting.

Burton Joyce

The first task was to seek out somewhere to live. Burton Joyce had been suggested. Leaving the Nottingham conurbation the river Trent meanders eastwards along a trench two or three miles wide, through the water meadows of Stoke Bardolph, Burton Joyce, Bulcote and Gunthorpe. By road, the A 612 takes you up over Carlton Hill, through the suburbs of Carlton, towards the villages of

Netherfield and Gedling. Once independent entities, they have now been engulfed in the sprawl of expanding Nottingham. Going further east under the old Railway Bridge the road then opens out into countryside for a mile or two before reaching the outskirts of the village of Burton Joyce on the north bank of the river Trent. Some told us to avoid this village because of the smell from Stoke Bardolph sewage works but we decided to take that chance.

Burton Joyce, now a village of some 3,000 folk, had begun to expand in the middle of the 19th Century with the introduction of the framework knitting industry. The opening of the Nottingham to Lincoln railway in 1846, built over a period of eight months, allowed easy access to Nottingham, encouraging business men to travel to the city daily and often back home for lunch. The journey into the lace market took 10 minutes, about half of the time it takes by car or bus today!

In the 21st century, it retains a rural atmosphere with an active village life and a good mix of professionals, upper management, commuters, tradesmen, local workers and retired folk. Its main claim to fame is that it was the birthplace of the famous cricketer Alfred Shaw who bowled the first over in the first ever Test Match in Melbourne in 1877.

Lambley Lane

From the War Memorial in Burton Joyce a little wooded valley runs northwards. Locally these valleys are known as dumbles. At the head of this valley Romano-British pottery was found suggesting that it was the site of an early Roman encampment. Along the course of the stream running down this valley are the houses making up Lambley Lane. Tucked away amongst the trees is the house we bought and where we still live. (see colour photos: fig 2)

When we came to Lambley Lane money and houses were in short supply but we splashed out on the asking price of £12,500 on a family house, pushing our mortgage as high as we dared go. At that time few professionals starting their careers would want to spend much more. On reflection this was probably my best-ever financial speculation. My generation of junior doctors had earned minuscule salaries during their early years and a consultant's starting salary was only slightly better. Fortunately 1970 started the escalation of house prices, which has continued unabated, except in the late 1980s. Soon it became apparent that the seemingly large mortgage was a relatively small one.

So Rosemary and I, our tiny daughter Claire and Dalmatian bitch Pepper moved into a large house built in the solid style of the 1930s with an acre of garden and an orchard. It was a much-admired secluded site with southward facing sunny lawns and rose beds sloping down to the drive. It was clear that, amongst other things I would need to be a gardener myself and possibly employ one. (see colour photos: fig 3)

We have lived there happily ever since - and the smell from the sewage works has never been a serious problem!
(see colour photos: fig 4)

A New Consultant

It was time to start the new job. You expect to feel different as a new consultant. In fact I quickly learnt that I was exactly the same person that I was a few weeks earlier with no new magical source of knowledge, any more diagnostic skills and certainly no additional wizardry to perform therapeutic miracles. And to some I didn't look the part either. On my second day a grumpy schoolteacher asked, "When am I going to see a proper consultant?" He rightly identified me as a recently jumped-up senior registrar. Then, thirty to forty years ago, most patients still had their own image of the archetypal hospital consultant: a middle-aged, sober-suited, grey-haired, gravely spoken patrician exuding gravitas.

What I had not been prepared for was the torrent of work and the speed at which it had to be performed. Decisions were made there and then; there was usually no going back. How different from the leisured pace and pattern of work in the old London teaching hospitals where I had trained. Sadly the East Midlands, including Nottingham, was a medically deprived area short of money, short of hospitals and short of doctors. Those of us working there had to make up the shortfall by seeing more patients and working harder and faster!

My base was the General Hospital, Nottingham. I had last worked there ten years earlier and it hadn't changed much since. I was even allocated beds on the wards where I had worked as a junior. My patients, strictly segregated by sex, were on two separate wards. A few years later we moved to the Queen's Medical Centre, where the mixed wards were divided into four or six bedded male or female bays. This was thought to be progressive and politically correct. A few years later still, after many complaints from patients, our political masters decided that mixed wards were degrading and unacceptable! I had to agree that it was much easier to manage men and women on different wards! Nevertheless most of my admissions came as emergencies and were often very seriously ill. Many were just thankful for care in a hospital bed and weren't too concerned about the sex of their neighbours.

My Sister, Mo Hodder, on the male ward was straight out of "Carry On, Nurse"- starched cap and collar, rustling stiff apron, busy, tight-lipped, soft hearted, and Nottinghamshire through and through. No patient ever died on her ward. He just "clocked his clogs." Both she, and our other efficient Sister, Daphne Fenton, ran their wards like clockwork.

At the General Hospital I looked after the in-patients, co-ordinated their investigations, directed them, where necessary, to more suitable units and ran two outpatient clinics weekly.

I had similar but somewhat less arduous commitments at the City Hospital in north Nottingham. This was the old Poor Law Hospital that had been expanding and modernising since the 1950s and which had become the second District General Hospital in the town. It had in excess of a thousand beds, more than the General Hospital, but a larger component of long-stay beds. Because of its humble origins as the Workhouse, many potential patients were reluctant to be admitted, fearing, quite wrongly, that they would receive inferior service and care. Working at the two hospitals could be embarrassing and confusing. One patient, who had been under my care at the General, found himself readmitted with recurrent problems to the City Hospital a few weeks later. He didn't recognise me and I didn't recognise him. When I asked him why he hadn't been readmitted to the General where he was before, he proclaimed "Not bloody likely if that butcher of a doctor I saw there was going to look after me again!"

The major difference between the two hospitals was that the General Hospital, situated in the centre of town, had one of the busiest Accident and Emergency Departments in the country. Because of this it was bustling, chaotic, exciting and we never knew what was going to come in through the door. One of my colleagues there described it as working underground at the coalface whereas it was all opencast working at the City. On reflection this was an unkind jibe as the City took on a rather different workload.

My other two commitments in these early days as a consultant were Highbury Hospital in Bulwell and a somewhat nebulous duty as physician to the Psychiatric Hospitals, Saxondale and Mapperley. I understood later from my colleagues at my appointment committee that these two duties were added in to my job description to keep me busy!

Highbury Hospital was a folksy little hospital with about a hundred beds of which two wards were for medical patients. Its function has now been changed but in those early days it performed a useful function housing the sub-acutely ill, such as folk with respiratory problems, heart failure and neurological disease, and offering rehabilitation to those with mobility disorders. I always felt that such hospitals performed an extremely useful function in the NHS but they were phased out because they were inefficiently expensive and they lacked support services. My two sisters there were gems. Both were middle-aged ladies of the old school who, in addition to running the ward, acted as efficient resident doctors, mother confessors, councillors, dietitians, social workers and shoulders to cry on. One was plump, bustling and very kind. The other was slim, occasionally sharp of tongue but highly efficient and knowledgeable. Where could the NHS get such a bargain these days?

One Session a Week Psychiatrist

Perhaps the most illogical and inappropriate of my duties when I arrived in Nottingham was to act as consulting physician to the two major psychiatric hospitals, Saxondale Hospital, near Radcliffe on Trent, and Mapperley Hospital, within the city. I was contractually obliged to spend one session (half a day) per week seeing patients with medical problems referred by the consultant psychiatrists or their clinical assistants. It soon became clear that the arrangement was something of a dog's breakfast and that my time could be better spent elsewhere. After 2 or 3 years it was agreed by all that my attendance on a regular basis was superfluous and this commitment lapsed. Nevertheless my visits to the psychiatric hospitals were an education for me and gave me an insight into an unfamiliar and neglected sector of the NHS.

This was a time when media attention, patients' groups, politicians and doctors realised that this was a service in neglect. Because its work was not dramatic or heart rending it had been allowed to moulder. Unless they had vociferous relatives or friends, the public was not too interested in mental illness.

Like geriatrics the vast "asylums" had been at the end of the queue for re-building, modernisation, re-staffing and re-organising. Those in Nottingham were no better and no worse than many others in the country. The buildings were vast redbrick Victorian edifices - presenting imposingly exteriors to the front with polished, echoing public corridors leading off to the wards. Outside there were gardens lovingly tended by squads of patients supervised by staff gardeners. The serried rows of salvias and geraniums outside accentuated the scruffy, run down barrack-room wards inside often smelling of musty toilets, stale bodies, and dirty underwear.

In those wards schizophrenics jostled with depressives and pre-senile dements. The young, middle aged and elderly shared the limited facilities whilst the over-pressed staff struggled to keep order, comfort and some degree of cleanliness. I certainly saw the whole spectrum of psychiatric illness. Some had been institutionalised so long that many, including the staff, had almost forgotten the reason for their original admission. I was asked to see one because of a complex anaemia. He was a dried-up husk of a man, reluctant to communicate and unwilling to leave his ward. In hushed tones the charge nurse whispered that 30 years earlier he had been the central villain in a seemingly motiveless horrific triple murder. This was now depersonalisation by institutionalisation.

But there were episodes that lightened the gloom.

At Saxondale an extroverted schizophrenic always met me at the door and greeted me with a cheery "Good Morning, Jesus Christ." He then generously thrust a large cigar into my top pocket. As a non-smoker I collected many of these expensive cigars, as I didn't have the heart to refuse them. Then, for some weeks he failed to appear. On enquiry I was told that he had collapsed and died suddenly. He had no relatives and died intestate, leaving £60,000 to the exchequer. In the early 1970s that was a substantial legacy and I did not feel too guilty about the cigars.

One genteel elderly country lady was admitted to the psychiatric observation ward in a confusional state with a severe anaemia. I was asked to see her to define the cause of the anaemia, which seemed likely to be due to blood loss from the gastro-intestinal tract. In training we are always taught that it is essential under these circumstances to perform a rectal examination to exclude a bleeding tumour in the rectum. This I did as part of my general examination. As I left the dear lady queried "Are you the vicar?"

Living in the House on the Dumble

Whilst there was more than enough to do professionally our family was expanding. Helen was born in the summer of 1969. I remember the day well. It was early on a Saturday morning on 9th August 1969 when Rosemary went into labour. I had tickets for the Test Match against New Zealand at Trent Bridge. But things couldn't have worked out better. Helen Louise arrived safely before lunch - and I was able to see the rest of the day's play! Joanna Mary arrived in 1972 to complete our family of three girls. So there is no son to carry on the rare family name of Toghill. But that is a small price to pay - we have three lovely daughters.

My son is my son till he gets him a wife
But my daughter's my daughter all the days of her life.

Learning to Grow Roses

I soon learned that one of the problems of being a consultant at a busy hospital in those days was that one was nearly always on call, even when not on take-in. We were always tied to the phone at home and when it rang we were involved. There were no mobile phones then of course. One of my older and highly conscientious colleagues, Reggie Twort, claimed that his home phone was never left un-manned during the whole of his consultant career. No answer phones then either. Such was devotion to duty.

This meant that it was essential to find another interest to replace cricket, which had been my summer relaxation. In any case I was getting too old to play. The selection was not too difficult as my garden needed a lot of time and I couldn't afford a gardener. But I could be on the end of the phone!

I soon discovered that the soil in our part of the Trent Valley transmutes from a tenacious paste in winter to cracked concrete in summer. Fortunately this maligned soil has two virtues: it creates admirable batting wickets and it grows exquisite roses. Between the wars when Nottinghamshire cricket was in its heyday, giants like George Gunn and Joe Hardstaff plundered the visiting bowling on the notorious strip of red marl at Trent Bridge. One wonders if their exploits could have been reproduced on the more lively turf of other county grounds. Modern groundsmen have been able to liven up the old unresponsive plumb wicket and in 1981, 1987 and 2005 the County Championship found its way to Trent Bridge again - with the help of New Zealanders and South Africans!

But the second virtue of the soil means that roses grew well. After all, the gaitered Dean Hole, father of the English rose, was born at Caunton and was later Vicar there, only a few miles away from Burton Joyce. More recently our commercial rosegrowers have prospered with the be-whiskered Harry Wheatcroft leading the way. When I arrived in Nottingham I was encouraged to see that in the summer Nottingham was ringed by dozens of fields brimming with blooms, adding a new industry to a city more famous for cycles, cigarettes and pharmaceuticals. Clearly roses were the answer to my gardening dilemma. Not knowing a floribunda from a hybrid tea I set about filling the garden with roses. It was sound economics and for me, not getting much exercise in the week, sound ergonomics. (See colour photos: fig 5) What started as a necessary task flourished into a consuming hobby which threatened, but never ousted, cricket as a summer relaxation. Now some 40 years on, the good old faithfuls planted then, like Arthur Bell, Queen Elizabeth, Mountbatten and Iceberg are still blooming vigorously. Last year Rosemary and I celebrated our Ruby Wedding by planting a lovely bed of David Austen roses named L D Braithwaite. They are of course ruby reds!

The Queen's Medical Centre Opens

It was always anticipated that the new Teaching Hospital would replace the General Hospital to become, with the City Hospital, one of the two major District Hospitals in the City. The building of the new hospital began in the early 1970s but it was not until 1977 that Her Majesty opened the new hospital formally on 28th July as part of her Silver Jubilee celebrations. (See colour photos: fig 6)

I was clinical sub-dean at the time and was one of the parties responsible for showing the Queen and the Duke of Edinburgh round. Meeting the Queen at close hand made me realise what a tiny person she was - impeccably cloaked in blue and heavily made up. We had been told that she did not enjoy meeting ill patients so she was shown round the impressive buildings of the medical school. My remit was to look after the Duke of Edinburgh who was, I believe, genuinely interested in the scientific exhibits and had to be called sternly to heel by the Queen when he began to lag behind!. He didn't obey immediately and I was impressed and touched that he found the time to walk back to thank me for looking after him.

Fig 1: The south prospect of Nottingham in 1750

Fig 2: Our house in summer

Fig 3: Claire, aged 2, with a supercilious Dalmatian, Pepper, who didn't think too much of the photographer!

Fig 4: Burton Joyce fields in winter. From a painting by PJT in 2000

Fig 5: I set about filling the garden with roses – one of my favourites Just Joey

Fig 6:
The Queen opens
Queen's Medical Centre
on 28th July 1977

Fig 7: A view of the newly built Queen's Medical Centre from the University campus.
Note the passing John Player van. The Player family had been generous benefactors of
the General Hospital but had also damaged the health
of many patients with their products!

Fig 8: Professor David Greenfield, first Dean of the Nottingham medical School.
"A charming and saintly man."

Fig 9: An early structure on the site of the old woodyard. This is the first photograph that we have of a medical school building on the new site! Things did improve later.

Fig 10: In September 1982 the General Hospital Nottingham celebrated its Bicentenary with a procession through the City and a service at St Mary's.

From L to R: Mr J F Sheehan, PJT and Mr Brian Hopkinson

*Fig 11: Port Stanley – the most southerly capital in the world.
A huddle of brightly painted houses clustering round the harbour.*

Fig 12: Penguins at Volunteer Point

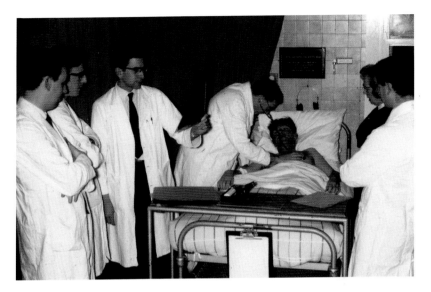

Fig 13: A ward round by the cardiology team at the General Hospital, Nottingham.
Left to right: Steve Talbot, Keith Morris, David Banks, John Hampton and, partly
concealed, Sister Mo Hodder. c 1970

Fig 14: The Physicians of the Queen's Medical Centre, Nottingham
on Prof. Tony Mitchell's Retirement
L to R: Back Row: Alan Cowley, Ian Johnson, Keith Morris, Bob Wilcox, Chris Hawkey,
David Hoskins, Robin Spiller, Peter Rubin
Front Row: Robert Tattershall, PJT, Tony Mitchell, Simon Allison, John Hampton

Fig 15: Iris and Michael Atkinson at their retirement home in the Lake District

Fig 16: Annie, my long-term secretary at the QMC.
One of the unsung heroines of the NHS

Fig 17: An examination candidate undergoing a viva voce examination at the RCP (Rowlands and Pugin 1818. Courtesy of the RCP)

Fig 18: Leslie Turnberg PRCP (Lord Turnberg) and PJT. A wet morning on the Great Wall of China

Fig 19: Returning to the Firm Office with some of the team after my last ward round at the QMC

Fig 20: The Old Post Office, Hutton Buscel. Our bolt-hole for several years

Fig 21: Three daughters – Claire, Jo and Helen

Fig 22: Cricket at Peshawar University.
"There's still some dew on the wicket, professor."

*Fig 23: Fierce tribesmen at the Bab-el Kyber.
Everyone carried a gun, except me!*

Fig 24: The Kyber Pass. Kabul in the distance.

Fig 25: One of the townships outside Cape Town in 1998

Fig 26: A buxom barmaid and her mini-brewery in one of the townships.
The brew from her rusty water butt tasted foul!

Fig 27: My good friend Eddie Carr,
surgeon turned sheep farmer, Cowra, NSW, 1989

Fig 28: A short cut to the beach, near Jo's home in South Adelaide.
Acrylic painting by PJT 2003

Fig 29: The Dingle Peninsula.
I much enjoyed my years as external examiner in medicine to the Universities of Dublin,
Cork and Galway as I could combine a few days holiday with the work.

Fig 30: Two old men on the river in SW France (David Banks and PJT).
Actually we were on a cycling holiday.

Fig 31: Windy Brittany Café. Acrylic Painting by PJT. 2005

Fig 32: Our four grandchildren.
L to R: Sam, Sophie, Katie and Thomas

PJT as Clinical Sub-Dean showing the Duke of Edinburgh round the Medical School at the opening of the QMC. Mr Ian Massey FRCS on the L

It was a great day for Nottingham. From the QMC the royal party went on to the Test Match at Trent Bridge in blazing sunshine. This was a time when Derek Randall was at the height of his popularity with the local cricketing fraternity. The following day the back pages of all the newspapers reproduced photos of the large banner displayed from the popular stand at the ground - "Randall and the Queen rule - O.K."

The first transfers to the QMC were from the old Children's Hospital, an outlying unit in Chestnut Grove. There followed a gradual shift of adult patients from the general Hospital during the late 1970s. Chris Pegg, one of the consultant surgeons resplendent in black coat and striped trousers, celebrated the move by pushing a medical student in a hospital bed, all the way down the Derby Road to the new hospital.

As the Queens' Medical Centre began to fill with adult patients the General Hospital was relegated to a sub-acute hospital with a rump of medical and surgical beds and, for a few years, the existing ENT, eye and radiotherapy departments, out-patients and the Private Wing (Pay Bed Wing). This meant that the medical staff in Nottingham had to polarise to one or other of the major hospitals. I always anticipated moving to the QMC and by then had shed my duties at Highbury, the City Hospital and the Psychiatric Units. Concentrating resources at one large district General Hospital made sense and allowed more efficient usage of time. At the Queen's Medical Centre I would spend the next twenty years of my life as a physician and teacher. (see colour photos: fig 7)

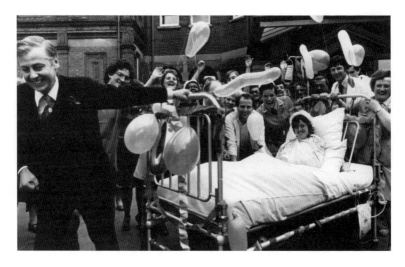

Mr Chris Pegg FRCS, resplendent in black jacket and striped trousers, leads the way in the move of surgical beds from the General Hospital to the QMC

Chapter 10

Nottingham's New Medical School

The exciting prospect of being part of a team creating a new medical school at the hub of middle England was one of the reasons why I was enthusiastic to get back to Nottingham. But it was a few years before the new clinical students actually arrived in the existing hospitals.

Clinical Apprentices weren't new to Nottingham

It had always been assumed that the medical students in Nottingham would be the first ever trained there. In fact, with the passing of the Apothecaries Act on 15th January 1815 a number of provincial hospitals, including Nottingham, had been recognised as approved teaching schools in which a medical apprenticeship could be served. The Statutes and Directions of the General Hospital, passed in 1834, allowed provision for at least six pupils for a three-year period of study on payment of a fee of twenty guineas. The physicians and surgeons were entirely responsible for the teaching at all times and the fees were divided amongst themselves. These pupils or apprentices continued to be taken on until 1860 when, what had become a formal medical school in Nottingham foundered for lack of support. Nevertheless other medical schools in several provincial cities such as Bristol, Manchester. Birmingham, Sheffield, Leeds and Newcastle, which were set up in the early 1800s survived and flourished.

Life was hard for those early medical students in Nottingham. They were bound to strict contracts, which defined harsh conditions of work. The wording of one indenture for a Nottingham apprentice, Joseph Thompson, in 1828 sounds quaint now but it laid down rigid conditions: -

Taverns, Inns, Alehouses he shall not haunt;
Cards, Dice, Tables and other Unlawful Games he shall not play;
Matrimony he shall not contract;
Not from the service of his master day or night shall he absent himself......

Not many of our house physicians would have signed up to these conditions now.

The stamina of those early teachers and pupils must have been tested strenuously too; on Wednesdays and Saturdays they started the day with a surgery lecture at 7.00 am and finished with a midwifery lecture at 8.00 pm. Even the most enthusiastic modern student would have difficulty with these grinding conditions of work

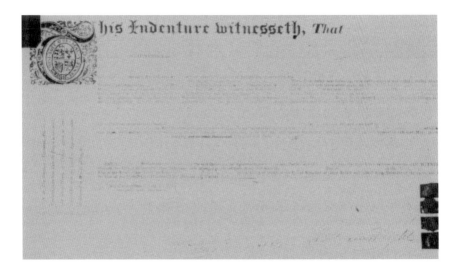

The Indenture of a Nottingham apprentice dated 1828.
An extract from the faded small print is quoted in the text

Plans for a new Medical School in the UK

For several years we had known that we could expect students and a new medical school in Nottingham. In 1964 Mr Anthony Barber, the Conservative Minister of Health announced in the House of Commons that Nottingham was to be the site of the new Medical School. He had proposed a new teaching hospital of 1,400 beds linked with a medical school and conveniently situated adjacent to the university campus. Its construction was eagerly awaited. This was the first new medical school to be established in the UK since the Welsh National School of Medicine was set up in 1893.

There were two reasons why Nottingham was chosen, one good and one bad. The good reason was that Nottingham had already an energetic and thriving University with faculties as old as theology and as new as social sciences. The bad reason was that since the inception of the National Health Service, it had been a deprived region. It was short of doctors, it was short of hospitals and it was short of money. The injection therefore of at least £12,000,000 for the new hospital and medical school was more than welcome. Looking to the future, many of the locally trained doctors would be likely to stay in the area to practice.

The more detailed plans for the new Nottingham Medical School were laid in 1967 by a Committee chaired by Sir George Pickering, then Regius Professor of Medicine at Oxford. He was an autocratic, academically arrogant educationalist who had previously been Professor of Medicine at St Mary's. His Committee envisaged a fresh and uninhibited approach to the older concepts of medical education. The traditional pre-clinical course in the older universities and medical schools taught structure and function as separate and often unrelated subjects. Sir George's Committee reshaped the old 2nd MB course to offer, after 3 years, a B.Med.Sci. degree based on a study of the cell, man and his environment. By the time our new clinical students arrived on the wards they had already seen the full impact of illness in the home, in the workplace and in the hospital. Hopefully there would be a smoother transition from the basic sciences to the bedside.

The new medical school was remarkably fortunate in recruiting, at this time, Professor David Greenfield to the post of Dean (see colour photos: fig 8). This charming and saintly man welded together a team of disparate clinicians and scientists. The new medical school was to become a flagship for excellence and teaching in Europe. Throughout the whole of his Deanship I never heard him say an unkind word of anyone, though there were many times when he must have thought it! When he retired he was awarded a CBE for his services. Many of us felt he had more than earned a knighthood.

But though the preclinical students were on site at the University, by the late 1960s a series of planning disputes delayed the building of the new hospital. To anyone concerned with the project it seemed impossible that the misshapen tangle of iron girders and concrete on the site of an old woodyard would ever be transformed into a working hospital before 1980 (see colour photos: fig 9). As an interim measure to cope with teaching requirements the existing Nottingham Hospitals had to have face-lifts and extra units built on. This meant that the General Hospital Nottingham, an old Voluntary Hospital built in 1782, had wings added to accommodate the Professorial Surgical and Medical Units. A new Maternity Hospital was built at the City Hospital, which had been the old Poor Law Hospital and extra wards and new units were planned elsewhere. (See colour photos: fig 10)

What should they be taught?

With this first influx of students my colleagues and I felt that we should try to get away from the old style emphasis on rarities and concentrate on day-to-day medicine. Looking for some guidelines, we looked at the causes of admission to our own medical wards. It came as no real surprise that the majority were patients with degenerative vascular disorders with the unhealthy addition of some elderly folk over treated and many young folk self poisoned. Whilst it was easy to define the common and more obvious topics it was amazing how much argument was generated as to what each physician regarded as core teaching. Personal interests coloured our views enormously and we decided that we were all like the American professor, who excused himself any selection in his teaching material by claiming

"What I teach is core, what the others teach is crap!"

We had an advantage in Nottingham in that there were more than enough patients and, sadly, more than enough diseases, to allow each student to have his or her own extensive portfolio of "cases seen personally." None of us could have imagined that, by the turn of the century, the demands for vastly increased numbers of doctors in the UK would mean that we would run out of real patients for the expanding army of medical students to study. Novel methods of teaching history taking and eliciting physical signs would have to be sought using audio-visual aids, actors and simulated devices.

Our surfeit of clinical material in the early 1970s was in contrast with many of the older London Teaching Hospitals who were beginning to suffer shortages of clinical work by the population drift from the city centre to the suburbs. As a result the wards of the great metropolitan teaching hospitals were often starved of patients with everyday diseases and bolstered with patients with obscure disorders ready to satisfy the curiosity of the consultants and the appetites of the research workers. To combat these problems, much had been done to use the resources of the larger peripheral hospitals in the suburbs for student secondments away from the a*lma mater.*

New Students Walking the Wards

Our first batch of clinical students was scrutinised suspiciously by the older clinicians but everyone was delighted to find them eager, well informed and enthusiastic, with a disarming frankness which had been lacking in our own contemporaries. Mostly they were tidily dressed and, even if trendy, their appearance could not give offence to the patients. Looking back - and indeed it is only just over 30 years ago - we were concerned about trivial variations from conformity: for the men shoulder length hair, earrings, open neck shirts, gold necklaces and bangles. Curiously the girls chose to conform though I remember some of our older lady consultants weren't happy with female students wearing slacks.

We had a minor crisis on my ward when one of the new (male) students appeared wearing an earring. I can't remember the side or indeed the significance. My fellow consultant colleague on the firm, Mike Wells and I debated how we should justify a ban on earrings for male students on the ward. Fortunately our old style ward sister, Mo Hodder, came to the rescue before we were directly involved.

"For God's sake, don't let Doctor Toghill see you wearing an earring on the ward or you'll be eaten alive," she declared.

No one ever appeared again with an earring and I earned the reputation of being a tough disciplinarian!

There had been a deliberate effort by our student selection panels to choose a significant proportion of mature students. We had a solicitor, already in his 40s, who quickly became father figure to that first batch of students. In later years he utilised his medico-legal qualifications to become a coroner. One suave and older than usual student astounded me on our first bedside teaching session with his dexterity in testing the visual fields. I complimented him on his performance, only to elicit a round of suppressed titters from his peers. He turned out to be a qualified optician. Amongst others we had a chemist, a pharmacist, a qualified nurse, and an airline pilot. Another character appeared in a cat suit and nail varnish on the morning of the General Medical Council's Inspectors' visit. They chose not to notice this theatrical gesture! This strikingly attired student proved, in later years, to be the first Nottingham graduate to gain a university chair!

Watching these young men and women on the threshold of their careers I couldn't help feeling a little saddened that the constraints of the examination system and the necessity to absorb so much knowledge prevented them from enjoying life more. There were assessments every few weeks. Contrast this with my medical student life. We sauntered along until that dreadful rush in the last few weeks of the course when everyone mugged up their notes and midnight oil burned late. It had to be accepted that there was no place in the modern world for the perpetual student of the inter-war and immediate post war years. Not everyone now will remember Benskin, the sports coated, bow tied, plum-waistcoated, corduroy-trousered elderly student so superbly portrayed by Kenneth More in the "Doctor in the House films." His aunt had left him £1000 per year just for the time whilst he was a student - and he was going to enjoy every minute of it!

Introducing Students to Patients

Any initial contact between a patient and a doctor involves two basic processes: taking the history, that is finding out the reasons why help is being sought, and performing an examination. The latter may overlap with the patient's symptoms but often it provides additional information about them. This initial contact should give the opportunity for the patient to spell out his or her main worries but it also should give the doctor an opportunity to pick up non-verbal clues about the problem. Additional information perhaps not obviously important to the patient may be critical. As Wilfred Trotter observed "Disease often tells its secrets in a casual parenthesis."

It always seemed to me that this initial confrontation was absolutely critical to every thing that followed. How often have we heard the complaint that doctors never have the time or inclination to listen and are reaching for a prescription pad or requesting a blood test or X-ray without looking up from the desk. Nowadays they are glued to the computer screen. I believe that talking to patients and examining them is the grammar and vocabulary of the language of medicine.

One had to remember too, that the vocabulary of our working class East Midland patients might be different from that of our students from Tunbridge Wells, Carnarvon and Aberdeen; and it might be completely unintelligible for those from Kuala Lumpa, Sri Lanka or Hong Kong. In Mansfield "bonny" didn't mean good-looking; it meant plump going on to frankly fat. In Newark "my legs are giving me hammer," meant my legs are painful. And in Nottingham "Ey up, mi duck!" is a normal mode of greeting.

Jumping forward a few years, the first tiny cohort of 37 students graduated in 1975. They had not suffered from the delays in building the new super- hospital, later to be known at the Queen's Medical Centre. Instead this tolerant group of pioneer medical students received their education in temporary huts, jocularly known as the cowsheds, in the University and in the old General and City Hospitals.

Going further forward 30 years from the first graduation ceremony, the integrated medical school and hospital that now forms the QMC has established itself as an international centre of medical education and research. Major academic departments have been set up there and at the City Hospital. A new graduate entry medical school has opened at Derby and the total annual intake of medical students stands at 330. Perhaps more importantly - and something that is now taken for granted- is the staggering improvement in health care provision locally. The Nottingham graduates themselves have been at the forefront of this change, with 80% practising within 80 miles of the medical school, providing professional leadership and clinical care for the people in the East Midlands.

From little acorns .....

Chapter 11

A Journey to a Faraway Outpost of the Empire

In 1978, four years before they became the focus of world attention in an extraordinary war between Britain and Argentina, the Falkland Islands represented an obscure outpost of the Empire far away in the South Atlantic. I doubt if many living in the UK could accurately pinpoint their position. Even fewer cared.

It came as some surprise therefore that in 1977 I found myself tangled up in a review of their medical services. I had been offered a Travelling Scholarship to take my medical skills to any remote part of the world for the benefit of the local inhabitants and for the medical workforce. At the same time the Department of Overseas Development was anxious to review and improve the medical services for the Falklands which were, in every sense of the word, out on a limb. The Department was particularly worried about the standard of medical care that Falklanders might receive when they were evacuated to the nearest hospital in Argentina at Comodoro Rivadavia or to the British Hospital in Buenos Aires. They were also concerned about the expense and the criteria for sending Falklanders to the UK for medical treatment and were anxious to establish a clearer channel of communication between the Medical Department in the Falklands and the UK.

I had had contact with the Department of Overseas Development before and, to cut a long story short, it was agreed that the Department would supplement my scholarship if I would provide an up to date overview of the situation. Although relations between the two countries were at that time sensitive, the prospect of an Argentinean invasion was, to the Foreign Office at least, remote.

On a cold winter's evening in January 1978 I flew out from Heathrow by Aerolineas Argentinas to Madrid on the first leg of the long haul to Stanley, East Falkland. After Madrid there was the long flight over the Atlantic to Rio de Janeiro. South America was then still an infrequent destination for Europeans and the plane from Madrid was only half full. Three seats to myself, a steak and half a bottle of red wine allowed a good night's sleep and by dawn we landed in Rio. I had expected blue skies, a tropical sun, Brazilian music and a feast of colour at the Airport. Instead a damp grey mist wrapped itself round me - it was like a wet afternoon on the County Cricket Ground at Derby. The Brazilian airport staff, a pastiche of European, South American Indian and African cultures were surly and grumpy; no hint of the samba, the rumba, the throbbing music, the laughter or the infectious rhythm of carnival time. There wasn't even a decent cleavage or a flash of coffee coloured thigh. In homage to international travel the ubiquitous Tom Jones was belting out "It's not unusual...." in the background.

Buenos Aires

A quick change of plane and within a couple of hours we were up and away again, hugging the Brazilian coastline under what soon became a peerless blue sky. As we flew over Montevideo and into Buenos Aires, the estuary of the river Plate stuck out like a yellow tongue of muddy water into the Atlantic. Landing at Buenos Aires the blue and white national flag of Argentina was everywhere, mirroring the blue sky and white clouds. The airport staff were more cheerful and helpful though their heavily accented Spanish was difficult to understand. It was quickly apparent that this was more of a European culture, with a mix of Italian, Spanish, French, German and British lineage but, at first sight, very few indigenous South Americans. Downtown Buenos Aires was a city of wide avenues, spacious parks, palm trees and lawns surrounding imposing but faded, plaster-flaking, pink roofed public buildings. Further out there were tall blocks of flats, scruffy streets and dusty houses shuttered to the afternoon sun. Huge advertisements were plastered everywhere: cigarettes, petrol, wine, clothes, restaurants and watches all to be bought in this city - if you had the money! My first impression was of shabby Barcelona but maybe that was unkind to that fine Spanish City. Nevertheless for a South American country the people were well dressed, cheerful and gregarious; there was no obvious evidence of the undercurrent of political unrest, which had poisoned their society for so many years.

This was a different world with a parochial outlook. There was nothing in the newspapers of North American or European politics. The headlines were taken up with arguments with Chile about the Beagle Channel, the developing wine industry and, most of all, football.

I had been booked into the City Hotel, an old fashioned traditional hotel smelling of furniture polish and cigar smoke with candelabra, wood panelling, heavy curtains and oil paintings. There was no need to search for information as the reception manager quickly and enthusiastically introduced himself. His Cork accent gave him away. He was an Irish émigrée who had lived in Argentina for more than twenty years. Within minutes I had a verbal tour of the City, a list of the Irish Bars, two or three night clubs to visit and some phone numbers for ladies who did not speak English but who would know what I wanted! In fact my immediate needs were dinner - it was a huge peppered steak, what else, - and bed.

The Department of Overseas Development had warned me that a "Certificado Provisorio" was absolutely essential for my well being and ease of travel. So the first trip next day was to the British Embassy where I chatted agreeably with a fair-haired, pink-cheeked, public schooled Foreign Office bureaucrat who fed me coffee and biscuits, issued my "Certificado Provisorio" and warned me against getting involved in political arguments with the locals. I was surprised that he was already aware of my slightly undercover assignation at the

British Hospital Buenos Aires; it was reassuring that Government Departments communicated with each other at this distance. There was now a hint of James Bond!

The British Hospital, Buenos Aires was an impressive building dating from the end of the 19th Century when British influence in Argentina was at its height. We tend to forget that the British played a dominant role in the development of the railway system and that a large ex-patriot population settled here in the late 19th and early 20th centuries. In the 1970s the daily English newspaper in Buenos Aires had a circulation of 25,000. This was all brought home to me when I crossed into the entrance hall of the Hospital. There on the wall was a Board showing the list of consultants in gold lettering with an In/Out sliding panel adjacent to the names. The entrance hall was, as I remember it, identical with that of the old Radcliffe Infirmary at Oxford. The names on the list betrayed their origins: - O'Higgins, Mac Pherson, O'Grady, Mc Donald, Smithson, Brownlow and Sheehan, to name but a few. There was hardly an Argentinian (or should I say Spanish) name amongst them. I was to learn later that none of the owners of these British sounding names spoke English; they were second, third or fourth generation Argentineans.

I was ushered into the office of the Director of the Hospital. He would be with me in a few moments I was told. I settled to one of the international medical journals that was lying around. Out of the corner of my eye a small, slim, white coated, doctor with a pencil thin moustache looked furtively round the door seeking me out. Thinking I hadn't seen him he quickly slipped away to return a few moments later; perhaps he had been checking my credentials. He then greeted me enthusiastically and told me in halting English of the history of the hospital before taking me on a tour. This was clearly an expensive private hospital primarily for ex-patriots, but not exclusively British. As far as I could determine there was no obvious accident and emergency department. What I saw, on what was necessarily a limited tour, was a clean, modern hospital with adequate resources. I noted that the haematologist was a well-known name in the world literature and that several of the doctors I spoke to had worked in prestigious medical institutions in the USA. Nevertheless I could not avoid the impression that this was a hospital in decline and that deteriorating Anglo-Argentine politics might squeeze it out of existence. Future events proved me right.

To be fair I was allowed access to everything I wanted to see. At the end of the day I formed the conclusion that it was reasonable for Falklanders to be treated there for routine conditions such as elective abdominal surgery, straightforward orthopaedic surgery, gynaecological problems and ear nose and throat diseases. In fact only a few patients from the Falklands had used the facilities in recent years.

In Patagonia

The next stage was to get down the coast to Comodoro Rivaderia, the departure point to the Falkands. This took me over Patagonia, an area of some 300,000 sq. miles east of the Andes extending down to the Argentine port of Tierra del Fuego. I was to cover in a few hours the beginning of Bruce Chatwin's slower and unrestrained peregrinations through Chubut into the desert plateaux described so vividly in his award-winning travelogue "In Patagonia." It was Patagonia that represented to Chatwin, in his formative years, the last outpost of humanity, the only place on earth where he and his school friends, poring over atlases and studying prevailing winds, had decided that they could survive the chain reaction to a cobalt bomb. My air journey was more of a taxi service to Mar del Plato, Trelew and Comodoro where I was to stop overnight before catching the twice-weekly Fokker plane to the Falklands, or the Malvinas as the Argentines insisted on calling the islands.

Comodoro was a dry, dusty commercial and transportation centre bearing the air of an erstwhile oil boomtown. With a population of 125,000 its hotels were shabby and the bars were full of locals drinking rough red wine and watching the Argentine Grand Prix. Once again I had to suss out the local hospital because this was the first port of call for seriously ill Falklanders. It wasn't exactly a hive of activity. The two or three residents on duty were glued to the television. My impression was that Comodoro was something of a one-horse town a long way from anywhere else. My impression was right. It was.

But there was somewhere even further away, some 400 miles to the east, across the grey unwelcoming South Atlantic - the Falkland Islands, my destination after this long, fragmented air journey. By now I had met some real Falklanders or Kelpers as they were known locally. They had assembled in the hotel in Comodoro for the last leg of their journey home. A few had been on holiday in the UK or New Zealand. Some had been on holiday in Buenos Aires, shopping or sightseeing. Two or three farmers, going back after a business trip, already knew of me from the passenger list and were determined to make sure that I arrived in Port Stanley with one hell of a hangover. They succeeded.

The Most Southerly Capital in the World

The ancient Fokker taking the twenty or so of us across had seen better days and as we came in to land I was puzzled to see the Argentinian First Officer looking out of the windows under the wings over the windswept, scrubby landscape.

"Don't worry," said my phlegmatic companion. "He's only checking that the wheels are down!"

116

But with a few bumps and rattles we landed safely. The airport buildings were no more than a cluster of prefabricated huts where a uniformed officer, doing service as both policeman and customs officer, greeted us and checked our baggage as a matter of formality. After all, who would want to smuggle anything or anyone into or out of this isolated outpost of the Empire?

Surprisingly these islands, lying about 400 miles from the South American mainland, are at about the same latitude south as London lies north. It seems likely that the first British claim to discovery was a sighting in 1592 by Captain John Davis of *The Desire*. Captain John Strong of *The Welfare,* who navigated the sound between East and West Falkland in 1690, gave the islands their British name after Viscount Falkland, treasurer of the Admiralty. South Americans have known them as the Malvinas since the 1600s.

Bitter arguments about the islands' sovereignty have raged for 400 years. Argentina, then a Spanish colony, based their claim on a first sighting in the 1500s. The British claim rested on the first recorded landing in 1690 and subsequent settlement and administration from 1833. From the early 1960s the sovereignty of the islands had become an outstanding political issue in Argentina and relations with Britain remained at a low ebb, not helped by a United Nations debate on decolonization in 1964. When I arrived in the Falklands in 1978 the problem continued to grumble on and I had the impression that the British Foreign Office was keeping the issue on the back burner. Certainly no one I spoke to in the islands seriously feared an Argentine invasion.

The Senior Medical Officer, Dr Derek Cox and his wife arrived at the airport to pick me up in his Land Rover and took me to his home in Stanley a few miles away. Both he and his wife were Scottish Islanders who clearly loved the life of isolation and self-dependence there. On the way I could see, in the distance, the huddle of brightly painted wooden houses with green or red corrugated iron roofs, clustering round the harbour (see colour photos: fig 11). On the hillside were newer prefabricated houses forming "suburban" streets with their own neat but treeless garden plots. A little distance from the harbour and jetty were older houses from the early days of colonisation, with a hotel and few shops. I noticed the Church, dignified by the term cathedral with a whalebone jaw arch over the gate, at the centre of the town. There certainly wasn't too much of this southern capital city and I calculated that, if necessary, I could see and medically assess the whole population during my stay there.

I was touched that a party had been organised for me to meet many of the locals: the medical and nursing staff, the governor and his wife, local dignitaries and friends and neighbours. Although it was summer, there was a peat fire smouldering in the hearth and we remained inside for protection against the restless wind which swept across the islands night and day. I was to learn that summer weather was predominantly Scottish but that most days offered a taste of all four seasons. I learned too that anoraks were standard wear and that you took your shoes off when you went into peoples' houses! Gin and tonics were served very long and with increasing frequency during the evening. I was soon to get to know that the islanders were able to serve lamb or mutton in every possible combination of dish - roasted, curried, stewed, marinated, minced or boiled!

The next day I was introduced to the medical arrangements on the islands. There were three doctors; Derek Cox, a man in his 30s was the Senior Medical Officer and had trained in surgery and was a Fellow of the Royal College of Surgeons of Edinburgh. He had two colleagues, one a lady doctor who acted as anaesthetist as required. There was also a vet and a dentist in the town. The King Edward VII Hospital, from which they worked, was a white, wood built structure with the standard corrugated green roof, housing 30 or so beds, consulting rooms, a small lab, an operating theatre and a very primitive X-Ray machine. A small ambulance was garaged nearby.

The medical practice was spread far and wide because in addition to the two large islands, East and West Falkland, there were dozens of small islands, some of which had settlements. The distance from the most easterly point to the westerly outpost at the New Islands' settlements was over 170 miles. Land outside Stanley was termed "camp" and time there was an hour different from Stanley time! Communication between doctors and camp was by short wave radio but medical consultations could not be confidential since everyone on the islands listened to what was being said! The doctors had a rota for visits to camp and were taken there by one of the two floatplanes. The wrinkled, hard-bitten, chain smoking pilot of one of these must have sensed my unspoken concerns about his health when he started ferrying me around.

"Well, doc," he said, "there are old pilots and there are bold pilots but precious few old, bold pilots."

Standing on one of the floats, early one morning, arm hooked round a strut, an ECG machine under the other and cold blue water splashing over my legs reminded me that I was a long way from home.

In many ways the medical services on the islands were better provided than those in other distant parts of the world. Many of the problems were similar to those seen in the UK; it was the isolation that made their management different. The hospital patients were visited on a combined ward round each day. These included occasional maternity cases and some long-term geriatric patients, too ill to be cared for in their homes. As regards general medical care the emphasis was on preventative medicine and an extensive inoculation and health education programme was underway. Like many other isolated communities many drank too much, many much too much.

One of my jobs was to assess those chronically ill patients who might benefit from evacuation home and specialist treatment in the UK. This I did during my stay but two were particularly memorable, one at each end of the age spectrum. The first was a baby with an oesophageal stricture, later operated upon by my colleague in Nottingham Miss Lila Kapila; the second was an old man with a huge aortic aneurysm, dealt with by Professor Brian Hopkinson, also at the Queen's Medical Centre, Nottingham.

One unexpected source of work was the large Russian fishing fleet which was "hoovering" the Antarctic clean of fish during those years. The Hospital at Port Stanley was the nearest port of call for them for both medical and surgical emergencies. One evening I had to go out to the hospital ship attached to the Russian fleet to see a sailor who had had an emergency appendectomy on board a few days before. The operation, normally a few minutes job, had apparently taken an inexperienced surgeon two or three hours and had resulted in a faecal fistula (faeces draining from the wound). The Party Representative on board who organised these things (not the Ship's captain!) was reluctant to allow me to take the patient back to Port Stanley and expected me to perform extensive surgery on the ship. It is a reminder of how suspicious Russia was of the West during the Cold War. Eventually his resistance was broken down and we took the patient back to Stanley on a very rough sea. Happily the fistula healed spontaneously whilst there in hospital.

Local Diseases

Diseases relating to the sheep farming had always been endemic on the islands. Hydatid disease had been a serious problem in the Falklands in the past but was being eliminated in the 60s and 70s by deworming programmes in the sheepdogs. This very serious disease, seen world wide in sheep farming communities is due to the tapeworm *Taenia echinococcus* which forms cysts in sheep or man in vital organs. The adult worm lives in the gut of the dog and the eggs (ova) are shed into dog faeces. Sheep graze on pastures contaminated by dog faeces and ingest the worm ova. In the gut of the sheep the ova develop into larvae which then migrate to vital organs such as liver and brain where they form cysts. Dogs eating raw mutton containing the active cysts normally complete the cycle. In the intestine of the dog the cysts undergo digestion to become tapeworms which attach themselves to the lining of the dog's gut. In this complicated life cycle man gets infected, just like the sheep, by ingesting ova in food, usually vegetables, contaminated by dog faeces. Until the 80s and 90s it was impossible to treat the cysts other than by excision - a formidable surgical exercise. Now mercifully specific chemotherapy for hydatid disease is available.

One disease that I had never seen before was orf, a crusting pustular sub-acute skin lesion, due to a poxvirus contracted from sheep and seen on the hands of farmers and shearers. I soon came to recognise these lesions which usually healed spontaneously.

At the end of my stay I had to put forward suggestions as to what could be done to improve the medical services on the islands. It seemed to me that with better air travel serious routine operations, such as hip replacement, would be better carried out after evacuation to the UK rather than being transferred to Buenos Aires. As so often happens events overtook us and within four years the Falklands War hit the islands and made the direct UK evacuation programme mandatory. Now the presence of military doctors and supporting services on the islands allowed much more complex projects to be dealt with locally. In 1978 when I was there a new X-Ray machine was urgently required, basic endoscopy facilities and doctors trained to use them were also needed. The pathology lab was pretty basic. Sadly, after the Falklands War, a disastrous fire burned down the King Edward VII Hospital claiming as a victim a lovely girl who was having a baby there at the time. She was the laboratory assistant who had worked with me there.

Penguins and Diddle-dee Bushes

The Falkland Islands form a unique wild life ecosystem and I was delighted to see something of this. For those staying in the Falklands a trip to the shanty on Volunteer Point is a must. The shanty is an old shepherd's cottage with two up, two down, a lean-to kitchen, and a chemical closet round the back by the peat shed. It was impossible to miss because its red corrugated roof and white walls stood out strikingly two or three miles away; after all there wasn't another dwelling within 10 miles. It took us, Derek and family and myself, eight hours to reach the shanty by Land Rover from Stanley after a bumping, bruising journey over rugged windswept moorland, scarred by rocky outcrops and studded with diddle-dee bushes. We were lucky in having to winch the Land Rover out of the bogs only five or six times. I was told that we might have been unlucky and might not have arrived at all.

So why did my hosts go to so much trouble to get me to this isolated shanty? The explanation was that it overlooked Volunteer Point looking out across the grassy dunes towards the cold, blue South Atlantic where there are thousands and thousands of penguins. We were lucky enough to be there in the mating season. The little Magellan or jackass penguins were guarding their eggs in burrows spread out over the sand dunes, often several hundred yards from the sea. (see colour photos: fig 12) At our approach quizzical heads poked out twisting and turning myopically as if to get a better view and then pecking viciously at our boots if we drew too near. In the evening as we had our brew up in the shanty their donkey-like braying almost deafened us. It was hardly a haven of peace.

The gregarious gentoos were nesting in enormous colonies on moorland even further inland than the Magellens. These little chaps, looking just like miniature waiters, chattered incessantly as we walked amongst them but were neither frightened nor aggressive. Many of them spent their time toddling up and down well-beaten and tortuous paths to the sea. Most impressive were the king penguins standing imperiously and unconcerned, some incubating a single egg, covered by a warm apron of belly wall resting on top of their feet. The kings were a good deal less common than the gentoos but nested in groups in the same colonies, being distinguished by their greater size and by their scarf of bright yellow-orange feathers. In a few weeks the penguins would be gone, only to return to the same beach, to the same burrows on the same day next spring.

I counted myself lucky that I had been able to spend time on these islands of breathtaking beauty, seemingly immune to the ravages of modern life. One reclusive Stanley dweller that I met had emigrated there from Surrey and had transported a prefabricated Scandinavian type house to the site of his choice overlooking the entrance to the harbour. He believed, like the young Bruce Chatwin, that this would be a haven of peace well away from wars and disasters. He could never have imagined that within four years a war would have been raging around him.

Chapter 12

A Physician's Lot. Changing Life at the Coal face

What do Physicians Do?

Friends and family often ask me, "What exactly do physicians do?" It can be frustrating trying to explain and I felt a good deal of sympathy for Professor Krishna Somers of Perth when a diplomat asked him about his job. He replied that he was a physician and I reproduce the subsequent conversation reported in the London Royal College of Physicians Commentary: -

"So you perform operations."

"No, I am not a surgeon, I am a physician."

"So you are not a specialist."

"Yes, I am a specialist, my speciality is general medicine."

"Ah, so you are a general practitioner."

"No, I am a physician in internal medicine."

"Now I understand. So you are a gynaecologist."

That just about sums up the confusion! Everyone knows what surgeons do. They cure patients by operations: removing tumours, excising inflamed appendices, fixing broken bones and creating new blood channels. The public understand that gynaecologists deal with female problems - one of my large West Indian ladies described them as "lady's lower belly specialists." Most people know that pathologists examine tissues taken from dead or diseased patients. And geriatricians deal with health care of the elderly.

But what about physicians? Even the top newspapers and BBC News get it muddled. We hear or read about famous (or notorious) patients who might, for example, have acute medical illnesses such as pneumonia or a stroke and we are told that the surgeon (not the physician) in charge of the case was reported as saying this or that. We physicians get indignant when the media give the impression that all top specialists are surgeons with the courtesy title Mr and that physicians, when they become good enough or senior enough, are promoted from Doctors to Misters. It might be said that when surgeons make a reservation at a restaurant or book cars into the garage they use the term Dr!

So what do physicians do? Where does their work begin and end?

The truth is that physicians are hospital-based specialists who treat seriously ill non-surgical conditions with drugs or other procedures, diagnose complex disorders and direct patients to appropriate departments such as radiotherapy or oncology for further care. In fact these days, with radiologists, they undertake an extraordinary range of diagnostic, interventional and therapeutic activities - coronary catheterisation, biliary tract cannulation, endoscopic ablation of polyps and sclerosis of oesophageal varices to name but a few. All these have been made possible as a result of modern technological advances. Skill in these procedures requires long training and experience and this in turn has led to increasing specialisation. The general physician of yesteryear, who was expected to be able to deal with the whole range of human maladies, is now obsolete.

Until the 1950s most physicians were classified as general physicians but, because of their training or interests, usually had particular expertise in one speciality or another. In a busy District General Hospital in the UK 80 - 90% of a physician's in-patient work was and still is, generated from emergency admissions such as heart attacks, strokes, diabetic coma and asthma. Consequently every physician should have sufficient all round skills and knowledge to cope with this workload. In the early days therefore we were general physicians first and foremost and specialist system physicians secondarily.

Now in the early 21st century the reverse is true. Most physicians are primarily system specialists i.e. chest physicians, gastro-enterologists, rheumatologists but have also to deal on a day to day basis, with a hotchpotch of general medical emergencies.

Medical Changes in Nottingham - and a few of the Characters Involved

It is in the context of an evolving scenario that I have labelled this chapter "A Physician's Lot - Changing Life at the Coal Face." Its purpose is to describe what hospital physicians have been doing over the last half century and to highlight some of the issues that have dominated my life and the lives of my colleagues in Nottingham and elsewhere.

It is impossible to be comprehensive but I have concentrated on certain areas of general medicine where there have been remarkable and at times unbelievable, advances during my own career. Momentous changes have occurred in virtually every aspect of patient care in Nottingham over this period but I hope that this section will give a flavour of what has been happening. Unfortunately there is neither the time nor the space to deal with surgery, obstetrics and gynaecology, paediatrics and the many other specialities. I hope that my many other colleagues will forgive me for not writing about their particular interests.

From Faulty Valves to Heart Attacks

In the first half of the 20th century many of the cardiac problems affecting young and middle-aged patients were those related to valvular heart disease, following rheumatic fever or St Vitus' Dance. These two diseases were linked to poor living conditions. In my career in Middle England I saw no more than a handful of cases of acute rheumatic fever and in the Western world rheumatic fever is now something of a rarity. It is still depressingly common in the underdeveloped world. In my visits to Africa, the Indian Sub-continent and the Far East in recent years, I have seen many adults suffering from the long-term sequelae of childhood rheumatic fever.

As students we saw dozens of cases of chronic rheumatic heart disease together with advanced cases of congenital heart disease, many of which, at that time could not be dealt with surgically. Of course, 50 years ago there were, in addition, the routine cardiac problems that we still have to deal with today: rhythm disturbances, high blood pressure, pulmonary embolism, the vascular complications of diabetes, various types of heart failure and perhaps, most commonly, heart attacks. What we never see now is heart disease due to syphilis. Fifty years ago our teachers collected these cases to demonstrate gross cardiac physical signs including cardiac murmurs. The sight of a huge pulsating syphilitic aortic aneurysm seemingly on the point of bursting through the chest wall was one of the most frightening physical signs that I saw as a student.

As a medical student it became essential to become adept with the use of the stethoscope, the traditional tool of the trade. Buying a stethoscope was one of the highlights of the new medical student's shopping. Much time was spent (and wasted) on teaching sessions learning what particular sounds and murmurs were present. It was an important part of our training then but in my view given undue prominence. Now the interpretation of the heart sounds has been overtaken by echocardiography and sophisticated scanning techniques. They are more accurate, but a good deal more expensive!

The cardiac surgeons cut their teeth, if I can mix my metaphors, operating on patients with chronic valvular heart disease or, in the case of the paediatric surgeons, congenital heart disease. But new ground was broken when in 1967 the world heard the incredible news that the first human heart transplant had been performed in Cape Town by a South African surgeon, Christian Barnard. The patient, Louis Washkansky, died 18 days later but a second heart transplant performed by Barnard on another patient a month later survived 563 days. There was public outcry at the time. Many claimed that this was barbaric, unethical and contemptible. But the major scientific objection at that time was that there was inadequate immunological knowledge to support the procedure. Now cardiac transplantation is an accepted, though uncommon, procedure in special cases.

By the late 1960s, when chronic valvular heart disease was becoming much less common in the UK, resources were being diverted to the treatment of heart attacks. These attacks were termed coronary thromboses or myocardial infarcts and were due to blockage or narrowing of the coronary arteries (termed loosely thrombosis) carrying blood to heart muscle which was damaged as a result (myocardial infarction). Morbidity and mortality from heart attacks had been increasing since WWII and were, by mid-century, the commonest cause of sudden death in men.

Until then there was little that could be done for heart attacks apart from pain relief and efforts to treat any associated heart failure. The familiar picture I saw in my younger days was of a middle aged man, usually a heavy smoker, overwhelmed with excruciating acute chest pain, grey and sweating, pleading for relief of his pain. There were no coronary care units then and intensive care meant a bed near to Sister's desk. Many such patients died within minutes or hours. If the initial episode settled down a spell of complete (and it really was complete) bed rest was thought to be an essential component for recovery. This included being washed, shaved and fed. The whole process took up to six weeks in hospital. No one knew if it was really necessary and we ignored the hazards of deep venous thrombosis that complicated prolonged immobility.

Dealing with patients with heart attacks was a major problem for physicians working in acute hospitals (Colour photos: fig 11) and it was a long while before our political and administrative masters were prepared to allocate adequate resources for research or management. One cynical Minister of Health claimed that the best bargain in the NHS was for a middle-aged man to drop dead from a heart attack. No time in hospital and no expensive medical care!

So what could be done to tackle coronary heart disease which had become a major cause of premature death in our society? A three-pronged attack was required: prevention, improvement in hospital care and development of methods to unblock or by-pass occluded coronary arteries.

Firstly, education about the prevention of heart attacks was critical. Awareness of the link between smoking and heart disease began to emerge in the 1960s as a direct follow on of Richard Doll's work showing the association between smoking and lung cancer. Sadly even now 20 - 30% of the population are still smoking including, astonishingly, many nurses. There are commercial firms and individuals who still deny the association.

"Look at my father," people say, "he smoked 30 a day all his life and died at 90!"

The second approach followed an awareness that ventricular fibrillation (uncontrolled irregular fast beating of the ventricles) was a frequent cause of sudden death in the first day or two after heart attacks. With continuous electrocardiographic monitoring in coronary care units after admission the onset of this rhythm disturbance could be detected immediately and cured by an electric shock (electrical cardioversion). This was a major advance; certainly better than just being near to Sister's desk! So, by the 70s most District General Hospitals were establishing coronary care units.

Our own coronary care unit at the General Hospital grew from a side ward on one of the general medical wards. It was set up and supervised by Dr John Hampton (later Professor Hampton) who was Senior Lecturer in the Department of Medicine, which was in turn headed up by Professor Tony Mitchell, the Foundation Professor of Medicine. These two were a formidable pair.

Tony was a Lancashire man, who was a medical student in Manchester There his progress had been no less than triumphant. Effortlessly he won every prize and topped the examination lists time after time. After qualification he became, in turn, house physician to Sir Robert Platt in Manchester and, after National Service, Registrar and First Assistant to Sir George Pickering, Regius Professor of Medicine at Oxford. It was from that post that he was appointed to the Foundation Chair of Medicine in Nottingham. From his arrival in 1968 he built up a powerful team with John Hampton, Keith Morris, Stan Heptenstall and Bob Wilcox (one of my first registrars in Nottingham). This team, basing their work on the common cardiovascular diseases seen on the Coronary Care Unit and on the wards in Nottingham, showed the world how to conduct trials of therapy in cardiovascular disease. (See colour photos: fig 13) During the 1970s and 80s the group prospered and the flow of important papers to prestigious journals was but a trivial marker of the calibre of the team. Tony never missed an opportunity to make something out of virtually nothing.

For the other physicians in Nottingham, Tony was very much a father figure (see colour photos: fig 14) and he achieved national distinction. When Sir Raymond (Bill) Hoffenberg retired as President of the Royal College of Physicians in 1989 Tony agreed to his name being put down as a candidate for the post. He had much support in the country, particularly Nottingham, Oxford, Manchester and London. But we did not count on Tony's powerful left wing views. Shortly before the closing date for the candidature was due, he asked for his name to be withdrawn. A few days earlier Princess Margaret had attended a medical function there.

"I cannot bear the thought of having to kow-tow to the likes of that dreadful woman," he declared. Except that he used a different adjective to describe her.

Sadly he died unexpectedly in 1991. His bust, sculpted by a colleague Mr Kelvin Thomas, FRCS, stands in the entrance hall of the Medical School in Nottingham and bears this inscription: -

Si munumentum requiris, circumspice
(If you seek his monument look around you)

John Hampton was responsible primarily for the day to day running of the Coronary Care Unit. He was another Oxford man - studious, bespectacled, incisive and innovative. John had an alpha + brain and was a superb teacher. He was, in my view, the ideas man on the Professorial Unit and was instrumental in instigating many important trials of therapy dealing with heart attacks.

But I am drifting from my theme in talking about these characters and I must return to the general problems of tackling heart attacks. The third area of progress in the 70s and 80s was as a result of the technique of catheterisation of the coronary arteries feeding blood to the heart muscle. A fine catheter threaded retrogradely from the femoral artery in the groin, up the aorta and manipulated into the coronary arteries allowed dye to be injected to outline the vessels to show narrowings and obstructions. In those days coronary artery catheterisation was a difficult and potentially hazardous task. Time moves on and coronary angiography is now an everyday procedure in the hands of experts.

Visualisation of the coronary arteries enabled surgeons to turn their attention to methods of bypassing the blocked coronary arteries by grafts from other arteries or veins. The survivors of heart attacks, crippled by angina (chest pain on exertion) had their lives transformed; though at that time the expectation of life was not greatly improved. Bypass surgery became commonplace and survivors of the operation boasted of their triple or quadruple by-passes in the manner of describing three or four star hotels as compared with the humble one vessel operation!

Now interventional cardiologists, in our hospitals, are able to pass their catheters into the tiniest of coronary vessels to identify narrowings, which can be opened up by stents or expanding balloons. All this can be done within a few hours or days of a patient complaining of early symptoms with a quick return to normal life. Much of the interventional work and the cardiac surgery has been set up at the City Hospital where there is now a large team. These changes were scarcely believable 40 years ago when we had so little to offer other than morphine and prolonged bed rest.

Diabetes Made Easy

Insulin therapy is unquestionably one of the triumphs of 20th century medicine, converting a miserable wasting illness with an 18-month life expectancy to a state of well being. Sadly all those early hopes have been frustrated by the knowledge that insulin replacement therapy does not offer freedom from the disabling long-term complications. When many of us trained 50 years ago, diabetes was looked after by physicians for whom it was very much a secondary interest. We remembered large clinics with patients clutching their bottles of urine and scribbling on prepared charts with a variety of pens and pencils. What they were doing was filling in the urine testing charts that should have been filled in day by day over the previous weeks or months. We knew and they knew, that it was something of a farce. From the 1970s onwards the clinical management of diabetes underwent a sea change, putting patients in charge of their disease and simplifying its complexities. We in Nottingham were at the heart of those changes.

In 1970 I had the good fortune to appoint as my senior House officer Dr Robert Tattersall. He was a Cambridge and St Thomas's graduate who had flirted with the law before deciding on a career in medicine. A pipe-smoking soccer enthusiast with a huge intellect he later brought his many talents to bear on the practical problems of diabetes and put Nottingham at the forefront of the speciality in the UK. On leaving his junior post he worked at King's College Hospital with Dr David Pyke and published seminal work on the genetics of diabetes. After a spell at Bart's as a Senior Lecturer he returned to Nottingham as a consultant physician to run the diabetic department.

From that base he introduced home monitoring of blood glucose levels instead of urine testing, trained diabetic nurses, introduced foot clinics, and lectured and wrote widely. His research work with Edwin Gale (later Professor Gale) was widely acclaimed. Edwin, was remembered by us all whilst a Senior House Officer, not as a future professor but a kindly person always prepared to do something extra. On a blisteringly hot summer evening, labouring on a busy take-in, one of his patients complained,

"I could murder a pint of bitter, Dr Gale."

A few minutes later Edwin appeared with a foaming pint on a tray having been to the "Trip to Jerusalem" to get it!

Haematemesis and Melaena: Endoscopy now reveals all

As a gastro-enterologist this was my personal battlefield!

For patients, nurses and doctors haematemesis (vomiting of blood) and melaena (passing of altered blood per rectum) is an alarming symptom. It was a common cause of admission to medical wards being usually due to such diseases as bleeding peptic ulcer, hiatus hernia or bleeding oesophageal varices as the result of cirrhosis of the liver. In my early days as a house physician and registrar, management was based on attempts to make a clinical diagnosis of the cause of the bleeding by history taking and examination and to replace the loss of blood by transfusion. It was often a critical decision whether to continue with blood transfusion and to hope the bleeding would stop spontaneously or to tackle the problem aggressively with surgery. With profuse bleeding the mortality was often high whatever was done. In the event of continuing bleeding the surgeons were called in firstly to ascertain at operation (laparotomy) the site of the bleeding, and secondly to stop the bleeding by appropriate measures.

As a gastro-enterologist, many of these cases came my way. It was frustrating just to attempt to replace blood loss without knowing the primary source of the bleeding. In the 60s and 70s policies were adopted to attempt to define more accurately the source of the bleeding by barium meal examinations. Unfortunately clinical trials of urgent barium meal examinations for upper gastro-intestinal haemorrhage failed to establish this as a useful practical investigation.

What was needed was a method of viewing directly the inside of the upper gut, the oesophagus, stomach and duodenum whilst the bleeding was going on or shortly after it had stopped. The advance came with the introduction of the fibre-optic endoscope - unquestionably the greatest advance in gastro-enterology of all time. Rigid tube endoscopy of the upper and lower gastro-intestinal tract by direct illumination had been available for the previous 50 years. It suffered the major disadvantage of inflexibility (half metal and half rubber tube for the upper gut and all metal for the rectum and lower colon). Unfortunately as these instruments were rigid they caused patients much discomfort and not infrequently perforated the gut. It was Basil Hircshowitz, a South African who moved to Michigan, who in 1958 introduced a completely flexible gastroscope made up of multiple pliable optic fibres transmitting light. For the first time physicians and surgeons were able to visualise directly ulcers, tumours or oesophageal varices and to identify sites of bleeding. The enormous advantage was that this was all relatively safe and not too uncomfortable.

Those of us who had the responsibility for looking after "bleeders" (as patients with gastro-intestinal haemorrhage were known in hospital slang) adopted this new diagnostic tool which enabled us to quickly locate the site, severity and cause of gastrointestinal bleeding. We could then discuss with the surgeons whether an operation was required. With further progress we learned to inject sclerosant fluids into ulcers down the endoscopes through tiny catheters to stop minor bleeding lesions.

Our young trainees and registrars quickly learnt and adopted these new endoscopic procedures. Some of the consultants, like old dogs, were slow to learn new tricks. However one senior physician who was an absolute wizard with the endoscope was my fellow consultant on the firm, Professor Michael Atkinson. He was undoubtedly one of the most skilful wielders of the endoscope in the country and he taught us all a great deal, combining his technical expertise with an inventive talent, particularly in dealing with oesophageal lesions. I could not wish for a more loyal and supportive colleague on the wards. He and his wife Iris were also our near neighbours in Burton Joyce and we much enjoyed their good friendship, support and hospitality. (See colour photos: fig 15)

Shortly after Michael's retirement Chris Hawkey, one of our senior registrars, was appointed as gastroenterologist and began building a large and prestigious department under his headship as Professor of Gastroenterology. Now all gastro-enterologists are adept at manipulating their 'scopes both up and down the gut and threading catheters for diagnostic and therapeutic purposes into the biliary and pancreatic ducts.

Liver disease was a sub-speciality taken under the wing of gastro-enterologists in most large hospitals in the country until 20 or 30 years ago. Since that time it has become a significant sub-speciality in the UK. With other gastro-enterologists being appointed to the hospital in the 80s and 90s, I changed direction somewhat to concentrate on patients with liver disease which was becoming an increasingly challenging problem. We were beginning to see the dangers and consequences of Hepatitis B infection, an infection transmitted between drug addicts and homosexuals but also from mother to child. In the 80s and 90s we were able to identify another serious liver infection, Hepatitis C, a virus spread by intravenous drug abusers and blood transfusion. Whereas initially our wine and beer-drinking neighbours France, Italy and Germany always had alcoholic liver disease as a major problem, the UK was rapidly catching up. Now, in the 21st century, alcohol consumption matches that of our continental colleagues, with the added menace of binge drinking in the young. We are now seeing alcoholic hepatitis in our teenagers and alcoholic cirrhosis in 20-year-olds.

Nonetheless some of my older patients with alcoholic cirrhosis were likeable rogues. You could never believe a word they were saying. Elsie, a blowsy, peroxide blonde ex-barmaid made several valiant attempts to stop drinking. One morning she breezed into the clinic reeking of alcohol. I said nothing at the time but took the precaution of checking her blood alcohol level and asking her to come back next week. She duly arrived looking contrite. The blood level of alcohol had been astronomically high. She had her explanation ready,

"I know you found some alcohol in my blood last week, doctor. Well, I can tell you why. As I was leaving, the lady across the road called me over. Come and try the trifle that we are having for our silver wedding party on Saturday." Elsie turned to me apologetically, "I'm sure she put some sherry in it."

The Assault on Malignancy. From despair to hope.

Because I had had training in haematology in Sheffield and at UCH, I also had the task of looking after patients with haematological malignancies, including leukaemia, when I arrived in Nottingham as a consultant. This was in addition to the gastro-enterology. It would be an unthinkable combination now. But we were short of specialists of all varieties. During the 60s and early 70s haematologists in the District General Hospitals rarely ventured out of their laboratories onto the wards to undertake the holistic care of patients. They had not been trained as clinicians. Our old war-horse of a professor, Tony Mitchell was so antagonistic to laboratory haematologists that he refused to ever have them anywhere near his wards!

The diagnosis of acute leukaemia in an adult was then virtually a death warrant. I only recall one of my adult patients with acute leukaemia being cured and she is alive and well 40 years on. But scientific advances in leukaemia raced ahead dramatically and it became clear that a general physician had neither the knowledge nor the time to deal with such specialised problems. A new breed of clinically trained haematologists took over claiming the need for in-patient beds and wards. In the 21st Century, marrow transplantation and intensive chemotherapy in specialist units, such as that at the City Hospital, are producing cures that we never dared dream of 40 years ago. There was certainly no place for the likes of me looking after patients with leukaemia though I was touched when my old colleagues named such a specialist ward after me at the City Hospital Nottingham.

A particular interest in an unusual disease, lymphoma of the gastro-intestinal tract, led me into the wider field of management of Hodgkin's disease and the Non-Hodgkin's Lymphomas with my good friend and colleague Dr Eric Bessell. He had trained at the Royal Marsden Hospital as an oncologist and radiotherapist and we joined together to run a combined clinic for the benefit of such cases.

As part of our unit we recruited a Middlesex trained sister, Biddy Walker, as a chemotherapy co-ordinator and counsellor. This innovative appointment was one of the first of its kind and similar units in the UK followed suit. It proved a spectacular success and Biddy combined a sympathetic ear with practical advice for patients with lymphoma. She could more than hold her own with the senior medical and administrative staff! Regrettably, as with other innovations, many wanted to climb onto the counselling bandwagon. Now we can only call for two cheers for counsellors. Many so-called counsellors were untrained, ill suited and frankly dangerous. Bad advice was being given that was often unwanted. Now our feeble society feels the need to be counselled for burglaries, for failing interviews and for witnessing disagreeable events. A generation ago most would regard such unfortunate episodes as part of the ups and downs of life.

The way scientific progress in malignancy has moved on in the last 10 - 20 years was emphasised to me during the course of an illness of a near neighbour and friend. I saw her first at her home in the village when she had lost weight and was vomiting. Our investigations showed her to have bone lesions, a high calcium level in the blood and anaemia - all due to myelomatosis a rare form of bone cancer. The portents were bad but with intensive chemotherapy she went into good and lasting remission. Not unexpectedly the disease eventually relapsed, requiring more courses of chemotherapy. Later I referred her to my colleague Professor Nigel Russell who carried out bone marrow transplants. After a good quality of life, which had lasted for 15 years since the onset of symptoms she died, mourned by friends and family. Medical science had given her a worthwhile life, which would have been limited to weeks in the 70s and 80s.

An Invaluable Colleague in Respiratory Medicine and a Good Friend

It is impossible to list every speciality and to relate the changes but I must conclude this section by mentioning respiratory disease, which had previously taken a back seat at the General Hospital and the QMC. Until the advent of streptomycin therapy in the 1950s, respiratory medicine had been dominated by the care of patients with tuberculosis. With the development of streptomycin and other effective drugs, the need for tuberculosis doctors regressed and a new breed of respiratory physicians emerged to care for asthma, bronchitis, lung carcinoma, sarcoidosis, sleep apnoea and a multiplicity of breathing problems.

When Michael Atkinson retired, Ian Johnson was appointed to the staff as a respiratory physician to form a new firm with me. He came with glowing recommendations and has certainly lived up to them. Quiet, determined and with a wealth of specialist expertise he quickly built up a new department to which was recruited Dr William Kinnear and Dr Ian Hall. Ian Johnson has demonstrated that he has a very safe pair of hands administratively by becoming Clinical Director of the QMC, an unenviable but essential task.

The Medical Take-In

So much for the type of work that we physicians were all doing. How was it organised? For most physicians working in NHS hospitals, life in the last 50 years has been driven by the "take-in" - hospital jargon for emergency admissions. As I have said 80 - 90% of medical admissions are emergencies. This is obviously a major commitment. Take-in admissions comprise a ragbag of problems: patients with chest pain, asthma, pneumonia, stroke, bleeding from the gastro-intestinal tract, self-poisoning, fevers and coma. Some are life threatening; all are serious. You never know what will come through the doors next: a businessman returning from Africa with malaria, a gardener with tetanus or a member of the Royal Family who has collapsed whilst out shooting.

Three unusual cases admitted on take-in over the years illustrate the extraordinary range of problems.

A 17 year-old white Nottingham schoolgirl came in as an emergency with 4-Kg weight loss and several weeks of severe diarrhoea. The G.P's provisional diagnosis was ulcerative colitis. Shortly after her admission, our microbiologist rang us from the laboratory in a state of some excitement. She had found large numbers of the larvae of Strongyloides stercoralis in the girl's stools. The flurry of interest was because though common in Southern Europe and the tropics, no patient had ever contracted this gut parasite simply living in Britain. The common mode of infection is from a larval reservoir in warm wet soil. The larvae penetrate the skin of the feet and enter the blood vessels to reach the lungs. From there they migrate via trachea and pharynx to the gut where they multiply before being shed in the stools. This young lady had never been out of England, except for a day trip to Boulogne. She was, however, in the habit of walking barefoot everywhere including local parks. We thought that in walking barefoot she might have trodden in infected faeces from an infected dog or cat, which had contracted the infection abroad. An unusual hazard of being barefoot in the park!

A vet's wife, aged 41, was admitted in a coma from rural Lincolnshire. There were no obvious causes but she had had similar admissions to two local hospitals with unexplained coma and had recovered spontaneously. She slowly regained consciousness whilst with us. Screening of her blood revealed no poisons or sedatives. However our alert house physician was convinced that there were puncture marks on her thigh. Her husband was again challenged about the possibility of self-poisoning and he recalled that he had noted that the fluid level in the bottle of injectable cow tranquilliser had been going down inexplicably. It wasn't inexplicable; his wife had been injecting herself with it. The firm manufacturing the tranquilliser was able to identify the tranquilliser in a sample of blood that we had retained. I am glad the lady hadn't injected the full bovine dose!

A steelworker, aged 38, was admitted one Sunday morning in a confused state having attempted to strangle his wife in bed at 10am. His wife explained that he had been quite well except that on the two previous Sunday mornings under similar circumstances he had been confused and aggressive. Our initial tests showed that he had an extremely low blood sugar level. He recovered quickly when given glucose. Further investigation revealed that he had an insulin-producing tumour of the pancreas. The explanation of events was that on Sundays he had a lie-in and didn't have his normal big weekday breakfast. The situation was akin to a diabetic having a morning injection of insulin without breakfast. He recovered when the tumour was removed surgically.

These three patients were out of the ordinary run but most of the cases arriving through the hospital doors now are similar to those of 50 years ago. It is how it is managed now that is different. Numbers are greater, patients are streamed earlier to specialists and the technology is mind boggling.

Most District General Hospitals arrange their medical and surgical staff into firms, each consisting of two or more consultants, one or two registrars or senior house officers and housemen. The firms are often linked for ward location and deputising convenience. Depending on the size of the hospital, a firm is responsible for admitting and caring for all the medical emergencies in the area anything from two or three days each week to one day in ten.

Initially at the General Hospital Nottingham, when we were short of medical staff, the firm was on take-in for two or three days each week. The junior doctors were expected to deal with admissions during the night and to work normally next day. It was a gruelling task but as the years passed and we moved to the Queen's Medical Centre, numbers of staff increased and the rotas became less demanding. But this didn't mean the burden lessened because concurrently the numbers of emergency admissions escalated rapidly.

There is no doubt that this excessive workload sapped the physical and mental energy of the junior staff and stifled their enthusiasm. Not only that, it was dangerous for patients to be looked after by doctors who had been on continuous duty for many, many hours. They were no more than zombies. Thankfully the public and later the politicians recognised the long hours faced by poorly paid, over - worked juniors. And, as I was to learn, the consultants were working quite hard too!

Outpatients at the General Hospital, Nottingham in the 1930s

Outpatients at the Queens Medical Centre, Nottingham, 1990

Never enough Hospital Beds

A critical and on-going problem over the years has been to find beds for not only the take-in admissions but also the waiting list admissions. From the 5 to 15 medical patients admitted daily on a take-in to the General Hospital in the 1950s, numbers of admissions soared in the 1990s to between 30 and 80 each day to the two major Teaching Hospitals in Nottingham. On one horrendous Boxing Day my own firm admitted over a hundred patients. We had patients on 14 wards in the hospital.

These mounting admission rates in all large hospitals were fuelled by improvements in therapy, advancing technology, growing public expectations, medico-legal pressures and closure of smaller peripheral and cottage hospitals. The general practitioners, in response to all these factors were less inclined to care for patients in their own homes. This remorseless demand for emergency beds meant, of course, that patients had to be discharged earlier and earlier. They were often still ill with their work-up incomplete. Often incomplete investigatory procedures had to be performed on an out patient basis. Some patients, who were discharged before they were really fit enough to go, were quickly re-admitted as part of a "revolving door" syndrome.

During the middle years of my career as a consultant, the length of stay for acute medical admissions fell from 10.2 days in 1974 to 6.7 days in 1988 -89. Over this period the bed stock in England was cut from 158,000 to 123,000. Similar changes were reported in geriatrics and in units for the younger disabled; 243,000 cases treated in 1979, and 447,000 in 1989 -90 whilst the bed stock fell from 57,000 to 51,000. Statistics such as these were used by some to highlight an apparently increasingly efficient use of one of the most expensive resources of the NHS.

Unfortunately the hospitals with fast stream activity were assumed to be the most efficient. If they were anything like our hospitals in Nottingham the fast throughput was not efficient. It was forced on us by the excessive demand for beds from the surrounding areas. I believe that admitting patients into fewer beds and shortening their stays is fraught with dangers. A 100% occupancy produces a tight bed state which has inevitable consequences: patients on trolleys on corridors outside A and E Departments, patients housed in unsuitable wards, patients sent home dangerously early and time wasted by everyone searching for empty beds.

I believe that it is high time that we killed the myth that rapid turnover and high occupancy of beds equates with efficiency and that empty beds indicate profligacy. In busy hospitals there needs to be more flexibility and the acceptance of a less than 100% occupancy.

Ways of dealing with Admission Crises - Good and Bad.

In Nottingham we made some progress in dealing with the torrent of emergency admissions in the 1980s and 90s by creating a medical emergency ward. In theory this ward admitted all the emergencies but they stayed no longer than 24 hours, before being moved on to other wards. A duty physician was on duty for 24 hours and carried out a full ward round each evening and another round the following morning. Thus the laudable object of all emergencies being seen by a consultant within 24 hours was achieved.

This change was not achieved without manpower costs. The ward had to be staffed by junior doctors round the clock. To have a shift system over 24 hours meant more staff. With this emphasis on emergency admissions, work elsewhere was interrupted and the duty consultant had to cancel his or her routine work for that day.

Unfortunately because of this conveyor system patients may never see the same doctor twice. The admitting consultant transfers the patient after 24 hours to another ward under another medical team. There may be other relocations; for example a patient with a haematemesis (vomiting of blood) may be moved to the endoscopy unit, later to a gastro-intestinal unit ward and then, if the bleeding continues, to a surgical ward for an operation. Regrettably in this sort of system there is limited continuity of care. This isn't good training or experience for the doctors or nurses either as no one seems to take responsibility for the long-term care. Disease is seen as a series of snap-shots rather than a continuous sequence.

How the NHS Responds to a Disaster

There are times when events overtake us, staff have to be summoned quickly and beds found.

On 8th January 1989 I was sitting at home watching the beginning of the 9pm evening news. The horrific bulletin started

"A Plane has crashed on the motorway."

Within seconds my phone was ringing. It was the District Manager, David Banks.

"A plane has crashed on the M1 near Kegworth on its way to Dublin. You are the Physician on Duty. Will you mobilise the Major Disaster Plan?"

The physician on duty always had the responsibility for supervising and co-ordinating any major disaster. In fact David had read the rota incorrectly and I had to inform him that Tony Mitchell was the man he needed. Nevertheless it was clear that all hospital staff were required immediately. I was on my way.

British Midland Flight 092 had crashed on the western bank of the M1 and there were multiple casualties. Within a few minutes medical nursing and ancillary staff were converging on the Queen's Medical Centre. It was the nearest and largest hospital and received most of the casualties. David Daly was the senior surgeon on duty and I cannot improve on his description of events, which appeared later in a letter to the British Medical Journal.

It took some 15 minutes to reach the hospital, by which time the stream of ambulances had begun to arrive. In the Accident and Emergency Department were our three consultants and a host of junior staff of all disciplines, enough to provide each of the injured with several doctors. The injured were numbered on arrival, for many were unconscious and the remainder too shocked to speak, their clothing torn and without possessions with which to identify them; it seemed strange to check the cross-matched blood for "Patient 1405."

The major disaster plan was working well. Two wards had been evacuated and were ready to accept the injured while the intensive care unit was gathering staff and preparing its complex machinery. At 10 o'clock I went to the theatre unit and found the theatre manager there. He told me he had eight theatres fully staffed and ready. Within minutes my first crushed abdomen and chest was coming into theatre.

At no time did I see any shortage of medical staff. One patient, his face crushed beyond belief, needed specialist care and within minutes two consultant surgeons, dental and ear, nose and throat, were examining him and planning his treatment. Most of the injuries were skeletal, in particular leg and spine fractures, and all our nine orthopaedic surgeons, with their junior staff were there before midnight. We had so many anaesthetists that there were two with every patient in theatre.

I was pleased later to read the words of the BMJ's editor, "The medical care was exemplary." Indeed I believe it to have been so, but I know that it could not have been so without the work of the rest of the hospital staff. Ward F19 was evacuated to provide room for the casualties and I saw staff midwives pushing patients in their beds over to east block. I went into theatre and found my operating department manager there; he said,

"I heard it on the telly, so I thought I had better come."

Anything we needed for the casualties always seemed to be at hand: crystalloid and colloid infusions and blood cross matched seemingly in minutes for the drips, and no doubt this was due to the laboratory, blood bank, and pharmacy staff being there in large numbers. We had porters and our engineers............

...The injuries were horrific: compound leg fractures, with feet almost detached at the ankle, appalling cervical and lumbar spinal fractures, crushed chests with multiple rib fractures, haemothoraces, but few abdominal injuries. Some patients were unconscious, and often paralysed, and virtually all were deeply

shocked. Throughout the night all the teams I have described worked skilfully and gave devoted care to the best of their ability.........

As a physician on the spot I agreed that the medical and surgical care was exemplary. This was the NHS working at its best. Our only fault was in the identification of the dead. Of 118 passengers and 8 crew there were 47 fatalities with 79 with serious injuries.

Many of us had read in the Sunday Times earlier in the day a leaked cabinet review which had been highly critical of hospital consultant staff. The authors of the report were no doubt safely tucked up in bed during that hectic night.

Downsides - Bogged Down with Committees

Unfortunately as you become more senior you get landed with increasingly irksome committee work. It is the same in most other professions. I wasn't particularly keen on this as I never considered myself as particularly articulate and I wasn't quick enough "on my feet" to become a medical politician. Nevertheless it had to be done and some of the committees were important.

One of these more important committees was the Committee on Safety of Medicines. Our postman complained that the papers that arrived each month were the heaviest he had to deliver! If one read every word it would take 8 hours reading every day of the month. How many hectares of forest are destroyed each year just to keep the bureaucracy of the NHS ticking over? Nevertheless this was an interesting committee of important therapeutic influence. It also had powerful commercial ramifications. Though confidential, it leaked like a sieve and I was often able to read of our secret deliberations in the broadsheets next day.

I fear that I must have sat on dozens of Committees over the years, many trivial and time wasting. I could never understand why it was necessary to have a committee of eight or ten senior doctors to appoint doctors to relatively junior posts when two or three could have done the job perfectly well. Ludicrously the mandarins in Whitehall regarded Chairmanship of a Committee with administrative and political implications as being far more important than a lifetime of industrious clinical work or teaching. That's the way to get a knighthood!

Downsides - Litigation, a Canker in our Midst

Each year the Medical Defence Union (one of the profession's insurers) publishes its Year Book. In one section it describes several illustrative examples of cases of doctors who have been in trouble and who have been represented by the

138

Society. Some were in trouble with the law or were frankly negligent and the Union had to pay damages. Some doctors had made genuine mistakes. Others had been caught up in a series of unfortunate circumstances or chances which could have overtaken any of us. A number were the butt of malicious accusations and were cleared in the courts. Often after the publication of the Medical Defence Union's Annual Report colleagues would shake their heads and mutter

"There but for the grace of God........."

We are not all paragons of virtue. Like any other profession there are bad apples in the barrel. Unfortunately the medical profession has become a prime target, with lawyers, not wronged patients, as the prime benefactors.Litigation is on the increase in the UK fuelled by outrageous courtroom settlements in North America, sensationalism in the media and "ambulance chasing" by British lawyers.

Luckily, I was only sued once in my professional career. I say luckily because it is often as the result of a series of unforeseen circumstances or simple mistakes that we get entangled in the medico-legal net. An elderly diabetic lady had been admitted under my care desperately ill with acute heart failure due to a heart rhythm disturbance. She was resuscitated and given a powerful drug into a central vein near the heart to control the heart rate; which it did and the patient recovered. Unfortunately in the drama and hassle of resuscitation the catheter administering the powerful, but toxic drug slipped out of position and leaked under the skin causing, two or three days later, a patch of skin necrosis. This had to be dealt with by plastic surgery at a later date but all went well and the patient survived. We were later sued for malpractice (her son was a lawyer). I argued that this lady was lucky to be alive and that the leakage of drug was an unfortunate complication. The Regional Board solicitor advised that we should settle for damages out of court. Any legal battle would be far too expensive. I was bitter about the case as I felt we had saved the lady's life. The family claimed that they did not want the money but "wanted to be sure that the mistake was not repeated." This is not an unusual response in my experience.

Now I do not want to suggest that the profession is hard done by in the courts. The dreadful Bristol heart scandal and the Shipman case show that we have to put our house in order. Indeed in my later post as Director of Education at the College of Physicians I was closely involved with the General Medical Council in ensuring that members of the profession were answerable to their peers and to the public and that they were maintaining the highest possible standards of practice.

However litigation has become a canker in our midst. The profession is now spending too much of its time looking over its shoulder and practising defensive medicine. This is time consuming and formidably expensive. Litigation is escalating at a frightening rate and medico-legal authorities seem unwilling at present to differentiate between mistakes and negligence. And the public and the media must realise that there are times when death is inevitable.

Unsung Heroes of the Health Service.

The vast majority of those working in the NHS rarely hit the headlines. This is because they get on with their jobs conscientiously and diligently. They are the unsung heroes (or heroines) of the Health Service.

Annie (see colour photos: fig 16) was my secretary for the whole of the 30 years whilst I worked as a physician in Nottingham. Short, dynamic and combative, with at times a short fuse, she would surround herself with a barricade of hospital notes which spilled off windowsills and shelves and spread as far as the doors. Only she knew where things were! Though nominally a hospital secretary she performed many additional duties, shielding me from awkward phone calls, shuffling the waiting lists and organising outpatients for optimum efficiency. Given my own disorganisation this was an unenviable task. For hundreds of patients she was the mother hen, clucking a bit, but caring for them all with immense patience and pride. She, Liz and later Chris, Michael Atkinson's secretary in the same office, worked diligently and were paid a pittance. It is a disgrace that the NHS neglects such loyal workers.

She was one of many thousands who keep the NHS going: secretaries, ward receptionists, porters, cleaners, ward orderlies, laboratory staff, and filing clerks. The vast majority are ordinary people doing their jobs quietly and well. We are all in their debt.

50 Years of Progress

This chapter has tried to give a flavour of what it has been like to be a physician working in a large hospital at the hub of Middle England. Whereas medicine was largely an art in the first half of the 20th century, it has undoubtedly evolved into a science in the second half of the century. A profession which was therapeutically limited before World War II has now much to offer.

The changes have seen the QMC become one of the flagship hospitals in the UK and its Medical School arguably one of the best in Europe.

Chapter 13

Talking to Patients and Breaking Bad News

"They never tell you anything" is one of the commonest complaints that patients make about doctors and hospitals.

About 30 years ago E.E.Rawlings, a gynaecologist from Salford, wrote amusingly but perceptively about this problem in the British Medical Journal. He had referred a patient to a colleague for an opinion and she had returned before the report had been received. Rawlings asked what Dr X had told her.

"Nothing" came the laconic reply.

"Didn't he even say good morning?"

"No" said she, "it so happens that the appointment was in the afternoon. But he didn't say Good Afternoon either!"

This was an occasion when communication was unquestionably rated as zero!

I have to confess that I hadn't given the problems of "Talking to Patients" any serious or positive attention during my early career, simply because like so many others in the profession I arrogantly assumed that I was good at it. However, my own deficiencies were exposed in mid career when I had the task of explaining to a worried husband what was wrong with his ill wife. She had enlarged glands in the abdomen that were probably due to a malignant lymphoma. So far as we could determine there was no evidence of disease outside the abdomen. To make a diagnosis we had to take a tiny sample (a biopsy) of an enlarged gland in the abdomen with a wide bore needle, examine the excised tissue under the microscope and define the precise type of tumour. The selection of treatment and the prognosis would be dependent on the microscopic findings.

I spent the best part of half an hour explaining all this. As the husband got up to leave he shook me firmly by the hand and said

"Thank you, doctor. So the biopsy will completely cure her."

Now I may not be the world's greatest communicator but I had made a genuine attempt to convey my distressing and serious news in an accurate, honest and sensitive way. But this intelligent man's response made it clear that I had failed completely. I resolved then to try to do better in the future.

For those of us who have to talk about illness and death to patients and their families, our failures in communication are far too common. Even when we think we have spoken in simple and direct terms we later hear of bizarre and horrific statements attributed to ourselves that are utterly incomprehensible. All doctors have had the experience of telling wives, husbands, sons and daughters that a loved one was going to die. And on two or three occasions after the inevitable death of the patient the distraught relatives have said,

"I wish you had told us it was that serious."

We are usually to blame because we talk in technical language. We try to deliver too much information and we forget that one piece of catastrophic and disastrous news slams ears and minds shut. Further details are irrelevant.

Some of my older colleagues were unbelievably arrogant when dealing with patients. One orthopaedic surgeon refused to talk pre-operatively to a GP friend of mine who was going to theatre having sustained a serious lawn-mower hand injury.

"Mr X only talks to private patients before trauma surgery," Sister explained. Another colleague, a radiotherapist, refused to talk to his patients with malignant disease and always shifted that considerable burden to his juniors of the nursing staff.

Everyone, be they doctors, nurses, counsellors or medical students, who have to talk to patients and to transmit bad news, should read Cathryn Morgan's book "A Private Battle" which describes her husband's fatal illness. Cornelius Ryan was an Irish American journalist who achieved fame from such books as *The Longest Day* and *A Bridge Too Far*. At the age of 50, thinking that his symptoms were due to prostatitis, he had a prostatic biopsy and was told brusquely by his urologist that he had a carcinoma of the prostate. The surgeon recommended him to have a radical prostatectomy in two days' time. This operation would, he was told, almost as an afterthought, cause impotence, sterility and possibly incontinence. Ryan's subsequent illness, with its hopes, frustrations, anger and grief, are recorded in *A Private Battle*, which his wife, Cathryn posthumously edited from tapes and notes. This particular "private battle" was fought by a highly intelligent, questing, and aggressive journalist who, not only sought multiple opinions about his diagnosis but researched his disease and eventually selected his own surgeon and line of treatment. This was a man who was determined to win his own battle and whose fatal illness might have had a less turbulent course had he been given more peace of mind and less technical know-how.

Unfortunately, in spite of countless books, articles and advice from so called experts there are no established guidelines about talking to patients and we do not always have the opportunity of learning from colleagues who do it better. Each case is different and one's approach has to be modified accordingly. Many of our efforts are undermined by the misguided enthusiasm of the communications industry. In the past what appeared in articles and books was, to a certain extent, censored and refereed. The Internet is a miraculous source of knowledge and patients are able to access technical information for themselves. Sadly much of what finds its way onto the Internet is not only misleading but frankly wrong. There are many weeds growing there amidst the flowers. In the publicity given to the latest developments in medicine and surgery, the public is encouraged to believe that in the early 21st Century every disease, without exception, can be cured. The proviso is that the appropriate expert must be found and his sophisticated and expensive drugs, surgery or equipment utilised.

This makes it difficult talk to patients about the inevitability of death and to persuade families that the time has come to halt treatment and to concentrate on care. Even so, we have to remember that human beings are subject to marked variation in biological and pathological behaviour and that prognostications must be guarded and imprecise. I squirm when I hear of patients being given "six months to live." How can doctors forecast death so far ahead?

Now well on in my career, I feel that there is still much to be learnt about talking to patients - particularly when one is breaking bad news. I really have no way of knowing whether I am any better at it than I was when I was a house physician 50 years ago. I flatter myself that I am less gauche in my approach and less brusque in my contacts with patients. Each patient has to be treated differently. Sometimes a direct firm statement is all that is requested or required.

"Don't worry about wrapping it up, doctor," said a tough foundryman with carcinomatosis, fearing (and I think already knowing the worst), "What you're going to tell me is that I am going to snuff it." Then with unusual tenderness for a rough working man he said, "Your's is a rotten job, doctor, having to give such bad news to the likes of us."

Over the years I learned a few basic rules, more from trial and error than anything else. I learned that it is essential to find out first of all what your patient knows or thinks he knows about his illness.

"Tell me what you have been told so far" often avoids blundering prematurely into areas that may never have been contemplated by an off-guard, uninformed and unsuspecting patient. The lawyers, the media and patient pressure groups tell the medical profession that every patient has a right to know and must be told all. We are held negligent if we fail to do this. My experience has told me that quite often people prefer not to know all the details of their illnesses. A retired ENT surgeon, facing a laparotomy for carcinoma of the stomach, probably inoperable said,

"I've forgotten all the pathology I ever knew - so don't bother to tell me of the findings." I took his hint. He never asked any more and we talked of fishing, of Scotland and of rugby football on my visits until he died a few weeks later.

For others, even the simplest and most careful explanation can be misunderstood and has to be repeated again and again before it is eventually accepted. Information is better absorbed when offered in dribbles rather than in a gush.

The success or failure of communication or the breaking of bad news interview depends on your patient's response. You can only do what you can from your experience and from your knowledge of that patient and their family. We have to prepare folk for the worst but this must never exclude hoping for the best.

Chapter 14

The Teacher and the Taught

"When a simple earnest spirit animates a College, there is no appreciable interval between the teacher and the taught - both are in the same class, the one a little more advanced than the other."   Sir William Osler (1849 - 1919)

Students at the Bedside

I started my medical career being taught and I finished being a teacher. Like Sir William Osler I don't think there is a great deal of difference between the two.

Looking back on my career, a substantial part of my time has been spent teaching students, young doctors and established consultants. This does not imply that I was a clever doctor with lots of specialist medical knowledge; nor was I an expert in communication. It was just part of my job at a teaching hospital and I had to get on with it. I like to think that the teaching has concerned both the art and science of medicine but these days the emphasis is much more on science than art.

Traditionally clinical medical students have learned their skills in the wards. It was termed "Walking the Wards" and I have written about my own memories of this as a student at University College Hospital London. It was literally walking round after the chief to the wards, to outpatients and to the operating theatre, listening to what was said and watching what he or she did. It was learning by the apprenticeship system.

There were disadvantages to this arrangement and many now would disagree with students being taught at the bedside of a patient in an open ward within earshot of other patients, visitors and cleaners. In an attempt to make the teaching as inoffensive as possible and to smooth over distressing language, a vocabulary of pseudo-scientific terms was invented by doctors which we were all encouraged to use in front of patients. Thus cancer became "a mitotic lesion", a post mortem became "a total biopsy", dementia became "atrophy of the grey cells" and syphilis became "spirochaetal disease" (after the type of micro-organism causing it). But before long an increasingly knowledgeable public began to learn the significance of our naïve alternatives.

There is no doubt that for many students, learning about an ill patient in hospital is far more valuable than hours spent with a textbook. Nevertheless this style of bedside teaching had to take account of the need for privacy and sensitivity for the patient. It has to be said though that many extroverted patients enjoyed this way of learning more about their diseases. Occasionally there were embarrassing episodes that were not anticipated and the appearance of an unfamiliar face could cause unexpected distress. Our Professor of Pathology used to enjoy attending our ward rounds to see patients whose liver biopsies he had interpreted under the microscope. On one occasion he was instantly recognised by another patient on the ward who happened to work at the University. After the ward round had moved on, the university employee couldn't restrain from cheerfully passing on his own special local knowledge.

"You know who that fellow was who came on the ward round today? That was the Professor of Pathology. He likes to look at the cases who are going to finish up in his department!"

As the years went by, the higher numbers of student doctors training for the NHS meant that innovative methods of instruction had to be introduced.. Increased numbers meant creating special clinical rooms for demonstrations. Teaching videos were made to demonstrate specific features such as unusual gaits or postures, involuntary movements and speech defects. Actors were imported as surrogate patients. Audio-visual departments pioneered interactive computer programmes. To practice particular procedures, such as bladder catheterisation or lumbar puncture, ingenious life-like models were fashioned on which students could practice, before being let loose on real patients.

However it was not always possible to simulate physical signs in models. How, for example, could one reproduce the feel of a kidney tumour, the signs of acute appendicitis or the smell of diabetic coma in actors or models?

A Shortage of Home Grown Doctors

But it was not enough to have larger classes in the existing teaching hospitals; new medical schools had to be built.

Unfortunately the forecasts made after WWII for medical staffing in the future had proved hopelessly inaccurate. In 1957 Henry Willink, a Conservative Minister of Health from 1943 to 1945, chaired a Committee on the future numbers of medical practitioners and the intakes of students required. The Committee concluded that, with improving care in the National Health Service, fewer doctors would be necessary. A 12% reduction of doctors in training was proposed. This proved to be a serious misjudgement, and a costly one too. By 1970 it was obvious that the UK would need more rather than fewer doctors and extra training centres.

Nottingham was selected to be the first new medical school to be established since the Welsh National School of Medicine was founded in 1893. The reasons for siting a new medical school in the East Midlands were entirely pragmatic. The region was short of hospitals, it was short of doctors and it was short of money. In 1972 the first intake of students was 48. By the early 21st Century the intake had risen to nearly 400 per year. The new school at Nottingham was followed quickly by others at Leicester and Southampton and now, in the early

21st Century, additional schools have been set up in other parts of the UK, in the Southwest (the Peninsular Medical School), East Anglia (Norwich), East Yorkshire (Hull) and Sussex (Brighton).

But in spite of all these efforts, we remain short of doctors. Politicians urge us to train more doctors but they are incapable of understanding that doctors cannot be conjured up out of thin air. They take many years to train. The alternative and immoral solution which has been proposed to import qualified doctors from the underdeveloped world, is utterly repugnant to me. They are needed far more in their own countries and their training is ill fitted for modern British requirements.

Staffing our Hospitals - New Answers to Old Problems

Not only were we short of doctors in training at the undergraduate level, the length of postgraduate training was far too long. This proved a major obstacle in persuading young doctors to enter main line hospital specialities. Not only was there a formidably long period of training but there were limited consultant posts at the end of training. From the inception of the NHS to the 1990s there was a rigid training structure - houseman for a year, senior house officer for two years, registrar for 2-3 years, and senior registrar for 4 years. Grafted on to this training was often a spell in research and secondment abroad before the goal of a consultant post came in sight. Most trainees, or junior doctors as they were termed, were in their mid-thirties by appointment to consultant rank. Many in the 1950s and 1960s were even in their mid forties; they could scarcely be called "junior doctors." Often then a significant proportion deserted the NHS and emigrated to North America, Australia or New Zealand as there were limited or unsuitable vacancies in Britain.

There was a further problem that had not properly been addressed. Increasing numbers of women were entering the profession. In the 1950s 10% were women, whereas in the 1980s many medical schools were admitting more than 50% women. Because of inflexible training requirements many of these were lost to medicine during their early years whilst they had children and brought up their families. In Nottingham in the 1980s - 90s we estimated that 25% of our initial intakes were no longer in clinical practice, most of these being women. For those who wanted to re-enter hospital medicine after bringing up their families, the difficulties were particularly pressing.

This unhappy state of affairs could not be allowed to continue. In the 1960s and 1970s the responsibility for postgraduate education was shared uneasily between the Ministry of Health, the Universities and the Medical Royal Colleges. Their co-ordination left much to be desired. As well as training taking too long, there was no structure or flexibility in the programmes and the role of the postgraduate diplomas such as the FRCS and the MRCP had yet to be clearly defined. Were these diplomas to determine entry to or exit from training?

New Consultant Physicians

The Royal College of Physicians clearly wanted to occupy centre stage in the training of physicians. But if it wanted to occupy centre stage it had to extend its influence outside London by encouraging the growth of a network of postgraduate and continuing education facilities. The then President, Professor Max Rosenheim (later Lord Rosenheim), took up this challenge and worked tirelessly, travelling extensively, opening and visiting new centres. All this demanded close liaison with other medical colleges and organisations within the UK.

Concurrently and then over the following years the RCP, with the sister colleges in Glasgow and Edinburgh, began to refine and standardise what was to become the MRCP (UK) Diploma. In many parts of the world, possession of this diploma had equated with consultant status. This was not how the three Royal Medical Colleges viewed it. They wished it to be an entry examination for training towards consultant status. And with all these extra doctors in training a considerable expansion of consultant posts was required to satisfy the needs of the NHS.

So how did I get involved in this complex period of transition?

Change of Direction

After 15 or 20 years as a physician, I felt that I needed a change in direction. I was confident in my job with a large hospital practice, a continuing research programme and a significant teaching commitment with both students and postgraduates. It was satisfying to see the young men and women trained on the firm promoted to senior posts and taking up professorial chairs.

The Membership Exam

One chance to change direction came from Dr David Pyke, the long term Registrar of the RCP of London. For my non-medical readers the term Registrar here had a completely different meaning from the humble registrar training grade in the hospital service. David held more power in the RCP than even the President himself. He was nominally physician to the diabetic department at Kings College Hospital but knew everyone in the profession - concentrating on those with public school and Oxbridge backgrounds! His power was like that of the Government

Chief Whip. And he could always be relied on to dish out the dirt if he wanted to block a physician's elevation to the Fellowship!

David Pyke's request was to ask if I would become an examiner for the MRCP (UK) examination, the diploma providing entry for postgraduate training for physicians. This wasn't a time consuming task but it re-introduced me to the RCP and set in train a series of appointments giving me a significant role in College and National affairs.

Being an examiner demanded all round competence as a physician to generate and mark the Multiple Choice Questions, as well as conducting the *viva voce* and clinical examinations (see colour photos: fig 17). These were held in hospitals around the country and in other centres in different parts of the world. Frequently the patients that we used as testing cases were current admissions with acute illnesses, though there was also a mix of the rare and the extraordinary. It was a demanding event for all the candidates many of whom arrived pale, trembly and sweating. Some described it afterwards as the most stressful single event of their lives. We always tried to put them at their ease by offering a simple starter question but they often thought this was a trick!

Tough examiners (hawks) were usually paired with gentle ones (doves). Our performances were always monitored statistically by a complex calculation. I tended to be on the hawkish side but I had some informal feedback about my own performance after a visit to Cardiff. My senior house officer in Nottingham heard from his brother in Cardiff.

"Ah!" he said, "You work for Toghill, don't you? He was examining in Cardiff last week. We call him the smiling executioner; he always smiles - and then fails you!"

I wondered if the candidates regarded me in the same awe as I regarded the pompous, ignorant old buffers who examined me all those years earlier.

The MRCP was an exam that had been subject to much criticism over the years, being regarded as too chancy and subject to the whims of the examiners. When I was involved, much time and thought was put into its structuring. A full range of topics was covered and each candidate saw all six of the examining team at some time during the examination. We tried to ensure that the successful candidates had minds well stocked with medical knowledge and that they could communicate with patients and examine them accurately and sensitively. Eric Beck, a physician at the Whittington Hospital, masterminded the exam brilliantly over many years and it became a major mission in his life.

There were several overseas centres and Hong Kong was one of the places I visited. On my first morning there, before the candidates appeared on the scene, I chatted to an ill looking retired Chinese restaurateur. He had volunteered to be one of the cases. I complimented him on his excellent English.

"Yes", he replied "I ran a Chinese take-away in Nottingham for 30 years before coming home to Hong Kong to die." It has become a very small world!

148

I liked the Hong Kong doctors. They were well informed, hard working and madly enthusiastic. One evening when I was there I was asked to conduct some mock *vivas* for practice for the MRCP. I expected a handful of doctors but was astonished to find nearly 80 young doctors packed into a small hall. I was ushered onto the stage to sit at a table whilst my six "volunteer" candidates for the mock viva each underwent a 20 minute grilling. The atmosphere was electric - cheers for well-composed answers, hisses for candidates who floundered. Such enthusiasm for their work and careers. Afterwards the young doctor who had organised it thanked me, declaring

"That was better than the races!"

What a compliment in Hong Kong. I never came across such keenness in the UK.

Examining gave one an admirable opportunity of seeing the workings of large hospitals throughout England and also Wales, Scotland and Northern Ireland. Until well after WWII the MRCP (Lond) was always a London based exam, grounded in the old-established Teaching Hospitals. With increasing numbers of candidates, organising the exam became a logistic problem and it was later hosted elsewhere in the provinces. I found it encouraging that our provincial hospitals had levelled up with the London Hospitals.

Overseas Doctors

Figures show that more than 50% of junior doctors in the NHS have qualified elsewhere than in the UK. Our Health Service could not exist without them. Most come from the Indian Sub-Continent, others from SE Asia, Africa, the Middle East with now increasing numbers from Europe.

Another job I had was to examine overseas doctors to decide if they were fit enough to practise in the UK. The examination was termed the Professional Language Assessment Board (PLAB) of which there were two components. Linguists assessed the candidates in both written and spoken English and the doctors assessed the candidates' medical knowledge. There were no patients involved. We were asked to check if they were up to Senior House Officer standard to work in our hospitals.

I always felt very sorry for these doctors, many of whom had spent a great deal of money and time coming to the UK to take the PLAB to enable them to train and work here. However the standard of some was abysmally low, partly because of the basic training in their country of origin.

One of my colleagues, an obstetrician with whom I was paired, asked one male doctor from the Middle East,

"Tell me about pain relief in labour."

"We never give any," was the response.

This of course might have been correct in his country but was unacceptable in the UK. Another candidate, asked about the management of severe injuries after a road traffic accident offered a many times fatal dose of morphine for pain relief.

Sometimes it was comic relief. A young man, probably from East Africa, was struggling hard in his *viva* and I was beginning to run out of easy questions. Thinking that he would at least know something about malaria prophylaxis I described the following scenario, which was in fact true.

"My daughter is going back-packing in East Africa next week. What advice would you give her?"

There was a prolonged and puzzled silence. Then his face lit up.

"She should take condoms. HIV is very common there."

It is my belief that the GMC has pitched the standard of the PLAB exam too low and as a result we are allowing inadequately trained overseas doctors to work in the NHS. It is not fair on them and it is not fair on our medical services. If these young doctors want to come to the UK to train, then we have a duty to look after them and support them fully. They must not be used to patch up deficiencies in our NHS staffing structure without proper training and support.

College Affairs

At an earlier stage in this account of my life I wrote disparagingly about consultants who spent too much time on committees and other outside commitments and not enough time in their own hospitals. From 1980 onwards I was conscious that I, too, was spending a lot of time away from base. I became an examiner for the Conjoint Board and then its Chairman, an examiner for PLAB, and an examiner for the MRCP (UK). Then in 1989 I was elected to the Council of the RCP of London.

At that time the College was under the Presidency of Professor (later Dame) Margaret Turner Warwick, the first woman to hold that post in the 471 years following its foundation. Dame Margaret was a distinguished chest physician who had been Dean of the Cardio-Thoracic Institute at the Brompton Hospital. Her formidable intellect made her an imperious but somewhat distant figure.

After three years she retired, to be replaced as President by Professor Leslie Turnberg (later Lord Turnberg), the Professor of Medicine at Manchester. (see colour photos: fig 18) I knew Leslie well and could not have wished for a better man. We had been registrars together at UCH and had both worked as Research Fellows there. His election to the prestigious post of President was not without controversy. The election had always been held at the College with Fellows voting there personally on the day. Knowing that the London candidates had mustered their own local support, the Manchester Mafia bussed several coachloads of Fellows down for the day, knowing how they would vote! A precedent had been set when Sir Douglas Black, also a Manchunian, had been elected a decade earlier. In the event it was a close run thing - nearly as exciting as the Grand National for those there - but Leslie made it in the final ballot. David London, another man of our age group, became the new registrar, succeeding David Pyke who had been in the post for 18 years. John Bennett a physician from Hull, another old friend, became treasurer soon after.

As a new Censor of the College, responsible for the maintenance of standards, I felt at ease with my new colleagues.

Continuing Medical Education

Pressures to introduce formal systems of continuing medical education for consultants had been building up since the 1980s when doctors began to face criticism of their traditional methods of maintaining professional competence. In fact few other professions had formal systems in place at that time but the doctors were always being compared with airline pilots who had to undergo stringent and regular checks on their competence. When he was chairman of the Education Committee, Professor Turnberg set out the London College's views, which were later incorporated into general principles agreed by the Conference of Medical Royal Colleges during the summer of 1993.

I was asked to become Director of Education at the College in 1993 to oversee its development in the London College. This was an interesting challenge, something of a poisoned chalice, since the introduction of mandatory continuing education was an anathema to a profession which prided itself in always keeping up to date. Whilst this was a part time appointment, I found combining it with my duties in Nottingham arduous and unsatisfactory. After a few months I decided that I was doing neither job satisfactorily and retired from the NHS (see colour photos: fig 19). I was 61 and I had been Senior Physician at the Queen's Medical Centre for many years. There were no new mountains to climb there and I did not fancy chairing interminable discussions on car-parking, waiting lists and ward ventilation for the next few years. It was relatively easy to commute to London. The train journey from Newark to King's Cross took only an hour and a quarter and was usually comfortable. The college offered me accommodation in St Andrew's Place when I required it and this enabled me to continue living in Burton Joyce.

With my corresponding directors in the sister colleges in Edinburgh (Professor Neil Douglas, later President of the Edinburgh College) and in Glasgow (Mr Alan Mc Kay) a formal credit based system was established and physicians were encouraged to participate in approved educational activities as a professional obligation and to record these activities in personal diaries. In addition to their specialist knowledge it was recognised that doctors required an understanding of wider topics such as ethics, management, appraisal, peer review and communication skills (Continuing Professional Development, CPD). Similar programmes were already under way in Canada, Australia and New Zealand. We set up computer marked Multiple Choice Tests in the College Journal and set in train regional courses throughout the country.

It has to be said that until this time many doctors went on educational courses - "Freebies" as they were jocularly called. These "Freebies" were organised in attractive locations and subsidised by the pharmaceutical industry. Some were fairly thin in educational content and entries in the programme such as "Afternoon at Leisure" were common. We organised a "Code of Conduct" with the pharmacological industry ensuring that the educational programme and financial support was appropriate and that courses had the approval of the specialist societies and the employing authorities.

I was given a Department within the College and with Catherine Crossley, an energetic Gallic educationalist as assistant, we set about persuading consultant physicians to embrace the concept of CPD. This was not done without much cajoling and seduction on my part as colleagues refused to accept that they were not "keeping up to date." I travelled round the country lecturing and talking informally to professional groups. There was no doubt that if the profession did not put its own house in order, some less acceptable system would be imposed on us from above.

The other Royal Medical Colleges (Surgeons, Anaesthetists, Pathologists etc) were formulating their own plans for CPD and I was asked to Chair the National Committee co-ordinating the various schemes into a common, collective framework. The CPD bandwagon was, by the mid 90s, rolling into distant lands and I preached the gospel in Europe, North America, South Africa, China, Malaysia, Singapore and Pakistan. Eventually most consultants in the UK came alongside and accepted the need for a formal system. Though everyone in medicine grumbled about the bureaucracy, it was of interest that the lawyers later adopted a similar scheme very close to ours! An awareness of the importance of the role of the College in the training of physicians in all grades in the New Millennium led to the expansion of education into a purpose built department headed up by Dame Lesley Rees. CPD is now an accepted part of doctors' lives and computer technology has been utilised to supplement traditional learning methods.

Back to Student Teaching

My pre-occupation in persuading consultants to keep up to date in these later years did not dim my enthusiasm for teaching new medical students. From 1990 onwards and encouraged by the publishers Edward Arnold (later Hodder) I edited three textbooks for students and junior staff: - Examining Patients, Essential

Medical Procedures and, with David Gray, Symptoms and Signs of Clinical Medicine. These all had a direct "hands-on" approach encouraging students and young doctors to look to the fundamental problems in everyday practice. I like to think that they are being used throughout the English speaking world -we have even had French editions!

Part 3 A Change of Tempo

Chapter 15

Another Side of Life

Of course it wasn't all work and, during my professional life, I was lucky to have a healthy lively family to enjoy at home. The three girls went to Nottingham Girls' High School and were more than busy in term time with music, swimming, badminton and a host of other interests that came and went. Going on holiday with three daughters always posed something of a dilemma.

A Country Cottage - The Home of the Squire of all England

When I was a boy, my parents always took me to Scarborough. There were two reasons why we went there. One was that Uncle George and Aunt Nancy lived near the sea and took in boarders for bed and breakfast during the summer. The other reason was that it was wartime and many other destinations were out of bounds. Scarborough, between the wars was the archetypal northern seaside town visited year in, year out, by holidaymakers from the Yorkshire industrial towns and by the Scots in late season. The Scots regarded it as a southern resort!

There were the two bays. The North Bay was quieter with a large open-air swimming pool and theatre, parks, boating lakes and a gusty, wave battered promenade leading round the headland to the South Bay. This was the popular side: glitzy with amusement arcades, shops with banks of postcards depicting wives with huge bosoms and bottoms dragging round their pathetic little husbands, sandy beaches for invigorating swims, cockle stalls, boat trips, donkeys and, not the least, the Grand Hotel.

As the children grew up we decided we needed a bolt-hole for long weekend and summer holidays. We didn't fancy Skegness, the Lincolnshire coast or Norfolk. Scarborough and Filey were an easy two-hour drive away; so we looked there. We found a rundown old Post Office in a picturesque hamlet called Hutton Buscel, six miles from Scarborough in the North Yorkshire National Park. (see colour photos: fig 20) It had been put up for sale by the Post Office because it was no longer viable. It didn't have too many "mod cons" but father and I patched it up to make a habitable dwelling surrounded with a manageable garden and a tumbledown old stable at the back.

There was a bus every two hours, the odd tractor, and an occasional flock of sheep. Add to that the clatter and chatter of the children on their bicycles, stealing an extra hour before bedtime and you had the total day's noise at Hutton Buscel. The tiny hamlet hugging a ridge to the north of the Scarborough/Pickering

154

road guarded its peace jealously. Nevertheless this quiet village did have its claim to fame.

My mother and father on holiday at Scarborough after WWII

Hutton Buscel was the early home of a rumbustuous character who was to earn for himself the title of "Squire of all England." Born in 1786, George Osbaldeston gained fame as a boxer, cricketer, shot, steeple chaser, jockey and gambler. He excelled in every sport but squandered a fortune in making a reputation as a sportsman. Even as a young undergraduate he could not resist a wager - the Master of his college complained to him "I can't bear a Yorkshireman because he always offers to back his opinion with a bet." Late in life Osbaldeston admitted that he had lost nearly £200,000 by betting and keeping racehorses and another £100,000 by the misdeeds of his agents.

He was the best single wicket cricketer and fastest bowler of his time, but it was his horsemanship that brought him particular fame. He rode with "legs appearing to belong to the animal rather than him, so firm and steady was his seat." He bought the Mastership of the Quorn in Leicestershire for £20,000 in 1817 and hunted furiously until 1821 when he sustained a terrible compound fracture of the leg which forced his resignation. Such was his resilience that after 14 months he was mobile again and re-purchased the Quorn for a second time from 1823-1827. His obsession with hunting was insatiable and at various times he was Master of Hounds at Barton, Atherstone , Thurlow , and Pytchley.

At the age of 44, still unable to resist an attractive bet, he wagered 1000 guineas that he could race 200 miles in 10 consecutive hours. Using 50 horses and changing mounts every four miles, he succeeded in covering a planned course in stormy weather, at Newmarket, in 8 hours 42 minutes - thus averaging 22.99 miles per hour. He did not know that this astonishing feat would earn him a place in the *Guinness Book of Records*.

George Osbaldeston lived in Hutton Buscel until 1808 when he left, as befits his character, in a blaze of glory. In a noisy and indulgent party his home, the Old Hall, caught fire and by the time the fire engine had arrived from Scarborough, more than half the hall had burned down.

We enjoyed the North Yorkshire Moors, the Forests and the gorgeous coastline for several years but it was always dispiriting to hear that the south coast had enjoyed ten hours of sunshine while we had been encased in sea fret. We did not leave Hutton Buscel in such a blaze of glory as George Osbaldeston, but we sold the house in 1986. Perhaps the most important factor was that the girls had stayed at Palm Beach near Sydney and decided that swimming in the Pacific Ocean was preferable to Filey Bay!

A Personal Beneficiary of Medical Advances

Shortly after they returned from that trip to Australia I had an unexpected and serious setback. In 1985, at one of the busiest periods in my professional career I suffered a heart attack.

Having diagnosed dozens of heart attacks in my patients over the years I was hesitant to diagnose my own. On a snowy winter's day Rosemary and I walked over the hill to the next village at Lambley. Climbing briskly I noticed a burning in my chest. It receded on slowing down and I dismissed it as heartburn after a too good a lunch. That evening whilst watching Barry McGuigan boxing for the world championship, the burning recurred. A glass of milk helped and after a couple of hours I was better. More heartburn I thought.

But I began to feel nervous.

"No. It couldn't be angina. I was only 53, a non-smoker and with an impeccable family history."

I suppressed the uneasy suspicions. The following day, a Sunday, I had to visit an awkward patient in hospital with anorexia nervosa who was being more disagreeable than usual to the staff. On getting out of my car on my return home the pain brought me to my knees; there was no doubt then about the diagnosis.

To cut a long story short I was admitted to our own Coronary Care Unit where everyone was kind and sympathetic and, thank goodness, treated me as an ordinary patient. But the condition remained unstable and my friend and physician, Dr Keith Morris, decided that an isotope scan was necessary at St Thomas's Hospital London. Coronary angiograms had not yet become routine. We set off down the M1, with lights flashing, as a matter of some urgency, Unfortunately in

Northamptonshire the ambulance ran out of petrol! It could only happen to a doctor!

Though I eventually recovered well and was back at work, angina persisted and by 1990 I was struggling to cope, being limited by pain to walking only 100 yards on the level. But I was lucky. By now bypass surgery had advanced and was widely available. My destination was Groby Road Hospital, Leicester, which had been for many years a regional cardiac centre for the Trent Region. This single storey collection of seedy dilapidated red brick buildings did not at first sight strike confidence but the wards were welcoming and the care was excellent. I had been sending my patients there for years and I reckoned that if it was good enough for them, it was good enough for me. Richard Firmin, a first rate cardiac surgeon, took me over. A bypass was performed and apart for the heaviest snowstorm in years the next day, all went well. I am grateful to Richard's surgical skills and quiet confidence and to modern cardiological advances that means I am here today.

Flying the Nest

When we tired of the Hutton Buscel house, we started to explore Europe and learned to appreciate France. In my earlier visits I had regarded all of rural France as an extension of Gabriel Chevallier's Clochmerle, with villagers arguing about the upgrading of their pissoir! The new France was a revelation: good empty roads, innovative and well stocked supermarkets, decent plumbing and welcoming locals. We camped, as did so many French families, on the south-west seaboard and spent the long summer days lounging in the sun. Topless sunbathing was the order of the day and bottomless not uncommon! Unfortunately these idyllic holidays were nearly always spoiled, as they were for countless other British families, by having to phone home for exam results.

As the children became more independent, Rosemary retrained and went back to work as a mature physiotherapist at the City Hospital. Claire was the first to leave home, going to Oxford Polytechnic (later Brooks' University) to do Hotel Management. She married Mark, and they now live in St Albans with two lovely strawberry-blonde daughters, Sophie and Katie. Helen became a nursery nurse, married Adrian and lives in West Bridgford, Nottingham. She has two very lively boys, Sam and Thomas. Thomas, a potentially first class cricketer may yet get the Cambridge Blue that I hoped a son of mine might get - but they are the pipe dreams of an old man. (see colour photos: fig 21)

Jo, the opportunist of our brood, went into nursing at my old hospital, University College Hospital in London. I had hoped that she would see the best of British nursing there but was disappointed to see how the fabric of the hospital had deteriorated in thirty years. When we took her down to move in to the Nurses'

Home I sensed her disappointment. Gone were the gleaming brass fittings on the doors, a welcoming foyer, the burnished mahogany and the smell of furniture polish as it was in yesteryear. A bored fag-ash receptionist in the dowdy entrance hall tossed her the key of her room. "Number 35, first floor," she muttered, fag drooping from her mouth. Where was the starched Sister Tutor who ought to be on hand to greet the new arrivals? Perhaps the accommodation was not everything - Jo made good friends straight away and the training on the wards served her well. She has travelled the world - Africa, North America, the Far East, New Zealand and Australia. Now she is a specialist respiratory nurse at the Alfred Hospital in Melbourne. We enjoy travelling to Australia to see her.

Chapter 16

Recollections of Far Distant Lands

A Passport for the World

When I was on the threshold of my career, one of my mentors, Karl Nissen, the orthopaedic surgeon, advised me "A medical training is a passport to the world. With a few tools you can ply your trade anywhere."

He was absolutely right and, many years later, thumbing through my old passports, I was reminded that "plying my trade" had led me to some intriguing destinations. Plying my trade covered a multitude of tasks: dealing with the sick, advising about disease, teaching local doctors hands-on skills and delivering formal lectures. All I needed was a stethoscope, ophthalmoscope, auriscope and a few more diagnostic bits and pieces - with the omnipresent box of slides for teaching. In an earlier chapter I have written about my experiences in the Falklands and in the Antarctic near South Georgia but there were other visits to distant places that I was privileged to see.

Karachi

For some weeks at the end of 1994 the Foreign Office had been pussy footing about the advisability of a small group of us from the Royal College of Physicians of London going to Karachi; there had been political unrest and violent disturbances. Eventually, losing patience, we went on what was, to all intents and purposes, a good will mission. In fact since the 1980s the city had been the site of violent eruptions between the political, ethnic and religious groups. The present upset didn't seem to be particularly unusual and in the event we heard no shots or explosions.

Modern Pakistan was born in 1947 out of the ashes of Imperial India. Karachi was the first capital until replaced by Rawalpindi in 1959. Today it is the main entry point and most of the international trade of Pakistan and land-locked Afghanistan, passes through the city's port, centred on the island of Kiamāri. The larger highways and railroads focus on the city and the modern airport is a stopover and re-fuelling point for intercontinental flights. The city is what it appears to be at first sight, a sprawling metropolis seething with humanity - all sorts and sizes, all ages and all colours. The streets are full of fairground-painted buses and lorries mostly of the vintage of vehicles from wartime American films. Weaving in and out are the carts, groaning with produce, and pulled by scraggy, sabre-chested horses and donkeys.

The centrepiece of our visit was "Medicine 1995 - Achievements, and Aims, Individuals and the Environment." By way of introduction to the Congress on the first evening, delegates were entertained in the college gardens under canopies. Around the periphery of the garden were groups to amuse us: fierce moustachioed soldiers with flashing eyes and teeth performing a sword routine, brightly dressed midget dancers from the mountains and snake charmers. An accomplice of one of the snake charmers produced a three-foot snake from a hessian bag and ran off into the crowd. Another accomplice let off his pet mongoose from a leash. It homed in like a rocket on to the wriggling snake's neck shaking it like a terrier killing a rat. Not all the English group approved of this local form of entertainment!

I had not realised before arriving in Pakistan how very much of an Islamic Republic it was. Life was interrupted every day by the calls to prayer. Walking out in the afternoon I had my bare arms tapped by a policeman's baton, indicating that they should be covered. There was no alcohol but we soon discovered that this was available in the hotels "for medicinal purposes" on the production of a doctor's certificate. Well, there were plenty of doctors in our group who were prepared to perjure themselves!

One of my pleasures during the short cooler evenings, after work, was to stroll through the parks watching the dozens of overlapping games of cricket. There is no doubt as to the national sport here with hundreds of youngsters bowling as fast as they could or attempting to hit the cover off the ball. Nothing was half-hearted! This was, no doubt, a release from their dingy dwellings, strung around by bare electricity wires, leaking water pipes and reeking stoves. A Health and Safety inspector would have had a fit. But in every dwelling, surrounded by the family, there was the ubiquitous television set.

Before we left, a commemorative stone plaque engraved with our names appeared in the wall of the College. The stonemasons must have been working all night. My impression, meeting many Pakistanis, was one of a genuine welcome - politicians take note! Perhaps I was unduly flattered by some young doctors who told me that they used my textbook for their exams!

The North West Frontier

As children we all have dreams. Mostly they don't come true! Mine was to travel to the North West Frontier. Being in Pakistan I had to go there.

The gateway to the frontier is Peshawar, a dishevelled looking town with a mix of gaudy decorated trucks, camel caravans, market traders, craftsmen, sweet shops, bazaars and street side restaurants. You are greeted openly but you cannot escape the glance of guarded suspicion, laced with a modicum of streetwise cunning. We had learned some of Kipling's poems at school and his "Ballad of the King's Jest" is as true today as it was when it was written in the 19th Century.

When springtime flushes the desert grass,
Our Kafilas wind through the Kyber Pass.
Lean are the camels but fat the frails*.
Light are the purses but heavy the bales.
As the snowbound trade of the North comes down
To the market square of Peshawar town.

(* frails - rush baskets for packing figs, raisins etc)

You must not miss the Qissa Khawani. The old story tellers in the Bazaar have been squeezed out by radio and television but there is still the smell of every food available on the sub-continent - kebabs, curries, freshly baked bread, grilled meats and spices. Perhaps all these aromas are now more familiar to the English whose favoured meal is curry rather than the roast beef and Yorkshire pudding! When I was there, world-wide terrorism had yet to cast its long shadow into Pakistan but it was not difficult to appreciate how a suspect could melt into the crowd in seconds, never to be seen again.

As if to emphasise the contrast of life in this remote part of the world, we moved on to the Ismalia College built during the 1920s and now part of Peshawar University. (see colour photo: fig 22) There, fronted by verdant lawns and cricket pitches were handsome buildings shimmering in the morning sun. Shade your eyes and it could have been Repton or Marlborough or Winchester. And yet this tranquil scene was only a few miles from the hustle and confusion of the commercial centre of Peshawar. A group of students, immaculate in their whites, were assembling for an all day match. Someone must have told them that I was a cricketer because I was handed a bat and invited to face a few gentle but guileful balls from a giggling undergraduate. He was a cunning slow bowler, all wrist action rather than finger spin. And he spun the ball a long way. "There's still some dew on the wicket, professor," he said, "I need to be put on early." It could have been a summer's morning at Trent Bridge. Then we were off again to what for me would be a highlight.

It is a 55-kilometre journey from Peshawar to the Pass. I peered nervously at the bald tyres on the venerable bus. The driver saw me looking and tactfully stood in front of the wheel until I moved on. I was even more nervous when an armoured car with soldiers carrying rifles appeared to escort us to the Kyber Pass. "They, (unspecified), may take a few pot-shots at you as we go along. We don't want to lose you, you are a valuable cargo," the officer in charge explained.

Just 15 kilometres from Peshawar, the bazaar at Jamrud marked the southern entrance to the Khyber Pass. The symbolic gateway, the Bab-el Khyber, is modern, having been built in the 1970s. This is the land of the Afridi, fierce warring tribesman with strong chiselled features and smouldering eyes. But their most striking feature is that they are all armed - rifles, pistols or sub-machine guns, ranging from Webley revolvers, to the old British Lee Enfields of WWII, and modern Russian Kalashnikovs. (see colour photos: fig 23) This region is the armoury of the world where an exact working replica of any weapon can be fashioned on request. In this society the young acquire their guns early, as easily as our youngsters take to mobile phones.

Our minibus growled and groaned up the winding precipitous roads. I was less worried about the shooting practice by the locals than those bald tyres. There were other brightly decorated lorries and coaches moving people from village to village in a round of commerce and activity. On this route are the enormous refugee camps housing hundreds of thousands of displaced persons from Afghanistan but as far as one could see they were orderly and peaceful.

A memorable stop before the last frontier post was the Officers' Mess of the Khyber Rifles, clearly a showpiece as the billiards room walls were covered with signed photographs of every dignitary imaginable. At a glance, amongst dozens of others, I saw prominently displayed Bill Clinton, Jimmy Carter and Princess Diana. They were entertained I am sure, as we were, by twenty swirling tribesmen performing the Khattak dance on the carefully cultivated lawns.

A captain in the Khyber Rifles accompanied us on the last stage of the journey - tall, erect, a well-trimmed moustache and unbelievably handsome. He could have walked off a film set. A very senior lady physician confessed later that she had been on the point of swooning! From the last border post high in the mountains you could see the road winding through the valley into Afghanistan with Kabul in the misty distance. (see colour photos: fig 24) Then, as though on cue, a caravan of camels and donkeys laden with goods, emerged around a rocky outcrop plodding patiently on toward Peshawar. We were back two thousand years in time. "Don't go too far away," advised the handsome captain, "we are not out of range here."

Kipling's poem about the young public school educated British Officer, shot whilst on service at the Border Station, came to mind.

> *A scrimmage in a Border Station -*
> *A canter down some dark defile -*
> *Two thousand pounds of education*
> *Drops to a ten rupee jezail* -*
> *The Crammer's boast, the Squadron's pride,*
> *Shot like a rabbit in a ride*

*Jezail - long Afghan musket

There were no pot shots - and the view was daunting. Kabul disappeared in the haze on the horizon.

Dr W G Grace is appreciated in Lahore

My introduction to Lahore was a seething scrum at the airport. At the centre of this scrum was a tall, distinguished figure besieged by admirers, both cricketing and political. It was Imran Khan.

This was perhaps an appropriate sighting. We were attending another large medical conference there and at the end of the meeting, before lunch, I had been asked to close the meeting with a light-hearted historical talk linking the two countries. I decided that the audience might appreciate hearing a talk I had given at home several times on "Dr W G Grace - Medical Truant." I had been interested in WG for many years since learning that he had been my great grandfather's doctor in Gloucestershire. How much time WG had for his general practice I do not know but he certainly had to employ a series of locums in the summers. These were paid for by the Gloucestershire County Cricket Club - an unusual arrangement that would not have gone down well these days. The talk was an inspired choice for a cricket mad nation. I started by saying what a pleasure it was to talk to them at "the heart of this great cricketing nation in the land of Imran Khan." In itself this produced a round of applause and the rest of the lecture was rapturously received. When lunchtime arrived and I stopped, the Chairman asked me to go on - but I had run out of slides!

I think that even the non-cricketing President, Lesley Turnberg must have enjoyed it because I was asked for a repeat performance at the prestigious Samuel Gee lecture at the London College later in the year.

South Africa - a Land of Contrasts

The "Rainbow People of God" is how the former Anglican Archbishop of Capetown, Desmond Tutu, described the new South Africa - a conglomeration of races, traditions, faiths and heritages set in a country of stark contrasts of breathtaking natural beauty. This was the rebirth of a new nation which, in 1961, had been led by Prime Minister Verwoerd out of the Commonwealth and into political isolation. I never visited South Africa in the apartheid days but spoke to many of the medical/political émigrés who fled the oppressive regime, condemning the country to pariah status.

What the first time visitor to South Africa is not prepared for is the astonishing racial mix with eleven national languages. To me it was a surprise to see the street names in two languages, English and Afrikaans. The original apartheid classification of blacks, coloured and whites is too simple as there are countless other races - Malays, Chinese and West Indians in bewildering combinations. It is now the coloureds who appear to dominate the commercial life in the Western Cape. A visit to the District Six Museum, located on the edge of this former Cape Town precinct, shows what life was like in this largely Muslim Community before it was cleared under the notorious group Areas Act with thousands being moved out compulsorily. And the Vootrekker Monument approaching Pretoria offers some insight into the driving force behind Afrikaner Nationalism.

I was fortunate to be part of one of the first ambassadorial medical groups to visit South Africa in the post apartheid era. In the main there was an air of hope and expectancy in the profession and Fellows of the South African College of Physicians were enthusiastic about the future. Certainly there was a relaxed atmosphere everywhere we went in the Western Cape. The editor of the South African Journal was one of the black speakers who entertained us at the College. "I am now going to show some slides," he proclaimed. "When I put the lights out I will disappear - but don't worry I will still be here!" The larger hospitals we visited in Capetown were of a very high standard and, though busy, well staffed. One remembered that the Groote Schuur Hospital was where the first heart transplant was performed in 1967.

Unfortunately I was unable to visit the Johannesburg hospitals. I was keen to see Soweto where my friend and orthopaedic colleague Nicholas Barton from the QMC in Nottingham worked for a while. He described the Accident and Emergency Department in Soweto on a Saturday night as being like a major battlefield with an average of three heart stab wounds in the evening. He said it made the A and E department at the QMC (one of the busiest in the UK) look like an afternoon tea party.

There is still an enormous discrepancy in medical care in the country. I visited a clinic in one of the townships, a huge conglomeration of shacks built of corrugated iron, tin, wood planking and plastic sheeting. Prejudices die hard "Whatever did you want to go there for?" a white South African colleague asked when I returned home. In the townships, families live cheek by jowl in squalid conditions with huge spotlights shining down from above at night like an open prison, an essential contribution to security. The doctors visit once a week and cope as best they can. (see colour photos: fig 25) HIV infection casts its long shadow in South Africa as in the rest of that blighted continent. I see no prospect of any reduction of infection unless there is a change of mind as a result of the educational programmes. Alcoholism is also a major problem in the townships, fuelling and igniting violent and often fatal knife attacks. Scattered through the townships there were mini-breweries concocting noxious brews in rusting iron butts. The brown fluid was evil looking. In one hut I was persuaded by the buxom barmaid to taste some. It did not merit a second mouthful! (see colour photos: fig 26)

Following subsequent visits I am hopeful for the future for South Africa though not all the whites are so confident. The "coloureds" are working enthusiastically for the future, determined to make a success of life. South Africa is perhaps the most variably attractive of all the countries I have visited with the sub-tropical coastal belt, bushveld, high mountains, temperate forest and semi-desert. It is little wonder that, with its excellent climate and burgeoning wine industry, it is rapidly becoming a prime tourist destination.

After my earlier working visits I promised to take Rosemary on holiday there, to see Table Mountain, the Garden Route and to safari in the Kruger Park. For the safari we flew to Skukuza and landed in torrential rain. It was the only airport (if one could call it that!) where instead of a bus coming out to meet you they brought a truckload of umbrellas. We stayed at Kirkman's Kamp an old colonial style camp, which was sheer magic. South Africa has it all for holidays!

China - Dirty, Dingy and Despoiled

March 1997 found me on the second of my three visits to Mainland China, this time as an educational advisor in my capacity as Director of Education to the Royal College of Physicians. My brief was to talk about the London College's Continuing Medical Education policy with Chinese doctors and to travel to the interior of China to see something of their work.

There was no doubt that the health of the population was improving. In 1949 life expectancy was 45 and by the mid 1990s this had risen to 68 for men and 71 for women. They were training more doctors. In 1949 there was only one doctor per 27,000 inhabitants but by the early 1990s there was one for every 637. Successful campaigns had been waged against tuberculosis, malaria, and filariasis. A para-medical corps of health workers, the so-called barefoot doctors, had been mobilised to advise about hygiene and preventative measures as well as dealing with everyday health problems. More recently there had been a resurgence of interest in traditional Chinese medicine with herbal medications, folk medicine and acupuncture. The doctors were conscious of the need to control the population explosion but the rigid one child per family rule was being relaxed. It was disturbing to be shown a class of schoolchildren and to be told that none of these children had brothers or sisters!

But whilst these measures were in place in the large cities and towns, rural and isolated communities were bereft of significant health care. My ventures into the interior of this vast country and indeed I have to say I visited only a part, showed up the scale of the colossal defects.

China is a dirty country. Hygiene is poor and most of the working population away from major cities had hands and faces grimed with dirt. In one rural marketplace I attempted to take photos of a vegetable stall but was shooed away until the stallholder had carefully washed his hands; he at least knew what he should be doing. Toilets were primitive in the extreme: open ditches in a park that we visited and a foul smelling stained toilet bowl in the private lavatory of the director of a public hospital. In the wards they were worse. Sanitation everywhere in the country was appalling. And still everyone spits in public.

Smoking is universal. This is the modern epidemic in China and in ten to twenty years time they will have to reap the whirlwind. In the meantime the western tobacco giants pump cigarettes into the entire Far Eastern world where virtually everyone seems to have a cigarette drooping from their lips.

Pollution is rampant. Every effort is being expended in boosting the economy but little thought is being given to the long-term effects on the environment - the atmosphere, the soil and the rivers. The size of some of the cities is startling. Xian, a city I had never heard of before has more than 5 million inhabitants and its dirt and smoked stained streets and houses left me thinking that it must be one of the most polluted cities in the world.

Many of the larger hospitals in the cities are undertaking high quality medicine and surgery. Some attitudes cannot be understood in the Western world. For example the growing trade in organs of executed prisoners has caused revulsion in the west but, despite its sensitivity, raises few eyebrows in China itself.

Perhaps I have been harsh because China itself is very much like the curate's egg - good in parts. Those who have read *Wild Swans: Three Daughters of China,* an autobiographical family history written in 1992 by Chinese writer Jung Cheng will have been given a unique perspective on modern China and the lives of families during the Cultural Revolution. The shabby buildings everywhere and the despoiled, desolate countryside bereft of wooded vegetation are markers of the wasted decades of war and revolution

Unique is an overworked word but applied to the Great Wall certainly is not! The aggregation of shacks and cheap souvenir outlets at each entry point somewhat spoils the foreground. You need to screw up your eyes and look into the distance at the Wall winding up over the hills and mountains in the distance. Leslie Turnberg and I stretched our legs and lungs walking briskly over two or three sections. It really is an incredible structure. (see colour photos: fig 18)

Now that Hong Kong with its finance and medical expertise has been successfully reabsorbed into China as a jewel in the crown, there is an immense rebuilding programme underway everywhere. Now in the 21st Century we are seeing the rebirth of a new giant in the east - let us hope it will not be a monster?

Malaysia

Some of my contemporaries served in Malaysia whilst doing their National Service. Much of the hinterland was violently and aggressively anti-British and in the sweaty heat of the jungle it was an inhospitable posting. During 1951, when the terrorist campaign was at its height, over a thousand civilians and security forces were killed. General Sir Gerald Templer, a hyperactive, bristling man with a high pitched voice, whom I met some years later, was appointed High Commissioner. From then on the tide began to turn. Fighting the guerrillas was loathsome work for the soldiers, many of whom were National Servicemen. They spoke of the steaming, insect ridden jungle and of their patrols from which they returned stinking, covered with jungle sores.

Visiting the now independent Commonwealth country 46 years on, it is difficult to reconcile our presence in the two eras; then unwelcome, now appreciated. One cannot help comparing the success and affluence of Malaysia and Singapore with the chaos, confusion poverty and failure of so many African States who embraced independence at the same time with such enthusiasm but who have moved backwards rather than forwards. Is it their natural resources, their choice of leaders or the industry of the populace? So little medical progress in central Africa, so much in Southeast Asia.

The University of Nottingham has, over several years, established educational links with Malaysia and we have had many students from there. In September 2000 the University of Nottingham Malaysian Campus became reality. My own task, in representing the RCP in April 1997, was to forge educational links and to introduce our own ideas about postgraduate programmes. It might be added that with well over 50 Fellows of the London College and similar numbers from the Edinburgh College, the postgraduate bodies in Malaysia were vigorously enthusiastic. I met many old friends there including one of my ex-house physicians from Nottingham.

Later, in 2003 Rosemary and I visited Malaysia again, enjoying the pleasures of Langkawi, a tropical island off the extreme northern border of the country. Little did we know that a year later on December 2004 it would be engulfed in one of the most terrible natural disasters of the modern era, the tsunami.

Chapter 17

I Love a Sunburnt Country

I make no excuses for poaching the title for this chapter from Dorothea McKellar's poem "My Country."

I love a sunburnt country,
A land of sweeping plains,
Of ragged mountain ranges,
Of droughts and flooding rains.
I love her far horizons,
I love her jewel sea,
Her beauty and her terror-
The wide blue land for me!

The stark white ring-barked forests,
All tragic to the moon,.........

And so the poem goes on, powerfully evocative of that sunburnt country. The country is, of course, Australia. And I have had a love affair with that "lucky country" since my schooldays.

I have lived through the grey austerity of the war years in England. Australia conjured up visions of cloudless blue skies, tumbling white surf and red parched earth in the outback. In those youthful days there seemed no prospect ever of visiting that distant land except by emigrating permanently. In the last fifty years the world has shrunk and now it is but 24 hours away by Jumbo jet.

I have to say that my first links with that sunburnt country were not auspicious ones. The Second World War was over and through the English winter of 1946-47 we schoolboys listened on the wireless at breakfast-time, to the crackling, screeching, buzzing commentaries of the Test Match series. The last match before the war between the two countries in 1938 at the Oval had produced England's biggest victory over Australia (or indeed any other Test Match side). We optimistic and perhaps naïve, English youngsters had high hopes of repeating that success over a largely unknown Australian side even though it was captained by the legendary Don Bradman, perhaps the most famous Australian of all time.

Frustratingly we strained to catch all the details of those early commentaries. On the first day of the First Test at Brisbane on 29th November 1946 I crouched at the sideboard with an ear to the wireless and toast and marmalade in my fist. The sound wheezed and faded at critical moments but I heard enough to tell me that England were in trouble. The 38-year-old Bradman had had a nervy start and survived a hotly debated "not-out" decision to a ball apparently caught by Ikin at slip. There were no action replays then. But the fragmentary commentary told me that Australia had a bagful of runs with only two wickets down by close of play. It was all depressing news to a youngster starved of Test Match cricket since the age of 6! And all went from bad to worse over the next few days. Australia made 645 and England, caught on a spiteful pitch after torrential rain, were dismissed for 141 and 172. Australia won by an innings and 332 runs.

The cricket news through the rest of that dark, wet and post-war English winter was generally depressing but, surprisingly, my love affair with Australia smouldered on.

It was re-kindled when, through work, I met Eddie Carr. He was my Senior House Officer when I was a House Surgeon in my first job after qualification. A Sydney graduate, he had come to England to get some more surgical experience and to obtain his FRCS diploma - cutting experience he described it. This was no ordinary Australian. In 1950 he had won Gold Medals in the 400m individual and the 400m relay in the Commonwealth Games in Auckland. Though not well known in the UK he was a prominent personality back home. Never one to boast of his athletic achievements he was, nevertheless, a man of immense pride in his country. During the long night hours we spent together patching up the surgical emergencies that were wheeled through casualty, he yarned about Australia - the whole kit and caboodle! We became good friends. Later he married Janet, a bubbly and irrepressible Northern Irish pathologist and I became godfather to their son Edwin Carr, Jr. Eddie later became a consultant surgeon to Parramatta Hospital in Sydney. Years later, in semi-retirement, he took on an even busier job as a sheep farmer near Cowra in NSW, some 250k west of Sydney. Over many years we have visited the Carrs at their homes in NSW.

In 1981 whilst on a holiday with us in Burton Joyce, Eddie and Janet sneaked a look at our engagement calendar. They decided that during a quiet spell at work and through the school Easter holiday break, there was a long enough period for the whole family to go out to see the country for ourselves. To ease the financial pain of a longish stay they generously offered us the use of their holiday home at Palm Beach, 20k north of Sydney, as a base. This left us with little option but to go!

Nothing can match the thrill of arriving in Australia for the first time. For hours we had been flying over the seemingly unending outback - a backdrop of red barren red earth criss-crossed at rare intervals with dead straight roads pocked by isolated outposts and homesteads. Crossing the Grey range into New South Wales the land below began to change and merge into various shades of brown; a painter's palette of yellow ochre, raw umber and burnt sienna. Here the cattle and sheep, we were told, were counted in acres-per-head rather than heads-per-acre.

It was here that the pilot, almost as a throwaway line, gave us the astonishing news that Argentina had invaded the Falklands. Until then most

Britons and Australians had regarded the Falklands as a distant group of islands of uncertain location, probably near Orkney and Shetland. We were to hear much more of them in the weeks to come. I heard the news with incredulity. Only four years earlier in 1978 I had been there as a visiting physician assessing the medical services and attempting to suss out the quality and safety of the hospital support given to the Islands by the Argentinian base hospitals at Comodora Rivadaria and Buenos Aries.

As our plane began its descent into Sydney Airport we craned our necks to get a first glance at the harbour. Yes and there it was with the Opera House, sparkling white in the early morning sunshine, looking exactly as it did in those hundreds of photographs everyone had seen earlier. And to put us in the mood "Waltzing Matilda" came over loud and clear on the intercom. It was just the melody but the words were familiar to me: -

Once a jolly swagman camped by a billabong
Under the shade of a coolabah tree.

The reason for that familiarity went back 50 years to when our headmaster at Ashfield School, Mr Brothers, conducted a class of scruffy, down at heel, wartime urchins singing loudly, in a cacophony of sound, words that they scarcely understood.

Eddie and Janet were there at the Airport to greet us and to lead us out to Palm Beach, our base for the next few weeks. My hired car had an automatic gearbox - the first time I had used one - and the Sydney traffic needed careful negotiation. I have to say that my first impressions of Sydney were disappointing. First there were the zones of factories, warehouses and wholesalers that led into the streets of the shabby suburbs. They weren't too different from Muswell Hill or Clapham or Edgware, with Woolworths, DIY stores and fast food takeaways. What was different was that many were of clapboard and the slightly posher shops were on the shady side protected from the fierce sun.

Downtown Sydney was different: impressive tall buildings, parks, attractive shops and a harbour of sparkling blue that was worth coming 10,000 miles to see. We crossed Harbour Bridge, visible from almost every corner of the city, massively riveted, solid, utilitarian and looking like a relic of the Industrial Revolution - though it was completed relatively recently in 1932. There is over 500m of it from end to end and to get on you toss a coin into a receptacle, which activates one of the gates barring the entrance. Such tolls were new to us. But whilst Rose, Claire, Helen and Jo were savouring the sights of this new city I was occupied with more mundane tasks, watching the road and keeping my feet in the right place to deal with the automatic gear box.

Our destination was Palm Beach, an affluent resort on the coast 20k north of Sydney. We expected it to be idyllic - and it was! It was the archetypal Australian beach resort with rolling breakers, fine sand, a Lifesavers' station and an old-fashioned swimming pool built in the rocks and filled with sea water. Some years later the resort was to become the location of a popular TV series.

Just off the beach was our temporary home, a holiday house with a huge gum tree sprouting through the sundeck. Jo ran round to the back.

"Come and look" she called excitedly "It's just like the jungle." And indeed it was - a tangle of bamboos, palms, ferns and banana trees.

"Are there snakes?" she asked breathlessly.

"Well there are," replied Eddie in his slow Sydney accent, "and the browns are very poisonous. But if you don't attack them or corner them and allow them to get away they won't harm you." Jo wasn't too convinced.

On this our first visit there was so much to see that we never left NSW. Sydney itself covers a vast area and it takes an hour or two to clear the sprawling western suburbs, which merge into the semi-rural region bounded by the Hawksbury/Nepean river system. Many of the suburbs have a familiar ring to the English visitor, Liverpool, Richmond, Sutherland and St Ives and some have the orderliness of the gin and Jag belt of the affluent Surrey suburbs.

In a New World country nowhere has more Old World charm than the small towns and villages of the Blue Mountains. Turn of the century guesthouses, antique shops, galleries, restaurants and "Old English" tea-rooms created a familiar scene. But for the visitor the appeal is the magic of those mountains, which first appear as a misty blue haze viewed from the western suburbs. From the higher points of the range the stunning vista stretches out into the distance with deep ravines, waterfalls and rainforest. Their haze comes from the bluish vapour released by the eucalyptus trees overrunning the whole area. Like all good tourists we took the trip on the cable car, said to be the steepest in the world.

"How many bloody Poms here today?" called out the conductor. No political correctness here thank goodness; in some parts of the world similar derogatory comments about racial background would have been met with howls of protest.

During the 80s the medical profession in NSW was hit by a series of rows about insurance payments which led to many surgeons leaving the profession. Disquiet about this was perhaps one of the reasons why Eddie later gave up his surgical practice to take on a new venture in semi-retirement - a sheep farm (see colour photos: fig 27). In fact many professional Australians seemed to nurture an ambition in their mature years to revert to the more basic lives of their forefathers on the land. So a move by the Carrs to a small sheep farm, a few kilometres out of Cowra, a tidy and compact town south west of Sydney, gave us another opportunity to see more.

Despite its relatively small size, 10-20,000 inhabitants, Cowra is well known to Australians as the site of an infamous prison camp breakout. During the Second World, Cowra was the site of a prisoner of war camp holding 2,000 Italian and 2,000 Japanese soldiers. The Italian soldiers were no trouble, as indeed was the case in the prisoner of war camps in the UK. The Japanese were a completely different kettle of fish - surly, uncooperative and hostile - they resented bitterly their incarceration, so great was the shame of being captured. In the middle of the night in August 1944, over 1,000 of them staged a suicidal breakout attacking the guard tower with whatever weapons came to hand. What they hoped to achieve by escaping was uncertain. They were on a hiding to nothing. After 9 days they were recaptured, the furthest having got 15 miles. During the escape and subsequent round-up 231 were killed and 112 wounded.

The years that have elapsed have softened memories and the bizarre episode is forgiven on both sides and commemorated in a delightful Japanese garden in the visitors' centre in Cowra which also houses a perfect little museum which has a wonderful example of a holograph. It was the first that I had ever seen and I was captivated.

Incessant downpours for several days had filled to overflowing the Wangela Dam and lazy brown rivers in the region were converted to swirling torrents. To get to the Carr farm we had to cross a ford. Normally a few inches deep, the river was cascading past and we needed a towline to be pulled across; this was just as well because in mid stream the hire car began to float downstream and we were glad to be pulled quickly to the other bank.

Living on an outback farm with several hundred sheep, a few kangaroos, many rabbits and little help was a romantic ideal. But with wool prices plummeting and the physical work of farming proving increasingly arduous, Eddie and Janet sold up and moved to a bungalow with several hectares of land (plus one emu) just outside Cowra. For 60+ year olds this was a prudent move.

I am not sure why our dear daughter Jo decided to relocate to Australia. Perhaps her appetite had been whetted by our visits to Palm Beach and to Cowra and then to Perth. Maybe it was an Australian boyfriend! Nevertheless she made the decision after some years of nursing training in the UK and disillusion with the NHS. She is currently carving out a new career for herself in Melbourne as a respiratory nurse specialist.

Selfishly, we were disappointed when she left her first location in Adelaide. (see colour photos: fig 28). Without the high rise buildings and hustle and bustle of an international centre it is a city which seems at ease with itself. We found Adelaide, named after the wife of King William III, smaller than we expected but this probably comes from the central square mile grid of wide streets and fine buildings contained by the belt of parklands, lakes and playing fields.

Melbourne, where Jo lives now is a huge busy city with impressive high-rise buildings downtown. But to my mind it lacks the excitement of Sydney, the panorama of Perth or the graciousness of Adelaide. It is the Manchester of Australia - red brick Victorian buildings, an insoluble traffic system and endless suburbs. Like Manchester it has a cosmopolitan population; unlike Manchester, it has absorbed immigrants from Greece, Cyprus, Eastern Europe and more recently South Eastern Asians and Chinese.

Visitors to Australia neglect the other island, Tasmania.

"Why go there?" mainland Australians ask, "It's just like England!"

But it isn't. The east coast weather is undoubtedly better, the scenery is superb and much of the island untamed. Snap shot memories are often better preserved than longer scenarios. Mine was of the Tasmanian Devils; fearsome, aggressive little black creatures the size of Jack Russell terriers. Their jaws are said to be stronger than any other mammal weight for weight. I can still hear the bones cracking as they crunched up the carrion meat that is their staple diet.

By the early 21st Century, Australia and New Zealand have become the premier long haul holiday destinations for the Western World. And many thousands are emigrating there to live a more relaxed life style in countries where there is space for all to live comfortably. It is a sad reflection that a liberal European democracy such as the Netherlands is now rebelling against the overcrowding that unbridled immigration has brought in the last twenty years. The indigenous Dutch are emigrating in droves. And where are they going? To Australia and New Zealand.

I suppose that it was the showpiece 2000 Olympic Games that really opened the eyes of the world to the wonders of the Australian continent. It was an event that had been eagerly anticipated by everyone there. The meticulous preparation over a long run-up period with splendid weather contributed to the enormous success, praised by the President of the Olympic Association as the "Best Ever Games." Many out there felt that the secret had been the enormous army of volunteers who had boosted every event in every sport. They all wanted the world to see their "Sunburnt Country." Who could blame them?

Chapter 18

Retirement

My good friend John Byron, who lives in the village, gave words of wisdom when I retired.

"Make sure that your diary has something in it for every day ."

Certainly he follows his own advice, being involved in every village activity, organising trips for the elderly and being a nuisance to the authorities whenever they attempt to foist their latest piece of bureaucratic nonsense on us.

On retirement I made up my mind to make a clean break with my private and hospital work and not hang around looking over the shoulder of my successor. So often, in my early days, I had watched the pathetic sight of older retired colleagues toddling up to their consulting rooms to see a handful of loyal private patients. Deprived of the day-to-day care of hospital patients, I was astonished how quickly one lost touch and became out of date. Nevertheless I continued with my quasi-medical associations. The presidency of the Nottingham Hospitals' Choir gave me enormous pleasure, even though some members threatened to make me sing! And the Nottingham Medico-Chirurgical Society, of which I had been president, gave me the opportunity of meeting medical friends on a regular basis. It is now perhaps the largest and certainly the most prestigious of such societies in the land. We have a wonderful programme of education and entertainment.

Holidays

In retirement we look forward to holidays that we have been unable to fit in during working lives (see colour photos: fig 29). Currently the Government is attempting to raise the retirement age, one of their arguments being that we are all living longer. The basic flaw in this argument is that the years from 70 to 80 are more blighted with illness and decline than from 65 to 75. Indeed a significant proportion of the male population will be dead before the age of 70! Like all schemes put forward by Governments there is a hidden agenda - except that in this case the agenda is obvious, they have got their sums wrong and cannot afford to pay the promised pensions.

Get on your Bike

After my by-pass operation in 1990/1 our friends David Banks and his wife Judith suggested that we might embark on some therapeutic exercises. I might add that David had been my physician. Cycling was the favoured option. A 25 mile trial run on a sponsored Heart Foundation ride round the magnificent Vale of Belvoir confirmed that we were all fit enough to cope and set in train some of the best holidays we have ever enjoyed.

"Bike Bavaria," a family run firm based in Shropshire, provided us with several idyllic cycling holidays in Bavaria and Austria. The idea was and still is, that the firm provides you with bicycles and a route through spectacular scenery, along rivers and lakeside looking up into the mountains all around. The journeys are mainly on tracks or lanes vetted by the organisers and charted on route plans with Boy Scout-like symbols: -

......*so thru* <u>*MITTENWALD*</u> *2.3 (21.30), at far end of town, R SP* <u>*LEUTASCH*</u> ↗ *3.0(24.30) cross border into Austria*......

We soon learned to interpret the instructions, which gave rise to much fun and not a little argument! Each day we covered 30 - 60 Km to arrive at an inn or guesthouse. Baggage was transported by the firm and after 48 hrs we moved on again. Bavaria is one of Europe's best kept holiday secrets and over the years we saw Gamisch-Partenkirchen and the romantic castles, including Mad King Ludwig's Neuschwanstein castle, the ornate Rococco art of the Weis Church, and the Ettal Monastery. Then there were the Bavarian Lakes and the Austian Tyrol, the Enns Valley, vineyards, meadows brimming with wild flowers, sombre forests, babbling streams, rivers and lakes.

For variety, in other summers, we went with "Cycling for Softies," a similar organisation run by Susi Madron from Manchester. The difference is that Susi's holidays are in southern France, we carry our own luggage on the bikes and the emphasis is on "gustatory delights." We explored the Dordogne, the Tarn, the Garronne and the Dropt valleys, staying anywhere from isolated rural hotels to magnificent chateaux. (see colour photos: fig 30)The sun shone most of the time, though we did get a soaking or two, but we enjoyed every minute - even the headaches from too much wine the night before. Red wine is said to be good for the heart anyway!

Long Hauls

Being retired also means that you can get away to distant places for several weeks during the English winter, particularly at the fag-end of the year in February and March when the garden can be left. We are lucky to have a splendid local travel agent, Vanessa, at Mainline Travel whom Australia House nominates as the expert in the Midlands on "Down-under." She gets us marvellous bargains to the Far East, Australia and New Zealand, and I have written about some of these trips already. I never like the long hours in transit but a good book, a comfortable pair of slippers, 75 mg of aspirin daily, some gentle exercises and plenty of fluids keeps us out of trouble. One piece of advice I always give is to break the journey for 24-48 hours somewhere like the Middle East, Singapore, Kuala Lumpur, Los Angeles or San Francisco.

The National Trust

We believe this is one of our great national treasures and have now visited most locations in the Midlands, the South and the Southwest. Our dacha at Burton Breadstick on the coast and amidst scenic Dorset countryside is a superb base for exploring. Wherever we go to look round National Trust properties we bump into people just like us! Urbane, sensibly dressed in anoraks, sturdy shoes, flat caps and sweaters, they emerge from their cars and set up their picnic tables with thermoses of coffee, sandwiches, Scotch eggs and pork pies before setting out on the tour. Our generation is reluctant to pay good money on food bought away from home- a leftover of the wartime stringencies I suppose.

Painting for Fun

Over the years I fiddled around sketching and trying to paint. But there was never time except on holidays - my spare time was taken up with the garden. I don't think I have too much talent but I was looking for a hobby that I could continue even when I became decrepit. You can't play golf or hill walk forever. Peter Burgess, a local artist, was encouraging and claimed that he could teach me the tricks of the trade which would allow me to paint competent pictures that I would enjoy, even if no one else did (see colour photos: fig 31). I chose acrylics because someone said they were easy and didn't make a mess. Well, they didn't make a mess! I soon became completely hooked and derived enormous pleasure from selling my first painting and exhibiting round and about. I will never be an R.A. but it gives me enormous fun.

A Comfortable Village

When you retire you have a number of options. Do you downsize? Do you move elsewhere to that idyllic bit of England that you have discovered on holiday? Do you move to be nearer the children? Or, like a few people we know, do you move to get away from the children?

I have to admit that many of my patients had retired to Norfolk or the South coast only to lose their partner after a year or two, then to return home to the

176

Midlands. We, with many friends in Burton Joyce and a scattered family, took the easy option to stay put. We had a prime site and when we looked around we didn't see anywhere better!

Like many of our age group we took on voluntary jobs locally. A new Abbeyfield home, Carnarvon House, sheltered accommodation for the elderly, had opened in the village and Rosemary became heavily involved. In theory the volunteers were just concerned with social support. In practice, as we soon learned, we were general dogsbodies when there were problems, which were most days! Elsewhere I found myself as Chairman of the Millennium Committee, the Village Gala committee and Burton Joyce Preservation Society. I soon learned that chairing a committee of village folk, all with passionately held views and all wanting to talk at once, was a good deal more difficult than chairing a major committee of national importance.

We have been fortunate to live in a village community. In the early part of the century Burton Joyce was a country village visited by the townsfolk of Nottingham who arrived by train and charabanc, to enjoy the riverside walks and to take their refreshment at the popular Rosary Tea Rooms - the site now of a Co-op store. The Village has grown but it remains a pleasant place in which to live. Most living here would agree that it is a good place to bring up children and enjoy family life, (see colour photos: fig 32) a convenient base for work and an agreeable spot to spin out the evening of your life as we intend to do. For more years than I care to remember we have been blessed with kind and loyal neighbours who have always given us their complete support. Michael and Iris Atkinson lived opposite for many years before moving to the Lake District and nearby are John and Vibeke Hamilton (Boots/historian and nurse), Kevin and Ann Gibbin (ear, nose and throat surgeon and physiotherapist) and Patrick and Jenny Bates (urological surgeon and diabetologist). They are our dear friends and I hope they will continue to be so for many more years.

177

Chapter 19

Fifty years on

It is now some 50 years on since I enrolled as a medical student and this seems an appropriate point to wrap up these autobiographical recollections. I hope to go on for a bit longer myself!

A 50 year re-union

By chance this proposed closure coincided with a re-union of former students of UCHMS who had joined 50 years ago. To be accurate they were students who had joined from 1949 to 1951 but to gather together a reasonable number, 70 or 80 as it turned out, we had lumped the three years together. Theoretically there ought to have been about 200 but some could not make it, many were living abroad, mainly in North America, Australia and New Zealand, and sadly a quarter had died. The great umpire in the sky had raised his finger and there had been no disputing his decision.

It was perhaps a sad reflection of the stresses of our profession that a number had taken their own lives at an early stage of their careers. I do not know the exact figures but I suspect that a similar proportion of today's young doctors end their own lives prematurely. Add in the problems of alcoholism and drug addiction and it makes medicine a hazardous profession to practice.

Many of us had not met for 20, 30, 40 or even 50 years and it was a shock to be unable to recognise close friends from the old times. Those smooth, lively, expectant faces of young manhood and womanhood were now crumpled and wrinkled by lines etched by years of exposure to the tribulations of the world; though to be fair, I doubt if they were any worse than other comparable age groups. Bald heads, white hair, expanding paunches, hearing aids, false teeth, bent backs and sagging breasts combined in some to provide an impenetrable disguise. I have to say that I was disappointed when an old friend, looking me up and down for a few seconds, declared in astonishment

"Good Lord, it's Toggers!"

In my vanity I was hoping that it would be

"Good Lord, you haven't changed a bit!"

A few had changed for the better. One rather plump lady medical student who was plain at 20 was stunning at 70. She had benefited from the Californian way of life!

But whilst the habitus of many had changed, those earlier mannerisms were precisely the same: the tilt of the head, the lift of an eyebrow, the gurgling laugh, the expressive flick of the fingers and the rock back on the heels. Within minutes of meeting, the years had melted away and the chatter became both excited and reflective. It is strange how memory for distant images and events overrides the stimuli of a recent meeting. Now some weeks on, the picture in my mind's eye of those old friends' faces is still as they were 50 years ago, not as they are now with wrinkled skin and creaking joints.

On our re-union day we heard from others what they had done with their lives. Compared with some, my life seemed rather pedestrian. Peter Lachmann, now Sir Peter, had fulfilled his early promise, as we expected him to, by becoming President of the College of Pathologists, Biological Secretary of the Royal Society and President of the Academy of Medical Sciences - and he still looked to be in his 30s. A Professor of Obstetrics retired earlyish and went into the church. In view of his previous profession, his Bishop shortened his ecclesiastical training to two periods of nine months to run consecutively. Most appropriate! There cannot be many Reverent Professors of Obstetrics about. I had been told that the House of Lords is proof that there was life after death. One of our number, a noble lord himself, enlivened us with secrets of the Upper Chamber. A surgeon told us of his life's work in a most primitive and isolated hospital in Nigeria; we were all humbled.

In complete contrast we moved to visit the new University College Hospital opened earlier in the week by the Queen. Successive governments have been struggling for more than 20 years to rationalise the health care provision, medical student teaching and nursing training facilities provided by the old run-down Middlesex and University College Hospitals. The unsatisfactory union, which resulted in what was jocularly termed the "Unisex" Hospital, had provided an uneasy temporary solution. When Jo our daughter started her nursing training, initially at the Middlesex Hospital, Rosemary and I were shocked by the squalid conditions in which the nurses were expected to live and to train. Quite frankly, having a nurse's view of the two hospitals whilst she was training, convinced me that our erstwhile great London Teaching Hospitals, the Middlesex and UCH had deteriorated beyond redemption. I hope that the new University College Hospital will rise from the ashes.

Developments such as the new UCH are encouraging and the enormous investment in health care in this segment of London long overdue. Sadly its problems are mirrored elsewhere in the country. But many share my concerns that we may not be able to sustain enormous units of this kind.

Some Reflections on the Management of the NHS

Whilst this book has been a personal story I have, of necessity, commented on the management problems that I have seen in my 50 years' experience of the NHS. It will have become clear from these comments that I am not an admirer of politicians, no matter what party they belong to. Their decisions are dictated more by political agendas than by patients' clinical needs.

Writing in the New England Medical Journal in 1988, Relman divided the evolution of health services into three eras. Whilst he was referring primarily to the USA his comments apply similarly to the UK. He called the first era, from the 1940s to the 1960s, the "Era of Expansion." Here, on this side of the Atlantic, this took into account the inception of the NHS, heralding some of the most significant and beneficial changes of the century. It was accepted then that there were inequalities both on a social and geographical scale. These inequalities were never completely resolved. Nowhere was this more apparent than in the tremendous gulf between the standards and finances of the London Teaching Hospitals and the hospitals of the East Midlands. In those early days, the East Midlands was near the bottom of the league for virtually every health parameter. Only in recent years has this gulf been narrowed. The new medical school and the growth of the teaching hospitals in Nottingham have led to a staggering improvement in health provision at a local level.

The second period described was the Era of Cost Containment extending from the 1960s to the 1980s. It did not take long to discover that supply created demand. In the 1960s health care provision was rapidly outstripped by health care requirements. In the UK there was a multiplicity of Reviews, Reports and Royal Commissions, all of which struggled to balance costs with improvements in the service. Much time and money was wasted with the recommended changes, none of which seemed, by themselves, to have provided any significant improvement. Some, misguidedly, believed that the NHS could be run as a business enterprise by re-organising managerial structure. Leaders of industry were brought in to provide leadership for the NHS - a concern that was second only to the Red Army in the size of its work force.

The commercial principles envisaged competition in the Health service to encourage efficiency. We became quickly aware of local difficulties in such a system here in Nottingham where two major hospitals, the QMC and the City Hospital, found themselves shedding the co-operation built up over decades to "compete for trade." The internal market did not work and now, in 2006, we are on the threshold of combining the two major hospitals in Nottingham into one large unit. Many of us felt, in the 1970s, that a United Nottingham Hospitals would provide a practical solution to many of our fiscal and logistic problems.

The third era of Accountability and Assessment started in the early 1990s and extends to the present day. It is undoubtedly right that as a profession we should make ourselves more accountable. It is also essential that our performance should be assessed carefully. The last years of my own career were spent attempting to ensure that doctors "kept up to date" and that they maintained acceptable standards. Nevertheless the relentless pressure to realise targets is often irrelevant in furthering the clinical needs of patients, as is the cascade of untested innovations.

An Essential Service

Whilst I believe that there is too much political interference with the running of the Health Service, it is essential to the life of this country. There is no reasonable alternative in a civilised society. Financially it will always be a bottomless pit. Unpalatable means will have to be adopted to contain the enormous expense. One of these is the unpopular option of rationing of health care. Currently our Health Service is attempting to treat everyone and everything. Consequently it is berated from all sides because it cannot do so. The high expectations of the public, fuelled by media coverage, cannot be fulfilled. We must remember that even in the 21st century, many diseases are still incurable, and more importantly, death is eventually inevitable.

Personal Responsibility for Health

What is disappointing is that individuals are prepared to take less personal responsibility for their health than they were in earlier days of the Health Service. Then, bruises and sprains were left to nature to heal without recourse to X-rays, physiotherapy and steroid injections. Colds, chills and mild 'flu like illnesses were treated with bed rest, aspirins or a glass of an amber fluid without requests for a course of antibiotics. Comfort and advice came from benevolent aunts and good friends not counsellors who often, in my experience, can exacerbate and extend a disturbing experience, which would regress with time.

A few simple changes in life style for all of us would reduce the burden of ill health: stopping smoking, eating less, not drinking too much alcohol and taking simple exercise. I remain unconvinced that organic foods, bottled mineral waters, skin foods, added vitamins and many alternative therapies contribute materially to our health and well-being.

Technological Advances

But on the whole, the NHS serves us well, no more so than in the management of major disasters such as that at Kegworth which I have already described. These last 50 years have, unquestionably, seen amazing technological advances from which we have all benefited. We have to admit, medicine is no longer an art but a science. Because of this some of the old doctor/patient

181

relationships have withered. Shift systems do not sit comfortably with continuity of personal care and teams of carers cannot hope to give individual attention.

I have always believed that the initial confrontation between doctor and patient is critical to all that follows. This involves taking a history and performing a physical examination. Sir William Osler encouraged students of medicine to

"Learn to see, learn to hear, learn to feel, learn to smell and to know that by practice alone you can become expert."

It was, therefore, disappointing to read in the New England Journal of Medicine in 2006 that Dr Bomback's examination, as a newly qualified doctor, had been condensed to roughly 60 seconds: a quick look at the eyes, a quicker look at the mouth, gross palpation of the neck, a cursory listen to the heart and lungs, a squeeze of the belly, another squeeze of both legs, and a touch of the hands to make sure they're still warm. In contrast he spent hours of each day checking laboratory values.......... and following various diagnostic procedures.

But I grow old and I must move with the times.

Four Pieces of Luck

At the beginning of this book I described three early pieces of luck. They have enabled me to live a busy and exciting life. I have watched medicine move to a highly sophisticated science. I have looked after thousands of ill patients whose gratitude has been humbling. I have taught medical students and young doctors and marked their progress with pride. I have also been part of a team establishing a huge and successful teaching hospital in the heart of middle England.

Great events have overtaken me

That has been my fourth piece of luck.